Europe's Industries

Cornell Studies in
Political Economy

EDITED BY

PETER J. KATZENSTEIN

American Industry in International Competition: Government Policies and Corporate Strategies, edited by John Zysman and Laura Tyson

Closing the Gold Window: Domestic Politics and the End of Bretton Woods, by Joanne Gowa

Europe's Industries: Public and Private Strategies for Change, edited by Geoffrey Shepherd, Francois Duchêne, and Christopher Saunders

Governments, Markets, and Growth: Financial Systems and the Politics of Industrial Change, by John Zysman

International Regimes, edited by Stephen D. Krasner

Europe's Industries

Public and Private Strategies for Change

Edited by
Geoffrey Shepherd
François Duchêne
Christopher Saunders

Cornell University Press, Ithaca, New York

© Geoffrey Shepherd, Francois Duchêne, Christopher Saunders 1983

First published 1983 by Cornell University Press

International Standard Book Number 0-8014-1706-6
Library of Congress Catalog Card Number 83-72884

Printed in Great Britain

CONTENTS

List of Tables and Figures

CONTRIBUTORS

Tibor Barna has been Professor of Economics at the University of Sussex since 1962.

Giovanni Dosi is a Research Fellow at the Science Policy Research Unit, University of Sussex. From 1978 to 1981 he was a researcher at the Sussex European Research Centre.

François Duchêne was until 1982 Director of the Sussex European Research Centre.

Daniel T. Jones is a Senior Research Fellow at the Science Policy Research Unit, University of Sussex. From 1977 to 1981 he was a Senior Research Fellow at the Sussex European Research Centre.

Mototada Kikkawa is Deputy General Manager and Senior Economist in the Industrial Research Department of the Industrial Bank of Japan. He was a Visiting Research Fellow at the Sussex European Research Centre in 1980/1.

Patrick Messerlin is Professor of Economics at the University of Lille and a Research Fellow at the Fondation Nationale des Sciences Politiques (Service de l'Étude de l'Activité Economique), Paris.

Peter Mottershead is a Senior Lecturer in the Department of Applied Economic Studies, North East London Polytechnic.

Christopher Saunders has been a Professorial Fellow at the Sussex European Research Centre since 1973.

Geoffrey Shepherd is Acting Director of the Sussex European Research Centre.

John Surrey, a Senior Research Fellow at the Science Policy Research Unit, leads its energy policy research programme.

William Walker is a Senior Research Fellow at the Science Policy Research Unit.

NOTES ON TEXT AND TABLES

Reference to Germany in the text or tables means the Federal Republic of Germany throughout.

Table conventions

— Nil or negligible
.. Not available
( ) Estimate

Minor discrepancies in table totals and sub-totals are due to rounding.

PREFACE

This book is one of two that report on a research project undertaken by the Sussex European Research Centre (University of Sussex) on Western European industry and industrial policy. The aims of the project were to identify the kinds of adjustment problems facing Western European industry, to understand public and private responses to these challenges better (and how and why these have differed across sectors and across countries), and to anticipate some of the adjustment problems and policy options that Western European countries, individually and collectively, would have to face in the near future.

These aims were pursued through a number of sector and country studies. The particular approach of the research was to get away from the usual division between self-sufficient sectoral studies— giving too little sense of some of the broader relationships in the economy—and broader studies on the trade and policy aspects of industrial development which fail to relate general principles to the range of particular cases.

This book contains eight sector studies while a forthcoming book, *Managing Industrial Change in Europe* (edited by François Duchêne and Geoffrey Shepherd), will look at the experience of four countries, Germany, France, Italy and the UK, and discuss the international implications of national approaches to managing industrial change. Some of the individual studies have already appeared in more extended versions in the *Sussex European Paper* series published by the Sussex European Research Centre.

The project was undertaken under the joint sponsorship of the Sussex European Research Centre and the Institut für Weltwirtschaft, Kiel, in Western Germany. It benefited from the collaboration of a number of different economists working at universities or institutions in the UK, Germany, France and Italy. The project was made possible by the foresight and generosity of the Anglo–German Foundation for the Study of Industrial Society, London, and the Volkswagen Foundation, Hanover. Their funds financed research at the Sussex European Research Centre from 1977 to 1981, as well as many of the costs of international collaboration. The Fondation Nationale des Sciences Politiques, Paris, and the Japanese Development Bank, Tokyo, gave important support to some of the studies.

Research collaboration between different institutions and individuals in different countries is not easy. But it can be very valuable indeed in multiplying resources relatively cheaply and, in a project making national comparisons, avoiding an approach that is too biased towards the experience of one country or another. To overcome the problems of international collaboration, a series of workshops was held from 1978 to 1981—mostly in Sussex, but also elsewhere in Europe—to work out common outlines for the sector and country studies and to discuss the resulting drafts. These workshops were attended by the project authors as well as a core of other people who made a notable contribution to the project. In addition to those project authors only appearing in the second book (Ernst-Jürgen Horn, David Marsen, Pippo Ranci and Margaret Sharp), we owe a particular debt to the following: Gerhard Fels, from the Institut für Weltwirtschaft, Kiel; Paolo Cecchini and Christopher Wilkinson from the Commission of the European Communities; Sir Arthur Knight, then Chairman of the National Enterprise Board, now at the London School of Economics; Peter McGregor (now at the National Economic Development Office) and Hans Wiener from the Anglo–German Foundation; Michel Sauzay from the French Ministry of Industry; Haruo Nakayama (a Visiting Research Fellow at the Sussex European Research Centre in 1979), from the Nomura Research Institute, Tokyo; and Lesley Cook, Ron Dore, Peter Holmes, Keith Pavitt, Joao Rendeiro and Angela Whelan from the University of Sussex.

The kind of research we have undertaken would not have been possible without a substantial amount of interviewing of businessmen and government officials. To these people we are also very grateful. We should like to thank Susan Joekes and Veronica McGivney for their help in editing the texts. Finally, Ann Curry and Terrie Russell typed so many drafts they might have been forgiven for becoming bored. Yet we are grateful and relieved that they were able to produce the final draft in record time.

Sussex European Research Centre, *François Duchêne*
University of Sussex. *Geoffrey Shepherd*
Christopher Saunders
1983

1 INTRODUCTION: INDUSTRIAL CHANGE AND INTERVENTION IN WESTERN EUROPE

Geoffrey Shepherd and François Duchêne

1.1 The context

The Western European industrial powers are no strangers to the threats of international competition. After 1914 a world war, political disintegration, recession and another world war severely weakened Europe while the relative industrial strength of the US grew. After 1950, in a new international context of trade liberalisation largely engineered by the Americans, Europe was able to arrest—even reverse—its relative decline, thanks largely to the powerful recovery of West Germany, France and Italy (more or less in that order of importance), which more than compensated for continuing British decline.

Since the 1970s Europe has become aware, as has North America, of a combination of new challenges. Post-war trade liberalisation and political decolonisation have led to the rapid spread of economic power outside the old industrial world straddling the North Atlantic. This became evident to Europe from the 1970s with Japan's rapid progress towards the status of a dominant economic and technological power and with the emergence of other new producers—most notably in East Asia—capable of competing in more mature activities.

The challenge to Europe may increasingly take on a technological character. If the widespread expectations of the impact of microelectronics are even partially confirmed, the industrial map could be reshaped in the next generation. The effects could be at least as great as those of the emergence of the electrical and chemical industries a little less than a century ago, a development closely connected with the rise of the industrial power of the US and Germany, both of which have since played a dominant part in world politics. The current electronics phase is becoming increasingly associated with the rise of Japan, the first major new industrial power to emerge this century in the capitalist world. This could imply far-reaching economic and geopolitical changes.

At the same time everyone's capacity to adapt has been

undermined by the two oil-price shocks of 1973 and 1979, the sustained recession since 1974, and the inflation that has compounded uncertainties about the future.

As with adjustment pressures, there are signs that national intervention has become more intense. Spurred on in part by a growing social resistance to change (itself the product of several decades of prosperity), in part by the alarming growth in unemployment in the 1970s, the state has been induced to intervene to protect the individual and the firm from the workings of the market. Such intervention very often further undermines national capacity to adjust. Some would argue that it encourages the very disease it is trying to fight.

But intervention has also been consciously adopted as a weapon of attack by countries seeking to improve their position in the world industrial league. In this sense we should perhaps view the experience of the Western industrial world in the quarter-century following the Second World War as historically untypical: a uniquely—and temporarily—powerful US, by imposing an international *laissez-faire* system on a temporarily weakened world, was able to suppress some national economic rivalry in the pursuit of a collective economic benefit. But countries with more interventionist traditions and less enthusiasm for the GATT rules of the game have gradually reasserted themselves. (Meanwhile, the relative weakening of the US has, not unpredictably, started to lead it in similar directions.) As a result countries compete with one another no less than firms.

Intervention, in both its defensive and offensive variants, may have a national logic, but it certainly creates difficulties in maintaining the international trading system and the European sub-system within it. Unlike in the 1930s, that system has so far held more or less, but in one important sense the situation is uniquely dangerous: the level of international trade relative to the size of national markets for manufactures in the industrialised countries is now, as best we can estimate, at least as high as in the previous peak at the turn of the century. It is significantly higher than in 1929. We estimate for 1978 that exports (including intra-regional trade) accounted for 17 per cent of manufacturing output in the EEC, North America and Japan combined. The equivalent figure for 1970 was 13 per cent and for 1960, 9 per cent. Our best estimate is that the 1929 figure was some 30 per cent lower than in 1978 and the 1899 figure some 10 per cent lower.[1] Thus a collapse of the international trade system could now have an unprecedentedly large impact.

A 'micro' approach to industrial adjustment

This book is concerned with a number of issues related to Western Europe's capacity to compete. How well are European industries surviving? What features of the industrial system—particularly public intervention—influence performance? What are the international implications, especially in the context of European integration? In recent years a substantial literature has been devoted to such questions.[2] The aim of this book is to lay the groundwork for providing more general answers by considering the problems at a 'micro' level, using as examples evidence from specific industrial sectors in Western Europe's major countries.

These sector studies mostly conform to a common outline which examines the nature of adjustment pressures, describes the reactions of industries (very often firms) and governments to them, and speculates on how pressures and reactions might change in the future. Within this outline some common characteristics have emerged in the way several of the studies have looked at industries.

First, the process of change is central: adjustment pressures require constant adaptation from firms and industries. The pervasiveness of change and the uncertainties associated with it make strategy (in the sense of the particular goals followed by firms in production processes, markets, location and so on) an important subject of study. Often it may be possible to associate certain more or less successful strategies with certain sectors in certain countries. This association is most likely to be made where a national industry is dominated by one firm or a few like-minded ones. But dominant or typical national strategies may, at the margin at least, sometimes also be identified in industries where there are many firms (see Chapter 2, Section 3).

It would not be wise to push this idea of national strategic homogeneity too far, but, to the extent that it has some value, it may be explained by the distinct character of national industrial systems. In the course of the research it became clear that public intervention could not be treated as an independent force operating on firms and institutions with homogenous characteristics. It had to be understood in the context of the performance of the industries or firms on which it operated. Was it, for instance, trying to reinforce private success or substitute for private failure? It also had to be understood in the context of distinct national economic and political institutions, such as labour relations, the banking system, the degree of centralism in government, which influence both it and the private sector. A better understanding of the relationship between government, industry and institutions has thus become an important part of the objective of this study. Shonfield's work on modern, mixed-economy capitalism, concentrating on the economic systems in Germany, France, the UK and the US, provides an important forerunner in this area.[3]

The importance of this three-way relationship is reinforced by the past—perhaps continuing—growth in minimum efficient scale of production in many industrial activities and in the length of investment lead-times. The consequent increase in risk and uncertainty and the spread of oligopoly tend to limit the reliability of market signals. In such activities, public intervention may be much less sharply differentiated from the 'normal' activity of the industry than it would be in an industry with many competitors. The government becomes one more in an oligarchy of decision-makers (including individual firms, groups of firms, banks and so on), rather than a *deus ex machina* sitting in judgment on strategies and breaking the rules of the market.

In spite of the common economic problems and similar resources of Western European countries, the common elements in their political and economic institutions, and the progress made in integration since the Second World War, Western Europe is still far from being a unified economic area (in the sense that the US is). It is for this reason that the study adopts a national, rather than regional, approach. The comparative-national approach, moreover, emphasises important differences in the 'industry-institutional' relationship between countries. (In this expression government figures as one of the institutions.) Limitations in research resources have restricted much of the study to considering the four major Western European economies (and their firms): the Federal Republic of Germany, France, Italy and the UK. (Together these account for about nine-tenths of the EEC, three-quarters of Western European, and one-third of OECD industrial output.) It is thus a study about industry and intervention in medium-to-large countries.

There is a particular merit in looking at differences between countries through the medium of sector studies. In addition to the intrinsic value of sector studies as detailed sources of information about and analysis of specific areas of activity, the level of detail in the sector study is often more effective in revealing the nature of the industry-institutional relationship than more general approaches. In particular it makes it easier to go beyond the 'cataloguing' approach to intervention common to many studies, in which national experience is contrasted by the amount of recourse to given instruments (R & D support, investment allowances, public government, and so on), or (more rarely) by quantitative comparisons of subsidy and protection. Instead the sectoral detail allows an approach to be adopted—perforce not very quantitative and necessarily speculative—in which judgments can be made whether, and in what sense, a specific instance, programme or pattern of intervention was effective; whether it was autonomously undertaken (or was itself the outcome of private pressures, for instance); and what private-sector and institutional conditions made it effective or ineffective.

In the following sections of this Introduction we first look at the breadth of adjustment experience met in the eight sectors covered in this book. We then try to characterise the national 'styles' that help explain systematic differences in the adjustment experience of the major Western European countries. We finally examine the limitations to the nationalist forms of intervention these countries are trying to pursue.

1.2 The adjustment process in Western Europe

Of the eight sectors studied in this book, three (textiles, steel and shipbuilding) are generally regarded as 'mature' or 'declining', two (process plant contracting and semiconductors) are new in the sense that they have only come into existence since the last war, while the remaining three (motor cars, electrical power plant and machine tools) are all long-established industries, though radical technical change has affected or may affect all of them. All eight sectors are among those parts of Western European industry where international trade is most important and competitive problems and trade frictions most salient. This is illustrated in the 'trade-intensity' ratios of Tables 1.1 and 1.2. In Table 1.1 ratios of trade to apparent consumption (that is, the magnitude of trade relative to the size of the domestic market) are expressed for certain EEC industry groups for 1968 and 1978. In Table 1.2 national ratios of imports to apparent consumption and exports to production are calculated, where available, for the sectors studied in this book for the years 1960, 1970 and 1980. (Note: since the Table 1.2 ratios are based on different sources, with some of them calculated on a volume basis, they must be used for purposes of comparing among sectors only with caution.)

The engineering (mechanical, electrical and electronic) industries, which account for about one-third of the EEC's market for manufactures (Table 1.1), include six of the eight sectors studied in this book (shipbuilding, motor cars, electrical power plant, process plant contracting, machine tools and semiconductors). The concentration

Table 1.1 Trade as a percentage of apparent consumption of manufactures in the EEC, 1968 and 1978*

		Intra EEC Trade	External EEC imports by origin						External EEC exports	Share of sector in total consumption of manufactures (%)
			North America	Japan	Other developed market economies	Developing countries	Other	Total		
1. Engineering industries†	1968	9.7	2.7	0.3	1.5	0.2	0.2	4.8	10.7	34
	1978	19.0	3.6	1.9	3.7	1.1	0.5	10.8	24.8	34
2. Chemicals	1968	10.0	2.6	0.2	1.7	1.0	0.5	6.0	10.1	10
	1978	18.0	3.0	0.3	2.8	1.3	1.1	8.5	17.7	12
3. Ferrous and non-ferrous metals	1968	9.5	2.7	0.2	2.6	4.3	0.7	10.4	8.5	9
	1978	17.0	1.4	0.4	4.6	2.4	1.7	10.5	15.8	8
4. Textiles and clothing	1968	8.3	0.5	0.2	1.3	1.4	0.3	3.9	8.7	10
	1978	20.8	0.9	0.4	4.4	7.1	1.7	14.6	13.0	8
5. Other industries‡	1968	4.3	1.0	0.1	2.7	1.2	0.6	5.5	3.6	37
	1978	9.5	1.1	0.1	2.5	1.7	1.0	6.5	5.5	38
Total	1968	7.6	1.9	0.2	2.0	1.1	0.4	5.6	7.9	100
	1978	15.2	2.2	0.8	3.3	2.0	0.9	9.2	14.8	100

* Nine members.
† Includes transport equipment; machinery; and miscellaneous manufactures not included elsewhere.
‡ Includes: food, beverages, and tobacco; wood products, paper and printing; rubber; petroleum and coal products; and non-metallic mineral products.

Source: Calculated from Table 7.1 of UNCTAD, *Handbook of International Trade and Development Statistics. Supplement 1981*, New York: United Nations, 1982.

Table 1.2 Major industrial countries: levels of trade-intensity for selected products, 1960–80

	Germany		France		Italy		UK		EEC[e]		US		Japan	
	I/C	E/P	I/C	E/P	I/C	E/P	I/C	E/P	I/C	E/P	I/C	E/P	I/C	E/P
Textiles: woven cloth (by weight)														
1962	12	13	6	25	5	15	31	15	3	13	4	1	..	..
1970	24	22	23	25	33	29	36	19	10	13	5	3	2	29
1980	59	59	59	46	62	56	74	51	35	20	7	6	8	36
Steel (by crude-equivalent weight)														
1961	16	32	27	41	26	11	3	19	3	20	4	3	2	10
1970	28	34	41	41	30	13	12[d]	19	9	18	12	7	—	24
1980	40	52	53	59	31	30	24[d]	26[d]	12	27	15	5	2	31
Merchant ships (by capacity in GRT)[a]														
1960	1	72	4	35	—	17	28	11	5	26	6	12	—	53
1970	41	56	27	38	—	14	61	15	12	29	13	1	—	61
1980	22	27	7	45	2	19	48	56	14	39	—	2	—	55
Motor cars (by no. of units)														
1960	9	46	4	42	5	33	7	42	—[f]	23[f]	7[g]	1[g]	2	4
1970	31	55	23	43	34	37	14	42	2	26	16[g]	1[g]	1	23
1980	42	60	36	46	62	35	57	39	16	20	30[g]	2[g]	2	56
Power plant: steam turbine deliveries (by capacity in GW)[b]														
1955–75	(5)	38	—	37	(5)	..	—	38	..	..	..	8	..	12
1975–87	(5)	50	—	17	(5)	24	—	55	4	25	9	7	9	52
Metal-working machine tools (by values)														
1960	21	48	35	26	31	29	30	30	..	..	6	23	31	3
1970	24	55	47	37	30	40	38	38	15	34	10	20	14	8
1980	33	63	56	54	29	49	58	61	20	41	29	22	9	38
Semiconductors: integrated circuits (by values)														
1982	..	..	..	..	..	..	..	..	66	18	8	19	14	31
All manufactures (by values)														
1960	11[c]	17[c]	..	..	..	..	10	15	6	11	4[h]	5[h]	5	10
1970	17	21	15	17	18	22	17	18	8	12	7[h]	7[h]	4	10
1978	21	28	20	22	22	31	25	25	9	14	10[h]	9[h]	4	12

[Notes and sources to Table 1.2 on p. 8.]

of the studies within this group reflects the importance of trade and trade conflicts in many of those high-skill industries generally thought to be the key to European survival in a world of spreading industrialisation. By the same token they are also the industries where Japan's impact, on both domestic and export markets, has been the most pervasive (although the figures for Japanese import-penetration in Table 1.1—albeit no more recent than in 1978— probably do not show the true magnitude of this).

Chemicals (not covered in this book), ferrous and non-ferrous metals (steel study), and textiles and clothing (textiles study) each account for one-tenth of the EEC market. For each of these four groups—engineering, chemicals, metals and textiles/clothing— the level of exports to other EEC countries virtually doubled its share of the market to about one-fifth, in the decade up to 1978 (Table 1.1). The levels of trade with partners outside the EEC have also grown for these four groups, most rapidly for the EEC's exports

---

Notes and Sources to Table 1.2

I/C: Imports/Consumption (Production + imports − exports) × 100.
E/P: Exports/Production × 100.
[a] Note that trade in this industry is 'lumpy' and that the use of flags of convenience makes definition of 'domestic' consumption problematic.
[b] 'Date of delivery' means the moment of the commissioning of completed plant. (Note: delivery lead times have now lengthened to as much as ten years.)
[c] 1962.
[d] 1979 (the 1980 figures, affected by a long strike, are: I/C 42 per cent; E/P 30 per cent).
[e] Nine members, excluding intra-member trade.
[f] I/C and E/P for all of Western Europe.
[g] Excluding trade with Canada.
[h] North America (including intra-US-Canada trade).

Sources: Textiles (woven cloth of cotton and man-made fibres): Textile Statistics Bureau, *Quarterly Statistical Review*, Manchester, various issues; UN, *Commodity Trade Statistics: Series D*, New York, various issues.
Steel: OECD, *The Steel Market in 1981 and the Outlook for 1982. Special Supplement*, Paris, 1982.
Merchant ships: Lloyd's Register of Shipping, *Statistical Tables 1981*, London, 1981.
Motor cars: Motor Vehicle Manufacturers Association, *World Motor Vehicle Data. 1982 Edition*, Detroit, 1982; Society of Motor Manufacturers and Trades, *The Motor Industry of Great Britain 1982*, London, 1982.
Power plant: Science Policy Research Unit, Turbine Generator Data Bank.
Machine tools: *American Machinist*, January 1972 and February 1981; UNIDO, *The Machine Tool Industry*, Vienna, 1974.
Semiconductors: *Business Week*, 23 May 1983, p. 83.
All manufactures: for Germany, France, Italy and the UK: Table 2.14 of Sharp, M. and Shepherd, G., *The Management of Industrial Change in Britain*, Brighton: Sussex European Research Centre, mimeo, 1983; for the EEC-9, North America and Japan: estimated from UNCTAD, *Handbook of International Trade and Development Statistics*, New York (Table 5.10a of *Supplement 1977*, 1978; Table 5.10b of *Supplement 1980*, 1981, and Table 5.10c of *Supplement 1981*, 1982).

of engineering goods and its imports of textiles and clothing. It is in textiles that the impact of the newly industrialising countries (the NICs) has been most heavily concentrated.

In the fifth category of industries—a miscellaneous grouping representing almost two-fifths of the market—trade is generally limited, due to such factors as transport costs (for example, in building materials), or protection (for example, in food processing).

The eight sectors studied in this book appear to have even higher levels of trade-intensity than the broader groups of which they are part (see Table 1.2). With the exception of textiles and machine tools they are characterized by the relatively small number of firms that produce in any one country. The degree of 'oligopoly'—albeit moderated by high levels of international trade—appears to be greater in these sectors than the average for manufacturing.[4] Our choice of sectors may have been biased towards oligopolistic cases for several reasons: industries with few firms may be more effective in putting their case for special treatment, they may be easier to intervene in, and they tend to be easier to study (in the sense that fewer firms represent a greater part of industrial activity).

The sector studies

One of the conclusions of the first sector study, on *textiles* (Chapter 2), is that, contrary to some perceptions, there has been substantial adjustment in Western European textiles towards the more sophisticated end of the market. As an agent of this change, trade among industrialised countries, particularly trade within Western Europe, has been more important than trade with the Third World (though heavy non-tariff protection against NICs has helped to make this so). Different Western European countries have typically found very different ways of surviving. Relatively successful survival in Germany and Italy appears to have been the result of the operation of market forces, consciously fostered by the government in Germany's case, induced by the weakness of government in Italy's. The British and French governments, on the other hand, were persuaded by their leading firms to encourage a process of concentration which helped undermine competitive forces. Yet even in these two countries the quantity of 'positive' adjustment, as seen for instance in the growth of exports during the 1970s, was substantial (see Table 1.2).

The problems first of modernisation, secondly of overcapacity in Europe's *steel* industry (Chapter 3) have been the result of the long-term declining trend in the elasticity of demand for steel— now exacerbated by recession—rather than of external trade trends.

Italy, with an economy catching up on Northern European levels of steel consumption, has avoided some of the problem. Germany's (and Luxembourg's) steel industry foresaw some of the problem and pursued strategies of specialisation and diversification from the 1960s. In France, the UK and Belgium—all now with nationalised steel industries—the process of adjusting to reduced demand was delayed by social pressures and over-optimism (and consequent massive government investment). But in France and the UK at least a drastic slimming exercise is now underway. The Community's enforcement of a cartel has made steel *the* industrial sector where Community-level intervention is strongest.

The *merchant shipbuilding* industry (Chapter 4) has faced a slump severer than in almost all other industries. This slump is the result in part of the decline in growth of seaborne trade, in part of over-capacity from many years of public subsidy in the world's industry. Japanese support to its shipbuilding industry in the 1950s was an important factor in unleashing the subsidy race. Since the recession OECD and Community attempts to regulate the level of competitive subsidy have been ineffective in the face of the slump. As a result intervention has become so endemic—in all the major sectors of Western Europe, as elsewhere—that national industries have effectively become 'captured' by their governments. Unlike textiles for instance, shipbuilding has not been notably successful in finding new products or activities to mitigate decline.

The European *motor car* industry (Chapter 5) has been subjected since the 1960s to restructuring pressures from US firms pursuing their concept of global integration of the car industry ('the world car') and to the intense competitive pressures of exports from Japan. The industry has changed (and will change) considerably under these pressures, but its rapidly deteriorating trade balance (Table 1.2) reflects the loss of its dominant position on markets outside Western Europe to Japan. The French, Italian and UK industries have for a number of years enjoyed substantial non-tariff protection against Japanese imports in their domestic market. The French car firms have been supported by the government in their bid to become full-range international producers. Italy's domi-nant producer has survived—at times precariously—with little government help beyond limiting imports from Japan. German firms have gone up-market or invested outside Europe. They have had comparatively little public support, although the Federal Government played a critical coordinating role when Volkswagen faced problems in the early 1970s. Large parts of the UK industry have survived only through heavy public support; cooperation with Japanese firms is now becoming more evident as a more positive approach to survival but this has created a source of potential dissension within Europe.

Western Europe's *electrical power plant* industry (Chapter 6) continues to face a domestic slump in world-wide power stations' ordering as a result of recession. Competition, intensified by this slump, is on export markets rather than domestic markets which are insulated by nationalistic procurement policies. Western Europe has so far held its position in the world market (Japanese inroads having largely been made at the expense of US exports). The extreme uncertainties about the future in this industry are intensified by the debate on the cost-effectiveness and social and political acceptability of nuclear power. If the French industry has so far weathered the recession better than other countries, this reflects the authority the government has been able to wield in pursuit of its commitment to nuclear power. At the other end of the spectrum the British industry has suffered from national pretentions to technological independence and the inability of the major interested parties (the firms, the utilities, and the governments) to reach consensus. The task of the Italian industry has more clearly been seen as that of catching up on the technological leaders, but in this it has been frustrated, as in the UK, by a failure to find consensus.

The *process plant contracting* industry (Chapter 7) is in reality a service industry building for process industries (mostly chemical and steel) and subcontracting from plant and equipment suppliers. Its strengths come from a close, 'synergetic' relationship with suppliers and clients. As a substantial exporter, the industry is therefore an agent of technological diffusion. The success of the European industry—up to the beginning of this decade at least—reflected European strengths in chemicals, the development of North Sea oil, and its ability to respond to Third-World industrialisation needs. Apart from the contribution of the state in building up an infant industry in France and Italy, the Western European industry, notably strong in Germany and the UK, was developed in the face of substantial competition from US firms in Europe and without government support. But, as in other industries which export in large 'packages', governments have inevitably become involved in competitive export subsidy and salesmanship.

The Western European *machine tool* industry (Chapter 8) is characterised by small firms. In the 1970s the Japanese industry was first to exploit the potential of using electronic (or numerical) controls to make general-purpose machine tools more flexible, thus to move the industry in the direction of producing more standard products. The historically strong German industry was rather slow to react to these changes in the nature of the market. The Italian industry, based in large part on very small firms and subcontracting relationships, was able to respond with some flexibility. The success of the industry was in part due to legislated tax concessions favouring the purchase of Italian machine tools, but also in part to the entrepreneurship shown by the industry's own association. Substantially less success in French and British machine tools largely reflected the narrowness of the domestic engineering industry in the former case and its relatively undynamic character in the latter case. Both governments intervened substantially, in particular by encouraging the emergence of larger firms, but this conspicuously failed to improve competitive performance. Yet even in the less successful countries adjustment is clearly in evidence: Western Europe has perhaps reacted faster to Japan's challenge in machine tools than in motor cars, partly through imitation, partly through the rapid growth of joint ventures with Japanese firms. But the success of this reaction still remains to be seen.

Semiconductors is at the heart of the fast-moving microelectronics industry; Giovanni Dosi argues (Chapter 9) that the existence of a strong producer-user relationship means that countries with firms at the technological frontier in semiconductors will be in the best position to encourage their application. Western Europe's problem, for several decades a technological lag *vis-à-vis* the US, is now also to catch up with Japan. This technological lag is reflected in a large and growing trade deficit (see Table 1.2). The US initially took the lead through demand derived from massive military and space programmes. Japan and the US now hold the lead through the dynamism of, and competition among, their private firms. The European industries have not benefited from massive public support, nor from effective competition among domestic firms. Governments have pursued nationalistic policies, although they have not always been able to impose their own objectives on the firms. Europe's two most powerful producers of standard devices, Philips and Siemens, have survived —without prospering—as semiconductor producers, but government support has probably not played an important part in this survival. French, Italian and British 'national champions' have only survived through public support.

The final chapter focuses on Japan, not Europe. Japan's growing competitive presence across a range of more sophisticated industries is often attributed to government intervention. The role of policy is put into its context in a review of the post-war development of the *shipbuilding, motor car* and *semiconductor* industries in Japan (Chapter 10). The government has continually played an important role in shipbuilding, first in the post-war rehabilitation of industry and promotion of exports, thereafter in helping organise an orderly contraction in the post-1975 slump. In the early stages of development of the motor car and semiconductor industries the government's role was important. The prospect of import liberalisation clearly provided a key incentive to firms. But as controls on imports became less important, so MITI's influence diminished. Many of the strengths of Japanese industry are thus attributable to the strengths of private firms and groups of firms, as well as to some of the forces of cohesion in Japanese society.

Sectoral generalisations

The structural peculiarities of each sector limit the value of typologies of or generalisations about sectoral patterns in adjustment. None the less, it is worth asking how far we can generalise about the amount, success and causal explanations of adjustment.

Perhaps the single most important generalisation is that change, whether in the form of new technology, new products or new forms of organisation, is a potent force for survival across a range of industrial activities. Textiles, motor cars and machine tools are mature or maturing activities that have experienced (or at least begun) a cycle of rejuvenation that steel, shipbuilding and electrical power have not (in the latter industry if only because the nuclear option went sour for a number of reasons). This capacity for rejuvenation undermines some of the notions of the product-cycle theory (as Jones points out for cars, Chapter 5, Section 4), including its deterministic implications for international comparative advantage.

How successful Western Europe has been in grasping the opportunities for change is more difficult to answer. Clearly it has been less successful than Japan, but on balance certainly no less successful than the US except—if we can generalise from semiconductors—in 'high' technology. If a sectoral pattern of success can be observed, or rather, hypothesised about, it is that, in addition to 'high' technology, the European industries most at risk appear to be those most susceptible to product standardisation and mass production, for instance, cars, machine tools, and standard semiconductor devices. Western Europe's greatest strengths appear to have been in industries such as power plant and process plant producing 'one-off' goods (often with a service content), or industries such as textiles and cars where the option was available to find 'up-market' niches when the mass market became threatened. Even in motor cars and machine tools, two industries where Japan's challenge in standard products has been very strong, there are encouraging signs of a positive response by Europe to secure its future position in the world market.

At a broad level, it is hard to dissociate the general process of change from the presence of strong forces of competition. This is perhaps most obvious in industries such as textiles and machine tools where many firms compete and where adjustment in the European industry has been considerable. In such industries adjustment has probably been more successful in Germany and Italy where the industry has been largely left to find its own solutions and less successful in France and the UK where the successful public encouragement of larger firms may well have undermined competitive forces.

In the remaining, more oligopolistic sectors we have looked at this is no less true. The world motor car and semiconductor industries are dominated by a small number of firms, but the opportunities offered by technical change, the high level of international trade, and Japan's ambitions as the newest entrant—pursued through both trade and investment—mean that firm (and country) rankings in the oligopoly can easily and dramatically change, even if the oligopoly persists. Indeed, there is even the prospect of technical change beginning to undermine some oligopolies. In motor cars, for instance, the application of electronics to the assembly line may, by permitting greater flexibility, enable smaller firms to survive profitably.

If oligopolies are most rigid in the steel, shipbuilding and power plant industries, this reflects a comparative absence of technical change, a relatively low level of foreign investment, and the extremeness of the slump forcing already oligopolistic industries further into the arms of national governments which are desperately trying to prevent further erosion of their national industrial base.

The association of change and competition—irrespective of the presence of oligopoly—tells us little about the direction of causation. It is true that a rigid oligopoly is likely to inhibit change. But, as long as the world trading system is as open as it has been up to the present, there is an even more forceful case to be made that industries and governments simply cannot escape the pressures for change.

Finally, what role did the NICs and Japan play in providing competitive pressures? The evidence of the sector studies does not on the whole portray the NICs as a major disruptive pressure for adjustment. They have been important in textiles and shipbuilding (although protection and subsidy have limited their impact), but in other sectors, where they have only been able to compete, if at all, at the bottom of the product spectrum, their impact has been limited. Far from constituting a threat, the NICs helped provide important markets for industries exporting capital goods (for instance, power plant, process plant and machine tools) in the 1970s. In the 1980s, it may be just these exporting industries that will pay the price for increasing European protectionism in more mature industries such as textiles and clothing. The challenge from Japan, concentrated in the engineering industries, appears altogether more formidable for several reasons. First it occurs on export markets (where European countries have traditionally earned a great deal of their foreign exchange requirements), as well as on Western Europe's home market. Secondly, it is increasingly occurring through investment, as well as trade. Thirdly, it is increasingly occurring in more sophisticated industries where it is difficult for threatened producers to 'flee' up-market.

1.3 The adjustment experience in four large European countries and in Japan

The evidence of the sector studies suggests far more useful generalisations by country than by industry. As a starting point, it seems more feasible to find general strategic similarities across sectors within the same country than across countries within the same sector; for instance, the promptness of German firms to move into more specialised markets (for example, in textiles, steel, cars and ships); the strong public role in French industrial development; the recent and growing British propensity to seek cooperation with Japanese firms (in cars, semiconductors, and machine tools); the success of small-scale, cooperative production in Italy. These 'strategic' patterns cannot be taken too far, but they are a useful device for underlining behavioural differences between national industries and governments.

In the following paragraphs we will attempt to give a brief and impressionistic picture of the nature of the adjustment process (and the influence on it of the government–industry–institutional relationship) that is suggested for the four major EEC countries, as well as for Japan, by the evidence of the studies in this book.

Germany

After the initial period of post-war reconstruction had passed, German industrial firms and industries clearly reclaimed the position of European dominance that they had enjoyed since the end of the last century. These firms had a strong market-, export- and future-oriented philosophy.

There has been a sense of greater competition among German firms than among French, Italian or British. Even in the privately cartelised steel industry and the somewhat protected textile industry, firms competed, not necessarily on price, but on strategies for the future. But, as the cases of steel and process plant contracting show, German firms were also capable of cooperation. The degree of competition reflects the size of Germany's industrial sector and the strength of its firms. It has probably also been favoured by Germany's federal political structure (see, for instance, the case of electrical power plant, Chapter 6).

German industry is also characterised by institutional consensus and cooperation. The harmoniousness of its labour relations is well known. Its large banks also play an important coordinating role. In some cases they may be oriented to planning for the future (as Jones suggests for cars in Chapter 5), but the evidence also suggests that they play a conservative role, sometimes rehabilitating distressed firms, sometimes trying to block inward foreign investment.

The Federal government is clearly more prone to intervention than its rhetoric would suggest. This intervention is at times critical and effective. None the less, it is light, not only in its quantity, but also in its objectives which tend to be to provide general support, rather than to engineer specific strategic objectives of firms or industries. Again, it can often afford to be light, given the role of institutions such as banks and the regional (*Land*) governments which are, for instance, often prepared to rescue ailing large firms. Whatever the *ex-post* realities of German intervention, German firms have had a far stronger sense than most of their European counterparts that the government would not bail them out if they got into difficulty. (However, it is also true that Germany's strong private sector has not in the past sought heavy intervention.)

The powerful combination of strong firms, powerful institutions, light public intervention and a strong competitive process has assured Germany a dominant position in the world industrial 'league' for many years, but there is an awareness in Germany that this position may now be threatened, particularly by Japan's strength in the engineering industries. Moreover, market forces do not appear to have whisked Germany to the forefront in the newest technologies: for example, information technology, opto-electronics and bio-technology.

France

After the Second World War France inherited a weak industrial base but a new public commitment to achieve political rehabilitation through economic modernisation. France has achieved considerable success in its efforts to modernise. Different observers have interpreted this achievement as the result either of planning and intervention or of the forces of competition as France joined the European trend towards trade liberalisation. The evidence from our sector studies does not permit definitive judgments. Nevertheless, government intervention in some of the sectors, particularly where technology was more advanced, has been heavy and methodical and has surely gone some way towards creating world-competitive firms.

The pattern of French intervention has certain important characteristics: first, post-war governments were able to build on a tradition of state authority and intervention to enable them to become full participants in strategic decision-making in many cases. Secondly, governments were often able to orchestrate a variety of powerful policy instruments, such as public procurement, non-tariff protection and control of foreign investment, to support the development of 'national champions'. In the absence of the large markets and the larger number of firms typical of Germany or the US, the French government was able to an extent to encourage producer–user relationships by encouraging the development of vertically related groups of companies. A number of these policy instruments, of course, fly in the face of the letter and spirit of the Treaty of Rome.

The main thrust of micro-economic industrial policy did not really change after the socialist election victories in 1981. In some ways, some of the nationalisations of leading French firms were the logical culmination of the policy of 'national champions' that had previously been pursued in some of the leading sectors.

It would, of course, be wrong to see nothing but successful intervention in France. For instance, intervention was not conspicuous for its success in textiles, machine tools or steel. In these sectors, to the extent that it was effective, it tended to encourage the concentration process without substituting any more dynamic objectives such as increased efficiency. Thus France's intervention record is at best patchy, greater success tending to be achieved in industries with larger firms and where long-established industrial structures do not already exist and in industries where public procurement can be used as a carrot.

The UK

The relative strength of UK industries has been waning for over a century. In recent decades the government has become increasingly involved in an effort to stem the decline. The weakness of UK firms perhaps helps to explain the importance of the US presence in some industries (for instance, cars and process plant contracting) and the potential importance of Japanese investment (for example in semiconductors and cars).

The UK industrial system appears to possess little of the 'cement' provided by government links with industry in France and by the banks, inter-firm cooperation and harmonious labour relations in Germany. Indeed, the poor relations among firms, unions and governments have often proven debilitating, for instance in the long-running debates on steel nationalisation and nuclear energy options. In addition, the longer-established industries (for instance, textiles, steel, shipbuilding and motor cars) have clearly suffered from poor labour relations or labour rigidities.

Industrial intervention in the UK has grown considerably, albeit at first unwillingly, against this unpropitious institutional background. It has taken several forms. First, a strong fixation developed in the 1960s with increasing the size of firms, principally through mergers. But this was accompanied by little effective integration of the merged activities and the results of 'unhappy marriages' took a long time to overcome (in the case of British Leyland in cars, for instance). Secondly, industrial intervention showed a strong attachment to technologically ambitious attempts to 'leapfrog' to the technological frontier. Thirdly, intervention has been very much preoccupied with employment, especially regional. It has also often shown itself to be a captive of perceived failures of the private sector. This has often meant nationalisation of failed firms (for instance, British Leyland, British Shipbuilders) and has sometimes resulted in state capitalism in areas that private firms apparently would not enter (for instance, the standard semiconductor devices in which INMOS invested).

However, there is some evidence that governments are learning to intervene more realistically and efficiently. Some technological ambitions are being scaled down (in nuclear energy, for instance), and there is a growing welcome to cooperation with, or investment from, Japanese firms. Governments have become more realistic—not to say ruthless—about problems of overmanning or excess capacity (for example, in cars and steel).

In spite of its public commitment to minimal intervention, the new Conservative government of 1979 hardly broke the continuity of Britain's trend towards widespread and gradually more effective intervention. On the contrary, there appears to be a new commitment to the support of high-technology industries.

There is likewise much talk of a new realism in British management, particularly since the deep recession for UK industry that began in 1979. Some improvements in productivity are no doubt partly the result of closer government–industry cooperation, but they also derive from a weakening of union bargaining power as unemployment has risen.

Italy

Italy entered the post-war period more underdeveloped than France. Its rapid subsequent development enabled it to enjoy some of the fruits of the virtuous circle of growth that Japan also enjoyed, for instance, the building up of a modern steel industry in tandem with the rapid growth of steel-using industries (such as consumer durables). Without the strong state apparatus available to the French, Italian efforts to catch up with North-Western Europe went in two directions: on the one hand, trade liberalisation to stimulate Italy's dynamic, often smaller-scale entrepreneurs; on the other hand, the development of infant industries through the state-holding formula (principally IRI which is represented in almost all the sectors covered in this book).

The development of industries new to Italy through IRI and other state-holding companies was a device to keep them clear of the political controversies in which Italy's weak central governments were continually involved. However, like the large firms of the private sector, such as Fiat, they could not altogether avoid these controversies (for instance, in cars and nuclear power). IRI, internalising some of the important producer–user relationships much like the French groups, has on the whole proven a reasonably successful formula for the development of risky new activities, such as semiconductors and process plant contracting, in somewhat difficult conditions. However, Italian public enterprises have also become captive instruments of government policies to develop the South and, during the 1970s, policies to maintain public employment.

Italy has also been remarkable for the role of 'decentralised production' in which small firms, often paying low wages, have engaged in competition and cooperation (through subcontracting, for instance) with other small firms in a kind of collective entrepreneurship. This has happened in a number of industries where scale factors have not been dominant, for example, in textiles and machine tools. Decentralised production is partly the product of Italy's political system—a succession of weak governments of the centre-right subject to clientelist pressures from within their own ranks and to substantial opposition from the political parties and the trade unions to their left. This system has made the operation of larger firms very difficult. It helps explain the emergence of a 'perverse' Italian specialisation in exports from the more labour-intensive industrial branches in the 1970s.

Japan

In view of Japan's phenomenal industrial success, it is useful to try to draw some lessons from its adjustment experience (particularly as it is represented in Chapter 10). It would be difficult to deny the importance of heavy, broadly-based intervention in the launching of many Japanese industries. Thereafter, however, this intervention appears to have given way (not always willingly) to a more general form of intervention creating an environment for industry (for example, through protection from foreign imports or investment), without specifically trying to guide it.

At this point, as the private sector takes over the burden, three crucial features should be emphasised. First, the private sector operates with strong and clear expectations about future government liberalisation of import and investment controls. Secondly, the level of competition among a number of strong Japanese firms on domestic, then export, markets appears to be marked. Thirdly, industrial capacity is powerfully reinforced by certain cultural features, particularly cultural homogeneity and consensus on national objectives, which help create an identity of interest between firms and the nation, and group loyalty, which helps create an identity of interests between the individual and the firm.

It has recently become fashionable to see France as that European country most following in Japanese footsteps. In our interpretation of Japan's industrial system, since the 1970s at least, Germany would perhaps come nearer as an industrial society, given its emphasis on broad policies for the industrial environment rather than specific structural policies, the importance of the process of competition among powerful German firms, and the coordinating role of the banks (somewhat akin to the role of the interlocking groups of Japanese companies, the *Zaibatsu*).

1.4 The dilemma of intervention

The subject of this chapter has been Western Europe's capacity to compete in a period when the pressures for change, and the risks of failure turning into protection, appear particularly great. The success of Europe's adjustment response has been patchy—neither all bad, nor all good—across sectors and countries. We have emphasised the role of competitive forces, both in transmitting pressures for change and in often providing the basis for a successful adjustment response. Because of the clear differences in the 'style' and degree of success of national adjustment responses, we have also chosen to emphasise the way the four largest Western European economies have responded, rather than to treat Western Europe, or the EEC, as one unified economy. This has been at the real risk of understating the considerable amount of economic integration that has taken place. But in the sector studies a salient point that has emerged is the extent of national intervention measures (in spite of the spirit and rules of the Treaty of Rome and the GATT in all four countries for virtually every sector. The intervention dilemma is that of four medium-large countries trying to engineer a competitive presence in a full range of industrial activities with instruments of public intervention that are not necessarily very effective and that threaten the well-being of the international economic system.

Our sector studies confirm much other evidence that Western European intervention is widespread and growing. It took a particular leap forward towards the end of the 1970s with the tightening of the EEC steel cartel (1977–80), the restrictive renewal of the Multi-Fibre Arrangement in textiles (1978), and Japan's application of restraints on its car exports to most major producing countries in the EEC (1981). The timing of these developments is, of course, bound up with the pressures building up since 1973. The increase in intervention in part reflects the unwillingness or inability of OECD governments to solve their macro-economic problems of recession and price and exchange rate instability. If these problems could be solved, the intervention process might be considerably diminished.

However, a substantial part of intervention is motivated by the objective of maintaining national industrial competitiveness. It would probably have grown even in the absence of recession. Indeed, the governments of the four Western European countries appear to seek to maintain a competitive, at least partly indigenous, industry in a full range of industrial activities deemed to be important.

It is useful at this point to draw a distinction between what we shall call *environmental* intervention, which changes the general environment in which firms, sectors or industries operate (for instance, by broad measures of protection or general tax incentives which may be effective at the macro-economic, industry-wide or even sectoral level), and *structural* intervention, which supports specific size-structures of industry, specific firms or specific strategies through more pinpointed forms of aid. For example, if a sector enjoys a regime of non-tariff protection (simply raising the domestic selling price for all firms), the intervention is, in our sense, environmental. If, instead, a government subsidises certain target firms whose strategy it wishes to support or influence, the intervention is structural. Of course, the distinction between the two cannot be rigorous, but it serves to make an important distinction in the 'heaviness' of intervention and the extent to which it replaces or reinforces competitive forces.

A good deal of German intervention has been environmental and has probably helped firms to pursue their strategies without influencing these strategies. It could be argued that this emphasis was appropriate in a situation in which firms were strong and sufficiently numerous to provide for some competition, even in more oligopolistic industries. France, on the other hand, has followed a policy of largely structural intervention. This has had a measure of success in building up some high-technology industries in areas where the private sector might not have ventured,but it has also had its notable failures. Structural intervention has also dominated the UK, with considerably less success. Italy, as ever, is hard to classify: the government was perhaps a would-be pursuer of structural intervention, but the state-holding formula kept governments at arm's length. Recent Japanese intervention appears to emphasise environmental, rather than structural, elements.

There are clearly many instances where intervention *can* be effective nationally. On the other hand, there are an equal number of instances where intervention is ineffective or wasteful. Moreover, intervention tends to beget more intervention, not only in the well-known sense that intervention in one part of the economy (for example, protection of a high-priced domestic steel industry) may create the need for intervention elsewhere (for example, subsidies to shipbuilders buying high-priced local steel), but also in the sense that governments risk becoming captives of the industry in which they intervene. For instance, governments may need to justify past investment decisions that have gone wrong by making further investments; alternatively, their structural policies may help create the large firms most capable of exerting pressure on them for further intervention (this was the case in UK and French textiles).

Finally, the evidence suggests that, from a national viewpoint, first-best policies tend to be those that combine competition with the 'right' environmental policies, while structural policies are second-best, resorted to in situations where strong firms are few on the ground and the prospects for competition among firms are poor —for instance, because of the size of the market (admittedly, the point being made here risks confusing cause and effect: structural policies can often be argued to be the consequence, rather than the cause, of the 'failure' of the private sector.)

National intervention at the level we have observed in Western Europe—both in its environmental and structural forms, but perhaps more particularly in the latter—is clearly at odds with the functioning of the GATT and EEC systems for trade in industrial goods. Both systems seek to allow market forces to operate internationally through a relatively simple set of rules emphasising non-discrimination and the need for minimal, transparent and predictable distortions of trade. Reconciling the interests of the international system and of nation states convinced of the need to intervene to improve their competitive position is not easy. Much economic history could be interpreted to suggest that nations rarely catch up from behind through market forces alone and that it is precisely the leading nations who most favour the unalloyed rule of market forces internationally.

In their individual efforts to catch up, Western Europe's large countries find themselves in some way in the worst of all worlds. They are not as large as the US or Japan and do not derive the consequent benefits of a large domestic market. On the other hand, they have a sufficiently illustrious history and a sufficiently large economy (unlike smaller industrial powers such as the Netherlands, Switzerland and Sweden) to have individual national pretentions to be 'full-range' producers. However, their national markets are simply not large enough for effective competition among domestic producers in all sectors. This goes a long way towards explaining the proliferation of industrial intervention in these countries.

The larger market of the European Community would seem to offer some ways out of the dilemmas posed by the partial ineffectiveness of national intervention and the growing international frictions it causes. But translating the structural interventionist approach from Member States to the Community level—that is, moving from 'national champions' to 'Community champions'—has not so far been very successful and is not likely to work in the future, if only because inter-governmental rivalries are so strong.

On the other hand, is there not a strong argument for replacing national structural policies with Community environmental policies; in other words, for trying to replace the entrepreneurial and 'picking-the-winner' activities of national governments with the forces of competition at a Community level? This, of course, is the original intent of the Customs Union and, indeed, tremendous progress towards more effective intra-Community competition was made in the 1960s and 1970s (see Table 1.1). This progress is now somewhat threatened by the growth of national intervention and internal barriers to trade. In any case, much more progress can still be made in the sectors we have looked at, but Western European nations would have to start by casting off the illusion that they can individually remain full-range competitive producers.

This plea for more Community competition is, of course, not new, but many Western European countries have so far failed to take much notice of the arguments behind it. This failure does not make the price to pay any less: the limitations and dangers of intervention and the impact of competition are certainly worth restating.

Notes

1. Our estimates for 1960, 1970 and 1978 are based on data in UNCTAD (various years). Maizels (1963, Table 8.11) provides data on a somewhat different basis for 1899–1959, but these can be linked, if tenuously, to the UNCTAD data by comparing figures for 1959–60.
2. Some studies have adopted a primarily statistical approach. See, for example, *European Economy* (1979), United Nations (1977) and (1981), and Saunders (1982). Others have looked in more qualitative terms at Europe in the international system; for instance, OECD (1979a) and Pinder (1982). OECD (1979b), Saunders (1981), and Turner and McMullen (1982) have looked at Europe's place in the international division of labour in the context of studies of industrialised and newly industrialising countries. Tsoukalis and White (1982) have looked at the evolution of Western Europe's relationship with Japan. Other studies on Western Europe have had a more policy-oriented approach; for instance, National Economic Development Office (1981) and Commission of the European Communities (1981). De Jong's (1981) book on the structure of European industry is notable for its sectoral approach. However, most of the sectors covered are different from those in the present book, while the approach in the individual sector studies tends to put less emphasis on a comparative-national approach and somewhat more emphasis on the structure-conduct-performance approach familiar from the literature on industrial organisation.
3. Shonfield (1965).
4. For example, the share of the ten largest firms in German manufacturing industry's sales in 1975 averages (on an unweighted basis) 42 per cent. Equivalent figures for sectors corresponding more or less with sectors studied in this book were: mechanical engineering (including machine tools), 18 per cent; road motor vehicles, 80 per cent; shipbuilding, 78 per cent; electrical engineering (including semiconductors and power plant), 48 per cent; basic iron and steel industries, 75 per cent; textiles, 10 per cent. (See Table A33 of Horn, 1982.)

References

Commission of the European Communities (1981), *Report of the Study Group on Industrial Policies in the Community: State Intervention and Structural Adjustment* (II/419/80-EN Final), Brussels.

De Jong, H. W., ed. (1981), *The Structure of European Industry*, The Hague: Martinus Nijhoff.

European Economy (1979), 'Report of the Group of Experts on Sectoral Analyses: changes in industrial structure in the European economies since the oil crisis, 1973-78—Europe: its capacity to change in question' (Special Issue), Brussels: Commission of the European Communities.

Horn, E.-J. (1982), *Management of Industrial Change in Germany*, Sussex European Papers No. 13, Brighton: Sussex European Research Centre.

Maizels, A. (1963), *Industrial Growth and World Trade*, Cambridge: Cambridge University Press.

National Economic Development Office (1981), *Industrial Policies in Europe*, London.

OECD (1979a), *Interfutures: Facing the Future*, Paris.

OECD (1979b), *The Impact of the Newly Industrialising Countries on Production and Trade in Manufactures*, Paris.

Pinder, J., ed. (1982), *National Industrial Strategies and the World Economy*, London: Allanheld, Osmun and Croom Helm.

Saunders, C., ed. (1981), *The Political Economy of New and Old Industrial Countries*, London: Butterworths.

Saunders, C. (1982), 'Changes in the Distribution of World Production and Trade', in Pinder (1982).

Shonfield, A. (1965), *Modern Capitalism: the Changing Balance of Public and Private Power*, London: Oxford University Press.

Tsoukalis, L., and White, M., eds (1982), *Japan and Western Europe: Conflict and Cooperation*, London: Frances Pinter.

Turner, L., and McMullen, N. (1982), *The Newly Industrialising Countries: Trade and Adjustment*, London: George Allen & Unwin.

United Nations (1977), *Structure and Change in European Industry*, New York.

United Nations (1981), *Economic Survey of Europe in 1980*, New York (see Ch. 4, 'Changes in the Structure of West European Manufacturing Industry in the 1970s').

UNCTAD (various years), *Handbook of Trade and Development Statistics*, New York (*Supplement 1977*, 1978; *Supplement 1980*, 1981; *Supplement 1981*, 1982).

2 TEXTILES: NEW WAYS OF SURVIVING IN AN OLD INDUSTRY*

Geoffrey Shepherd

2.1 Introduction

This chapter examines the record of industrial change in the textile industries of the major Western European countries, namely the Federal Republic of Germany, France, Italy and the UK. A comparison is also made with the US where a market of continental proportions has altered the problems facing the textile industry.

Textiles sit in the middle of a complex chain of production starting with the natural and man-made fibres and ending with making-up industries turning textiles into clothing (about one-half of the total market for made-up goods) or household or industrial goods (about one-quarter each of the market). Within textiles, individual branches retain much of their traditional separate identities: the cotton and wool industries (and smaller industries such as jute and carpets) spin, weave and finish textile fibres, while the knitting industry produces either cloth or fully fashioned knitwear.

Most of these branches use technologies that are not particularly sophisticated compared to other industrial activities in advanced countries, and employ relatively unskilled labour, often female or immigrant. Plant economies of scale are limited, especially in knitting, but economies associated with long production runs are more substantial. The industry produces a range of goods from highly standardised to fashion-differentiated, the degree of differentiation increasing generally with successive stages of production. Thus product innovation tends to be the result of design and marketing rather than technology. While the textile industry has a number of relatively large firms, often dominating narrowly defined submarkets, it has an essentially competitive structure: there is significant ease of entry for new firms on national markets, although such entry is more commonly the result of imports than of newly created home firms.

This chapter will tend to concentrate, within textiles, on the cotton industry as this is the part of the industry that has faced the most significant trade-related problems of adjustment. The clothing industry as such is not covered except inasmuch as it represents

* This chapter is a revised and shortened version of Shepherd (1981).

the most important source of derived demand for textiles. Both textiles and clothing show similar characteristics as mature industries, yet greater technological sophistication and average firm size in textiles mean that substantially different patterns of comparative advantage and survival options persist.

In spite of its apparent maturity and declining levels of output and employment, the textile industry in industrialised countries continues to be at the centre of change resulting from the intensity of international competition and the speed of technical change. (See Section 2.2.) The prospect of decline has brought forth a variety of 'survival responses' from the governments and firms. These strategies for survival, and the national environments which help shape them, are the subject of Section 2.3. The final part of this chapter is concerned with drawing some of the lessons from the case study about the past effectiveness of public policies and the relevance of these lessons to the future.

2.2. Change and decline[1]

The pressures for change

The massive liberalisation of trade since the Second World War has provided a continuing impetus to change in national textile industries. This impetus has come not only from the increasing importance of the Third World in global textile production, but also from enormous increases in trade among high-wage countries. The trade-intensity ratios (imports/consumption, exports/production) in Table 2.1 provide some summary measures of these changes for the cotton industry in the 1960s and 1970s.

The post-war development of 'low-cost' (that is, low-wage) producers (the developing countries, the low-wage countries of Southern Europe, and the centrally planned economies) has resulted in a significant growth of exports to industrialised countries. The major export thrust has been in cotton yarn and cloth (and some synthetic textiles). These products have become the object of a network of non-tariff restrictions (see Section 2.3). But this did not prevent a very large growth in low-cost imports which by 1978 accounted for 16 to 30 per cent of consumption of cotton and man-made-fibre cloth in the big four countries of the EEC. Very often restrictions on low-cost imports have merely tended to encourage imports from non-restricted sources.

In any case, the strengths of industrialised countries in areas such as synthetic textiles have meant *no* deterioration in their overall textile trade balances with the rest of the world. In clothing, on the

Table 2.1 Cotton industry: trade intensity ratios, 1962–81 (per cent, based on weight of production and trade of cotton and man-made-fibre woven cloth)

	1962	1969	1976	1978	1979	1980	1981
Germany							
P/C	102	96	103	103	104	102	123
IM/C	12	22	48	58	63	59	63
LCIM/C	1	4	14	16	17	17	..
ECIM/C	8	14	27	33	35	30	..
EX/P	13	19	50	59	64	59	70
France							
P/C	125	95	77	82	77	77	(82)
IM/C	6	25	51	58	61	59	(60)
LCIM/C	1	7	15	16	17	18	..
ECIM/C	4	16	28	33	34	31	..
EX/P	25	22	36	48	50	46	(51)
Italy							
P/C	112	111	87	115	93	86	(111)
IM/C	5	20	51	70	71	62	57
LCIM/C	2	8	21	25	27	23	..
ECIM/P	1	8	18	24	19	21	..
EX/P	15	28	44	74	69	56	(61)
UK							
P/C	82	78	64	55	53	54	..
IM/C	31	35	56	65	68	74	..
LCIM/C	19	23	31	30	31	29	..
ECIM/C	12*	13*	14	25	25	30	..
EX/P	15	17	32	36	39	51	..
US							
P/C	98	97	98	97	100	100	(96)
IM/C	4	5	6	7	5	7	(9)
LCIM/C	2	3	5	..	3	5	..
EX/P	1	3	5	4	5	6	(5)

P: Production.
C: Consumption (Production + imports − exports).
IM: Imports (including from EEC member-countries).
LCIM: Low-cost imports, i.e. from developing countries, Southern European countries (except Italy), and centrally planned economies.
ECIM: Imports from other EEC member-countries.
EX: Exports (including to EEC member-countries).
* All industrialised countries.

Sources: Textile Statistics Bureau, *Quarterly Statistical Review*, Manchester, various issues; UN, *Commodity Trade Statistics, Series D*, New York, various issues; OECD, *Commodity Trade Statistics, Series C*, Paris, various issues.

other hand, low-wage exporters have realised a far stronger comparative advantage. As a result the deterioration of industrialised-country
trade balances in clothing have tended to reduce their domestic
demand for textiles. Among the countries we are looking at, this
process has been particularly marked in Germany and the US. (See
Table 2.2 for the evolution of textile and clothing trade balances
relative to production in Western Europe.)

Contrary to superficial impressions, the pressure from increasing
intra-Western-European trade in textiles has been as important as
that coming from trade with the Third World. For instance, the four
large EEC countries now typically import between 20 and 40 per
cent of cotton and man-made fibre cloth consumed from each other
(see Table 2.1).

Table 2.2 The share of exports and imports in gross output of the textile and
clothing industry, 1970 and 1978 (per cent, based on value)

Country	Imports/Gross Output				Exports/Gross Output			
	Textiles		Clothing		Textiles		Clothing	
	1970	1978	1970	1978	1970	1978	1970	1978
Finland	55.5	70.7	9.5	11.8	22.9	36.9	27.8	51.5
France	14.5	29.2	6.3	15.3	22.6	26.7	13.6	17.4
Germany	27.0	44.0	13.4	37.3	23.1	34.2	5.8	12.3
Italy	14.0	20.7	1.9	2.5	35.1	49.2	25.6	35.3
Netherlands	74.4	97.1*	51.3	142.9*	63.2	82.1*	28.3	44.5*
Norway	107.4	117.1	59.3	158.4	21.7	24.0	8.1	9.1
Sweden	81.0	98.9	43.5	119.2	23.4	35.9	13.7	31.6
UK	12.7	27.9	9.7	24.6	17.5	23.3	9.2	15.2

* 1977.

Source: Table 4.3.10 of UN, Economic Commission for Europe, *Changes in the Structure
of West European Manufacturing Industry in the 1970s*, New York, 1981.

, Since the Second World War, substantial technical changes have
occurred in traditional textile processes, in substitute processes and in
raw materials. In the cotton system, for instance, a post-war backlog
in modernisation investments in Western Europe, continuous improvements in conventional techniques and the commercial availability from
the 1960s of new techniques (particularly in open-end spinning and
shuttleless weaving) have provided the opportunity for continuing high
productivity gains from new investments (see Table 2.3). Technological opportunities were far more restricted in clothing.

Table 2.3 Growth of output, employment and labour productivity in the
textile industry, 1963–81.

	1963	1973	1975	1978	1979	1980	1981
Index of production							
(1973 = 100)							
Germany	76	100	92	96	96	94	87
France	85	100	89	90	93	89	(81)
Italy	87	100	90	97	110	115	(112)
UK	90	100	87	87	83	70	64
US	56	100	85	96	101	97	95
Employment (000)							
Germany	568	431	354	320	309	306	281
France	(459)	406	371	329	318	307	285
Italy	..	377	352	315	..	295	290
UK	720	557	507	457	447	393	354
US	863	1,178	996	1,019	999	970	950
Index of Labour Productivity							
(1973 = 100)							
Germany	58	100	112	131	135	134	135
France	74	100	96	110	117	117	(114)
Italy	..	100	97	116	..	..	..
UK	69	100	95	102	100	104	97
US	76	100	101	111	119	118	118

Sources: Basic series for production (1975 = 100), employment, and labour productivity
were given for 1963–78 in Wilhelm Kurth, *Textiles and Clothing: a National and International Issue*, International Symposium on Industrial Policies for the Eighties, Madrid,
May 1980. These have been rebased to 1973 and updated on the basis of indices from
OECD, *Indicators of Industrial Activity*, Paris, quarterly.

Synthetic fibres, first commercially available after the Second
World War, have been the source of much technological change.
Initially, industrialised countries had a strong comparative advantage
in the production of these versatile fibres; proximity gave the textile
industries of the industrialised countries a comparative advantage in
their processing. Synthetics permitted a boom in knitting at the
expense of weaving during the 1960s. By the 1970s, with the most
significant new fibre developments long past, synthetics reduced to
commodity status, and increasing synthetic fibre production in many
developing countries, this advantage had been largely lost. Moreover,
the switch in consumption from natural to synthetic fibres has
slowed down.
  In recent years, undoubtedly the most important direct effect on
levels of textile production has come from the general recessionary

conditions that set in after 1973 and became particularly marked after 1979. Consumer expenditure on clothing in the EEC has stagnated in real terms since 1973.

Textile activity in high-income countries, and trade between them, has been sustained in recent decades by fashion changes. The opportunities offered by this kind of product differentiation have been crucial to the survival of Western European textiles.

The record of decline

Changes in levels of activity in textiles are most conveniently measured in output, and employment statistics (see Table 2.3), and changes in competitive capacity by changes in trade balances (see Tables 2.1 and 2.2). Since the Second World War, and up to 1973, textile output grew healthily in industrialised countries, but rarely faster than manufacturing as a whole. Since 1973, output has largely stagnated (Germany and the US) or declined (France and particularly the UK); the growth of Italian textiles in this period is the major exception.

In the 1960s and up to 1973, a strong productivity performance in Western Europe had meant a steady shedding of textile jobs (Table 2.3). Lower US productivity gains, on the other hand, had led to modest employment creation. The continuation of productivity growth in all five countries after the recession, but not as rapid as before and faltering from around 1979, combined with stagnating or declining output to create substantial labour-shedding in textiles: in 1973–81 Germany, France and the UK lost around one-third of their 1973 textile labour force and the US, almost one-fifth. On the other hand, Italy, whose industrial statistics tend to be out-of-date and to provide inadequate coverage of the thriving small-scale sector, appears to have maintained textile employment far better.

This acceleration in the rate of job loss has occurred in miserable circumstances, in a period when manufacturing employment was falling and the overall unemployment rate was rising. From 1973 to 1981, the four countries of the European Community lost well over half a million textile jobs, equivalent to well over 1 per cent of the total manufacturing labour force in Germany, France and Italy, and 3 per cent in the UK. US employment losses of under a quarter million represented 1 per cent of manufacturing employment. The spread of short-time working in recent years has added to the real loss of wage-earning opportunities. It is probably in the UK and France, with high regional concentration and, in the UK at least, a poor overall economic performance, that absorption problems have been worst.

Since 1973 Italy's textile industry proved the most successful survivor, achieving some growth in output (largely through growing textile and clothing exports) and minimising employment losses. US survival was not as spectacular, but both output and employment were maintained thanks to a continuing low level of trade compared to output. The poor output and employment performance of French and UK textiles, on the other hand, reflects declining trade balances *vis-à-vis* both low- and high-wage countries. Germany, whose government was among the least politically committed to the defence of its textile industry, was able to maintain textile output and exports as the result of a productivity performance that meant more rapidly falling textile employment than in any other country.

2.3 National strategies for survival

In a world of many adjustment pressures and an unknowable future, textile firms in industrialised countries have placed their bets for profitable survival or growth, sometimes for profitable exit, by adopting one, or a mix, of a number of possible strategies. Most of these strategies have been long in gestation, pre-dating the recession of the 1970s. Of these 'survival' responses to an almost permanent sense of crisis, the best known has been government intervention aimed at stemming the tide of decline with measures to protect and restructure. But large parts of the industries themselves have made substantial efforts to regain their competitiveness, variously through new technologies, new products, economies of scale, foreign investment, diversification, or the exploitation of dual labour markets.

Of course, national textile industries contain a mix of firms pursuing a mix of strategies. Yet I shall try to identify typical or dominant strategies that differentiate one country from another, at the margin at least, and relate these differences in strategic emphasis to differences in national 'business environments' and public policies. As a background to discussion of individual countries, I shall first examine the evidence on firm size-structure and briefly recount the international development of protection in textiles.

Size-structure

In spite of the similar size and openness to trade of the textile markets in the big four EEC countries, national firm size-structures have evolved very differently. Data from Table 2.4 (distribution of employment by different sizes of firm) and Table 2.5 (ratios of employment in the largest firms to total textile employment),

Table 2.4 Employment distribution by firm size in the textile industry, various years

Size category by number of employees	Germany			France		Italy	UK	
	1964	1970	1978	1970	1979	1975	1970	1978
0-19	*	*	*	} 20[†] } 23		*	} 12 } 14	
20-99	14	13	15			37		
100-199	13	12	14	12	15	18	8	8
200-499	25	25	27	18	21	21	13	12
500-999	18	20	19	} 50 } 42		11	11	11
1,000 or more	30	29	25			13	56	56
Total	100*	100*	100*	100[†]	100	100*‡	100	100

* Size category of 0–19 employees excluded.
† Excludes firms with 0–5 employees.
‡ A comparison of industrial census data (covering only firms with more than 20 workers) with labour force survey data for 1975 suggests that the Italian textiles and clothing industries combined employed roughly the same magnitude of workers in firms with more than 20 employees as in smaller firms, out-working and independent workers.

Sources: Michael Breitenacher, *Textilindustrie: Strukturwandlungen und Entwicklungsperspektiven für die achtziger Jahre*, Berlin: Duncker & Humblot, 1981; Lynn Krieger Mytelka, 'In search of a partner: the state and the textile industry in France', in S. Cohen and P. Gourevitch, eds, *France in a Troubled World Economy*, London: Butterworths, 1982; Eurostat, *Structure and Activity of Industry, 1975*, Vol. 1978-XV, 1979; Business Statistics Office, *1970 Report on the Census of Production, Summary Tables*, C 54 Business Monitor, London: HMSO, 1976; Business Statistics Office, *1978 Report on the Census of Production, Summary Tables*, PA 1002, Business Monitor, London: HMSO, 1980.

together with other indicators of the evolution of size-structure, tell quite distinct stories which can be summarised as follows:

—Germany: in the last two decades medium-to-large firms (typically employing between 200 and 3,000 workers, none employing more than 6,000) have been dominant, with a moderate trend to deconcentration evident in the 1970s;

—France: a pronounced concentration got underway in the 1960s, resulting in a highly concentrated industry, dominated during the 1970s by some four giant groups, each employing at least 10,000;

—UK: an even more powerful concentration process lasted from the 1960s to the mid-1970s to make it the most concentrated of the major world textile industries, dominated in the 1970s by five giant groups each employing at least 20,000;

—Italy: since the 1950s there has been a prounced deconcentration

Table 2.5 The concentration of large firms in the EEC, US and Japanese textile industries, 1965–80

	Germany	Belgium	France	Italy	Netherlands	UK	Total EEC	US	Japan
A. Cumulative ratio of employment in largest firms (by size of sales) to total textile employment									
1965									
3	4	7	10	6	23	16	8	16	6
5	6	9	12	9	30	21	9	20	8
10	11	11	14	..	..	28	11	29	12
1970									
3	6	..	13	8	23	45	13	15	6
5	10	..	17	10	25	52	15	18	8
10	15	..	23	14	..	57	19	25	11
1975									
3	5	..	17	8	22	40	12	15	6
5	7	..	19	12	26	53	16	18	8
10	16	..	21	16	..	70	17	26	10
1980									
3	4	(14)	22	(5)	22	43	12	13	3
5	7	(18)	26	(7)	25	56	15	17	5
10	14	..	30	(10)†	..	67	21	24	8
B. Number of large textile firms by size class of turnover in m. DM, 1980*									
More than 1,000	–	1	4	–	–	5	9	13	6
400–1,000	7	2	1	3	1	9	22	12	9
100–400	45	6	20	12	2	13	100	12‡	17
Total	52	9	25	15	3	27	131	37‡	32

* DM = $0.55.
† Nine firms only.
‡ Excluding size class of 100–200 m. DM.

(Notes and sources opposite.)

process leaving Italy with relatively few large firms and a dominant role for small firms of 100 employees or less (most of them far less).

Concentration appears to correlate with the dominance of typical large-firm strategies: mass production, foreign investment and diversification out of textiles. The dominance of small or medium firms can be associated with strategies of flexibility, product innovation and exporting. It is telling, if simplistic, to observe that the ranking of the four countries by their capacity for suvival in the 1970s (as measured by the output growth figures of table 2.3 or the evolution of the trade balance that can be calculated from Table 2.2) corresponds more or less with the ranking of 'unconcentratedness': that is, Italy as the least concentrated and the best survivor, followed in order by Germany, France and the UK. Thus size-structure appears to be related to firm conduct and industry performance but, as I shall argue, size-structure may be as much the result of conduct—or strategic choice—as *vice versa*.

The evolution of protection[2]

High tariffs were an important source of textile and clothing protection in much of Western Europe up to the early 1970s, by which time tariff cuts and the extension of the EEC and of its preferential arrangements had removed much of their effect. High tariffs continue to be important in the US. But by far the most important form of protection on both sides of the Atlantic since the 1960s has been provided by discriminatory non-tariff restrictions, mostly within the context of various international agreements negotiated with GATT. The original Long Term Arrangement for International Trade in Cotton Textiles (LTA), in effect for five years from 1962, was largely meant to allow the industries of the importing (industrialized) countries a temporary 'breathing space' to adjust to increased cotton textile imports from low-wage countries (which, until the mid-1970s, included Japan). The breathing space turned out to be too short and the LTA was twice renewed before it was replaced in 1974 by an agreement that embraced all the major textile fibres, the

Note: The ratio of employment in large textile firms (derived from firms' annual reports) to total textile employment (derived from public statistics) in Part A of this Table is not a precise concentration of the ratio since large-firm employment figures include employment in non-textile activities and foreign subsidiaries.

Sources: Calculated from: (i) large-firm employment data in *Textilwirtschaft*, Frankfurt, No. 15 of 13 April 1967, No. 2 of 11 January 1973, No. 8 of 24 February 1977, and No. 53 of 31 December 1981; and (ii) textile-industry employment data from same sources as Table 2.3.

Arrangement Regarding International Trade in Textiles, better known as the Multi-Fibre Arrangement (MFA).

The first wave of low-cost cotton textile imports, in the late 1950s and early 1960s, was largely borne by the US and the UK which both moved quickly to control it by quotas or negotiated 'voluntary' export restraints. US controls appear to have been tighter than UK controls which allowed substantial import penetration from developing countries (Table 2.1). Germany, France and Italy, until the mid-1960s at least, kept out most low-cost imports with a combination of tariffs and small quotas (a factor which added to the pressure on the US and UK markets), but the decade up to the mid-1970s saw a very substantial growth of their low-cost imports.

The first renewal of the MFA in 1978 saw the installation of a system of tight, global control in the EEC, negotiated under a Community umbrella, but based on bilateral quotas and administration. The onset of recession had helped remove the margins within which Community producers had previously felt able to absorb import growth. In 1982 the MFA was once more extended, until 1986, and the EEC obtained restrictive conditions.

Overall, the US appears to have emerged as the most consistently protectionist of the five countries in both tariff and quota policy. At the other end of the spectrum, Germany appeared to be the most liberal importer, to the point where cloth quotas were beginning to become redundant by 1976. Even after 1978, Germany's policing of low-cost imports was noticeably more relaxed than that of France or the UK.

Germany: liberalisation and competition[3]

In the period of post-war reconstruction, the German textile industry, having inherited a strong entrepreneurial base, enjoyed a reasonable level of import protection. But it was also very aware that trade liberalisation would increase intra-European trade, especially after the creation of the EEC in 1958. In the 1960s these liberalisation prospects came to include imports from low-cost sources as the industry, for instance, saw how the Federal government allowed a large growth in Yugoslavian and Hong Kong clothing imports. Apart from import policy, there was no other significant sectoral policy for textiles.

In the 1960s the industry embarked on a period of experiment and competition in strategies. Many leading firms adopted a strategy of vertical and horizontal concentration (both to exploit economies of scale and to achieve market power), and of capital-intensification. This *mass-market* strategy aimed at staying cost-competitive in the domestic market for standardised cloth through economies of scale and long runs. Other leading firms opted for a strategy of market niches—or *specialisation*—in fashion goods, household textiles and industrial textiles. This strategy emphasised flexible response (through a more modest scale of operation, but also through technological upgrading), marketing skills, and exports. On the whole, the mass-market strategy appeared to dominate German textiles in the 1960s, leading to some increase in the role of large firms (Table 2.5).

German textile exports were also helped in the 1960s by the substantial growth of the offshore activities of the clothing industry which was increasingly having German yarns and fabrics made up in Eastern European or Mediterranean countries through foreign investments or subcontracting arrangements. German 'outward-processing' tariff provisions, requiring duty to be charged only on value added abroad, were instrumental in this.[4]

In the early 1970s further liberalisation of low-cost textile and clothing imports combined with rapidly rising real wage costs (as a result of DM revaluation) to shift the balance of advantage against the mass-market strategy. In the course of the decade many of the practitioners of this strategy collapsed or converted to the specialisation strategy. This verdict of the market place is reflected in the 1970s in a mild deconcentration process and in the rapid growth of exports, to the point where Germany has become the world's largest textile exporter in spite of its high wage levels. Yet rapid productivity increases and the substantially faster shrinkage of the clothing industry have not spared Germany from a rapid loss of textile jobs.

Except for its import policy, which in 1978 took a turn towards greater restrictiveness, the Federal government has remained meticulous in standing at the sidelines. Politically this abstinence was made easier by the Regional (*Land*) governments frequently stepping in, often with the aid of the banks, to rescue ailing firms.

Compared to most other Western European governments, Germany is thus noteworthy for the success it has achieved by applying something approaching a competitive-market solution to the restructuring problem. Public intervention was noteworthy for the absence of a structural policy and the pursuit of a clear liberalisation policy, until 1978 at least. In this latter respect the German textile industry, even today, is notable for its strong commitment to market principles (that, however, stops short of accepting imports based on so-called unfair wages), and its continuing strong sense that the government would not act to guarantee its survival.

Yet I would argue that there are important features that help explain the success of this textile policy in the particular German context. First, Germany had an initially strong entrepreneurial base which was able to experiment in restructuring under the shelter of residual non-tariff protectionism and an undervalued DM until the end of the 1960s. Secondly, restructuring has clearly been helped by relatively harmonious labour relations, the result of a strong and unified trade-union organisation in textiles, of legislation on co-determination, and of the general consensual political ideology of post-war Germany. Thirdly, the relatively dynamic German economy has been able to mop up textile unemployment with little difficulty. These felicitous initial conditions enabled the German textile industry to explore the paths of successful restructuring before the world recession took hold. It is arguable that the initial conditions did as much to shape liberal policies in textiles as did these policies to create successful restructuring.

France: protection and dualism[5]

The French textile industry emerged from the Second World War relatively backward, dominated by the kind of smaller industrial units that had typified pre-war French industrial weakness. Government policy at first did little to change this; it provided heavy protection to textiles, supported marginal firms through subsidising short-time working, and encouraged the cotton industry to see an important part of its future in colonial markets in West Africa.

The 1960s saw both the gradual loss of these markets (after African independence) and new adjustment pressures created by membership of the EEC. In a competitive response a number of larger, more modern textile groups began to constitute themselves (particularly in the cotton industry) through merger and investment and to seek economies of scale, as well as to retain African markets through foreign investment. While some of the remaining smaller firms moved towards a European specialisation strategy, a rupture of interests began to develop from this period between large, typically modernising, and small, typically old-fashioned firms. At first the concentration process was largely autonomous, although it took place in a period in which the French industrial fashion for size, as a response to the 'American challenge', was particularly marked. But, reflecting the increasing importance of big textile firms and their comparative advantage in dealing with the government, the government began to support the concentration process with investment funds from 1966. Compared with other sectors this support was, however, modest.

The very large groups emerging by the early-to-mid 1970s were characterised by significant diversification: into textile production abroad; into clothing production and retailing; and into non-textile activities. Except for foreign investment, this diversification process was the opposite experience to that of German firms which have by and large remained dedicated textile producers. Indeed, to continue with the comparison, the counterpart of this French diversification appears to have been a failure to rationalise production, which continued in too many small, often under-modernised plants, or to stress marketing or exporting. For some firms, this suggests a strategy of exit from textiles.

The year 1973 and its succeeding years, marking the new liberalism of the MFA and the onset of recession, provided a turning point for French textiles. Smaller and larger firms united to call for protection and, after the liberal import years of 1973–77, the French government stepped in to play a leading role, with the British, in slowing the pace of trade liberalisation from 1978. In step with general industrial policy, the government also became after 1973 increasingly prepared to direct structural policy towards individual larger, more 'progressive' textile firms (thus bypassing the traditional intermediary of the trade associations). Such firms benefited from several of the many newly created entities for public financial aid. At first, such aid tended to support the concentration process, as well as to keep some large 'lame ducks' alive (notably Boussac in textiles). But, as the attitude to lame ducks cooled in the latter 1970s (and several very large firms collapsed), the government also came to put greater emphasis on specialisation, innovation and exporting. The outcome in 1981, was to add the textile industry to a scheme, which also covered six other industries of a significantly more 'strategic' or high-technology character than textiles, where individual firms would be eligible for aid through development contracts under the procedure of CODIS (Committee for the Development of Strategic Industries).

The new socialist government of 1981 has strengthened policy towards textile employment through a series of measures announced in March 1982. This includes a programme for reducing social security charges on a sliding scale for firms that agree on investment to maintain, or better still create, jobs. Thus structural policy has reverted to an emphasis on job-protection.

How much of France's failure relative to Germany can be explained by policy difference? First (and in spite of a superficial similarity in the post-war commercial regimes they both faced), French textile producers appear to have had far less clear expectations of trade liberalisation. Up to the 1960s, this was party the result of false (and diversionary) expectations about colonial markets. Secondly, a recurrent, if discontinuous, theme of French textile policy has been tax or subsidy measures to support employment. Thirdly, there was a growing structural element in textile policy from the second half of the 1960s supporting larger firms and favouring the concentration process. It is true that such structural policy has remained modest in financial terms, yet it was arguably part of a policy package which created an unhealthy kind of dualism: protection and employment-support kept smaller, marginal firms in existence, while structural policy encouraged size, but not the 'best-practice' (according to the wisdom of hindsight) of specialisation. In encouraging the two ends of the size spectrum, French textile policy thus discriminated against the medium-to-large size firms that have been associated with Germany's success.

However, intervention must be put into the context of political forces. As a mature sector consisting of a large number of traditionalist firms, making government intervention that much more tricky, it is unlikely that textiles would ever have been a focus for government modernisation efforts. Indeed, the very importance of these firms (nothing if not vociferous) made textiles a prime candidate for protectionist concessions. That no similar political force existed in Germany is partly the result of the unambiguous pro-market policies adopted in post-war Germany. French textiles faced other disadvantages. First, the inherited entrepreneurial base, the legacy perhaps of decades of protection, appears to have been weaker in France. Secondly, French labour relations did not display all the flexibility of those in Germany; in particular, and in spite of a weak union movement in textiles, legislation on worker protection and representation has, especially since 1968, given the workforce some job security and power.

Italy: 'decentralised production'

The outstanding survival record of Italian textiles appears to be the achievement of small-to-medium-sized firms with little outside stimulus, the result of structural changes that are unique in a European context. The two main interrelated developments have been: (i) the extensive exploitation of segmented labour markets; and (ii) the organisation of small-scale production in a cooperative-competitive mode know as 'decentralised production'.

In recent decades large employers have had to face rapidly rising real wages and the substantial organisational problems posed by a large labour force (such as absenteeism) and by unions powerful both in terms of membership and as a political force. Today, three textile and clothing unions, well-organised, well-informed and cooperating closely with each other, have a membership covering some two-thirds of employment in firms with 20 or more workers. Increased labour unrest since the late 1960s resulted in the passage of more stringent legislation on employment protection and worker representation. But much of this does not apply to firms of less than fifteen workers or to outworkers. Textiles and clothing, along with other sectors such as shoes and mechanical engineering where small-scale is viable, have seen a substantial devolution of production from larger to smaller firms to exploit lower labour costs and greater flexibility. Small firms are often based on family labour— families, moreover, of predominantly agricultural origin. This strengthens flexibility and makes union organisation particularly difficult. Small-scale production can compound these advantages through 'black labour' which evades taxes and social security payments (particularly the case for those activities such as knitting, sewing, some weaving—but not spinning—where low minimum viable scale permits out-working). Black labour has played a certain role in Italy's competitive strength, but the evidence is that its importance has declined. On the other hand, textiles and clothing which are predominantly located in the north and the centre, are slowly creeping south to areas where out-workers can most cheaply be employed.

The virtues of decentralised production go well beyond the labour-cost aspect. Prato's wool industry probably provides the best-known example of this.[6] The industry began a process of deconcentration in the 1950s in answer to problems of overcapacity and of trade unions. With time, it found that the new form of organisation conferred other advantages, those of flexibility and speed in product changes and in capacity to upgrade technology. The industry's structure is now one of small, subcontracting units highly specialised by stage of production: domestic and export marketing, and even many elements of design, are carried out by separate establishments. At the centre of this system are a few firms, not necessarily large or even manufacturers, which undertake the main entrepreneurial function. Working hours are typically long and there is little over-manning. Prato has become increasingly fashion-oriented over time.

In spite of its relatively long history of productive decentralisation, Prato shares important features with several other textile and clothing areas: for instance, Castell Goffredo (women's stockings), Como (silk-type fabrics and clothing), and Carpi (knitwear).[7] The structure is one of small, flexible, innovative specialists centred on one geographical area in a competitive-cooperative system that has some elements of central direction but which decentralises risks and many aspects of decision-making. It is akin to a firm with decentralised profit centres, but a central productive logic. Decentralised production has occurred in those areas of textiles where the fashion element (hence the need for greater risk and flexibility) is important. Italy's unique strength in Western Europe is to have created a kind of price-competitive mass-market in fashion, where certain products often enjoy an area 'trademark' (Como silk ties, Prato wool fabrics, and so on).

In product areas where fashion is less important, decentralised production has made less progress because of the economies of scale and long runs associated with larger plants; this has been the case of cotton textiles, for instance. Even here, however, firms are on average considerably smaller than in the other countries we are studying. One of the reasons is that, for flexibility, they also often subcontract substantial amounts of their business.

Decentralised production is the product of political conditions in Italy. In the absence of a social consensus enabling the formation of a strong central government, the vacuum is filled on the one hand by a clientelist system and on the other by a strong trade-union movement (as a kind of 'shadow' government of the Left). These two forces have helped to put pressure on larger firms to preserve employment at all costs with two principal and contradictory results. On the one hand, productive decentralisation and black labour were a private response (with some implicit help from labour legislation) to the difficulties of conducting business in large organisations. This has resulted in the emergence of a competitive textile industry. On the other hand, extensive nationalisation of ailing large textile firms, carried out by ENI since 1957 and GEPI since 1971, was the public response. Nationalised firms now account for 5 per cent of employment in textile firms employing more than 20 workers. This has resulted in the emergence of an uncompetitive segment that is a burden on the public purse, cannot be restructured, and distorts competition.

Other policy initiatives affecting textiles, particularly the 'intermediate' sector of more conventional firms standing between nationalisation and decentralisation, have been, on the face of it, considerable. Textiles, along with clothing, has been among the major sectoral beneficiaries of long-standing government support to workers on short-time. Moreover, since 1977, partial concessions on social security payments for female workers have particularly benefited these sectors. Law 1011 of 1971 provided subsidies for restructuring in textiles while Law 675 of 1977 included textiles among other priority sectors for restructuring; however, neither Law appears to have had much effect on structures. Policies to maintain a competitive lira in the 1970s have helped textiles, like other labour-intensive sectors, to maintain international competitiveness. Finally, MFA protection has helped some of the less fashion-oriented sectors to maintain their share of the Italian market. (Italy, like Germany, has also greatly benefited from MFA protection by other Western European countries.)

This policy package has been strongly influenced by the initiatives coming from a new-found cooperation in recent years between the trade unions and the leading trade associations (largely representing 'intermediate' firms). Yet the most interesting feature of the package is that it has not undermined Italian competitive capacity in the way that, I have argued, a similar set of policies did in France. Part of the explanation resides in a relatively ineffective Italian state, incapable of direct influence on restructuring or employment maintenance except through nationalisation. The other side of the coin with regard to the weak state is the Italian potential for labour market segmentation, as well as the flair and desire for independence of small entrepreneurs in Northern and Central Italy.

The UK: protection and concentration

The UK cotton industry has been in more or less continuous decline since its export heyday in the early part of this century. Up to the 1960s, more or less recurrent problems were posed by substantial excess capacity and the industry's inability or unwillingness to rationalise, modernise, or find new markets. In spite of some government attempts to help this rationalisation, the industry preferred to push for the protection of its colonial export markets (in the 1930s) and otherwise to exploit short-term expedients, such as short-time working. When the cotton industry faced substantial competition on its home market for the first time in the 1950s, it again turned to a short-term expedient in the form of privately negotiated (non-governmental) restraints for 1959–61 with the major Commonwealth suppliers. The government, unhappy to envisage permanent protection, offered the industry through its 1959 Cotton Industry Act a scheme providing partial financial assistance for scrapping and re-equipping, as well as for compensation for redundancies, but the results of the scheme were generally felt to be disappointing.

From the early 1960s an attempt to break the vicious circle of decline with a positive strategy was made by Courtaulds, the UK's largest producer of cellulose fibres.[8] Anxious to preserve its declining domestic fibre outlets, Courtaulds acquired during the 1960s a substantial share of the UK textile industry, particularly in the cotton system. It aimed to become competitive with the importation of standard cotton cloths in large volume from developing countries, a mass-market strategy of vertical and horizontal integration and the most sophisticated techniques of production. At the same time, in an attempt to orient itself towards the market, Courtaulds became active across a broad range of textile activities integrated downsteam into clothing and distribution. The UK's other giant fibre company, ICI, in a defensive response to Courtaulds, was instrumental in building up other large textile groups, largely through financial assistance. These groups came to pursue a similar set of strategies, emphasising the mass-market approach, vertical integration, and foreign investment.

Courtaulds argued that its strategy would require the continuation of protection for a period. This 'reborn-infant-industry' argument, buttressed by the substantial share of textile capacity Courtaulds came to control by the mid-1960s and supported by the other large groups emerging, clearly won over the government. The industry got the protection it sought, in a new comprehensive quota system for cotton textiles introduced in 1966, and many of the larger firms embarked on a substantial programme of take-over and investment.

As a result, the level of firm concentration rose steeply until about the mid-1970s, leaving the UK with an industry of unprecedented concentration (see Tables 2.4 and 2.5). This process also saw substantial modernisation as marginal, antiquated firms were driven out of business (although some of these still survive today as amazing relics of a bygone age).

The process of concentration and the creation of a 'band-wagon' effect favouring convergence in strategic approaches owe much to the entry of Courtaulds into textiles. Courtaulds was able to increase the government's commitment to protection and secure a permissive (until the early 1970s at least) anti-trust policy in textiles. The mass-market strategy may additionally have been encouraged by the high level of concentration in UK clothing retailing. By the 1960s a stable, contractual relationship had developed between the large retailers and textile producers.[9] The former played a dominant role in product choice, design and quality control. Reflecting their own view of the market, these retailers encouraged a production emphasis on long runs of standard, basic fabrics.

The evidence is that the mass-market strategy has failed on its own terms. Over time protection has certainly not proven temporary. In almost two decades since Courtaulds' launching of the idea of 'infant-industry' protection, quota restrictions have spread from cotton to all fibres, while tariff protection against Commonwealth imports has grown. Furthermore, textiles and clothing have been major beneficiaries of general employment subsidies introduced in 1975 and replaced in 1978 by short-time working subsidies. Some spectacular closures of highly advanced textile mills in the 1970s also suggest that the industry has not approached its goal of competing against imports of standard, basic fabrics with modest protection only.

Most obviously, the problems of UK textiles can be associated with an attention to marketing and innovation that, compared to Germany and Italy, has been insufficient. The UK market may have been neither large nor homogeneous enough to sustain a mass-market strategy. The UK's relatively low wage level, compared to the rest of the EEC, might have favoured such a strategy, but for various obstacles to rationalisation. One obstacle resides in the nature of labour relations. A high proportion of the textile work force is unionised. Textile unions are not militant by UK standards, but their organisation along craft lines, combined with a certain traditionalism among many workers and managers, makes incremental technical and organisational change particularly difficult and helps explain the relatively low productivity of UK textiles.

The industry's faltering competitiveness in the later 1970s has created a remarkable reversal in public policy from the liberalism of the early 1950s, through the 'offensive' approach of adjustment assistance, then temporary protection, to the more defensive and permanent protectionism of the late 1970s. The new Conservative government of 1979 has done nothing to change this.

Since 1979 there has been a marked collapse in levels of activity in the UK textile industry, primarily as a result of domestic recession, exacerbated by sterling revaluation. The large firms have drastically slimmed down their UK textile operations and pursued a policy of greater decentralisation, partly aimed at greater market awareness. This development, combined with an increasing fashion-oriented UK garment consumption, may yet lead to a more profitable survival for what remains of the textile industry.

Early post-war trade liberalisation by a British government strongly committed to world free trade did *not* produce the competitive response that liberalisation prospects did in Germany in the 1960s. It would seem that decades of decline had robbed the industry of its capacity for self-help. (The Commonwealth connection—both as export destination and import source—continued to divert the textile industry from the European dimension of market adjustment until the UK joined the EEC in 1973.) The vicious circle of decline was broken by Courtaulds' entry into textiles, combined with a strong government policy that was protectionist and supported the structure favoured by the industry's dominant firms. This policy package was probably a necessary condition of the industry's modernisation; yet it failed to make it competitive, partly because it encouraged a dominant strategy that underestimated the importance of marketing and the potential of specialisation, and partly because it never convincingly instilled the discipline of eventual trade re-liberalisation. It is tempting to criticise the package as pre-empting strategic experiment (à la Germany), yet the real choice was probably between this costly and imperfect form of restructuring and a very rapid decline in the 1960s leading to virtual extinction of the cotton industry. This last option, however, may not have been a bad thing at a time when Lancashire still showed a reasonable propensity for diversifying into other activities.

The US: a continental-size market[10]

By comparison with Western Europe US textiles have been little affected by international developments. This is most obviously explained by high US tariffs against all sources of imports and consistently tight quota protection against the most competitive low-cost import sources. Both imports and exports are modest in relation to the size of the market (see Table 2.1).

Moreover, prior to the 1960s, the US textile industry had already undergone major technological and structural changes that were still not complete in Western Europe. As a result of a large market where tastes are sophisticated yet relatively homogeneous, US textile mills are large and highly rationalised, producing long runs of a small number of products over long time periods. This rationalisation, rather than superior process technology *per se*, has been the basis for the US's world lead in labour productivity, a lead that has been eroded by Western European producers such as Germany which have invested in modern technology. Perhaps the most marked development in US textile firms' strategies has been an increasing emphasis on marketing. The industry led the world in promoting synthetic and synthetic-blend textiles and in turning household textiles into a fashion sector.

Slow growth in the economy and, in the 1970s, substantial devaluation have resulted in a slower rise in wages in the US than in any major textile country. Historically, wages have also been held down by the shift of the industry from the North-East to the South and by resistance to unionisation. Slow wage rises and high productivity have resulted in the US emerging as one of the lowest-cost industrialised-country textile processors.

Compared to those in Western Europe US firms seem to have enjoyed the best of all possible worlds. A large, homogeneous and well-protected market has created stable conditions for competition among a number of powerful firms (somewhat as in Germany), resulting in a dominant corporate strategy combining the mass-market approach with an attention to marketing. This strategy, together with low wage costs, has made the US a potential world force in textiles.

2.4 Some implications for the future

Adjustment and intervention

The historical adjustment process in Western European textiles has the following features: the role of liberalisation as a key 'transmission belt' for change, in spite of the propensity for protection in textiles; and the role of trade among industrialised countries as an increasingly more important adjustment pressure than low-cost imports. We have also seen that there has been a variety of opportunities (only partly foreseen in the collective wisdom of two decades ago) for restructuring, although commercially successful survival has generally involved large employment losses. The relatively successful performance of Germany and Italy can be associated with the emergence, through experiment by a large number of firms, of a strategy of product specialisation. Less successful performance in France and the UK reflected the protection-seeking strategies of a large number of marginal firms and the mass-market—sometimes exit —strategies of a small number of very large firms.

From the evidence we have been able to review, the nature of public intervention provides no simple explanation of performance. Both performance and policy are influenced by national environmental features such as the nature of labour markets and the entrepreneurial base. Indeed, there is a circularity and a reinforcing effect among all three elements. In Germany, for instance, the direction of causation between the strong entrepreneurial base and pro-market policies is not clear.

German and Italian performance was the outcome of a process of competition based on a strong entrepreneurial self-reliance. This was encouraged in Germany by the government's clear enunciation of a liberalisation policy and its abstinence from structural policy; in Italy it was induced by the private sector's lack of confidence in an interventionist, but weak, government.

The relative weakness of the competitive process in French and UK textiles largely reflected: an entrepreneurial base weakened in the UK by a history of monumental decline, in France by a history of protectionism; a less flexible labour market; a more equivocal government position than in Germany on trade liberalisation; and a structural policy which, partly because of the weak entrepreneurial base, favoured the emergence of a few very large groups and the kinds of strategies suited to such groups. Structural policy may have pre-empted what competitive experiment there might have been. Yet intervention probably did help modernise textiles in France and the UK, albeit at a large cost.

This kind of view of the interactions of performance, policy and environment is, like real life, potentially tortuous. At very least, it means that public intervention is far less exogenous than we normally assume. But this should not lead us to conclude that there is no such thing as independently determined policy. Both the French and the UK governments had the political strength to pursue different policies in textiles. One may speculate that had these governments followed a more clearly liberalising and structurally neutral policy, less of the textile industry would have survived than has been the case for Germany. The failure to restructure must surely have imposed costs on the rest of the economy in the full-employment conditions up to 1973.

Many of these costs are probably still being incurred in recession. Certainly, unemployed textile workers now face great difficulties in finding new jobs, but textile protection still ties up some new investment and scarce skills. And the standard resource-allocation arguments for free-trade still apply: that consumers benefit from cheaper imports and will spend more on other items; that the more supplier countries export, the more they can import (including many of the products covered in other chapters of this book). Moreover, textile protectionism plays an important role in further threatening an already weakened world trading system and continues to help sour North–South relations.

Possible future developments

The major constraint dominating the immediate future for Western European textiles is the depth and duration of the recession. Unemployment will worsen, until the mid-1980s at least. Among other possible important developments, the following speculations can be made:

(i)   in the next ten to fifteen years, the electronics revolution will probably not have sufficiently altered the core techniques in textiles (or for that matter clothing) to affect the present balance of comparative advantage, but the scope for large-scale diffusion of current best practice (for example, shuttle-less weaving) will maintain the industry's potential for productivity gain and job-shedding;

(ii) Europe will continue to maintain a comparative advantage in specialised products (for instance, fashion goods); while US and South-East Asian exports may increase their challenge in this area, the continuing integration of EEC markets may slowly enable domestic producers to move towards mass-market strategies of the US variety;

(iii) it is not clear how the industry's present very diverse size-structure will be affected by technological change, which promises both greater capital-intensity and greater flexibility; however, the very large textile firms of the UK and France may well shrink in size, unless they are maintained through explicit structural policies;

(iv) the MFA is likely to be renewed under very restrictive con-ditions for as long as the recession lasts. China and the US may pose increasing problems as suppliers: the Southern enlargement of the EEC, eventually giving relatively low-cost Southern European suppliers better access to northern Euro-pean markets, will add to the political pressures for a restrictive MFA;

(v) particularly within the context of an MFA that is increasingly restrictive towards Asian suppliers, parts of the European clothing industry will continue their slow move offshore to Eastern Europe and the Mediterranean.

These speculations notwithstanding, it is no more possible to forecast the future for textiles now than it was ten or twenty years ago. This being so, structural policies are no more likely to succeed in this industry in the future than in the past. To add to the specula-tion, however, it can be argued that structural change has reached a point from which it would be difficult to retreat: the level of international competition is now so great that unless it is reduced the restructuring process is likely to continue. The degree of liberal-isation towards low-cost imports is already substantial, but more important now are the competitive pressures maintained by the high levels of trade among Western European countries. Politically, this trade is far more difficult to restrict than low-cost imports.

While the amount of trade restricted through the MFA will no doubt have some effect on the maintenance of some textile jobs, the important policy choices are increasingly likely to involve intra-Western European trade. Already, subsidies to national textile industries have become an important issue because of their protective effects against Western European partners. Further pressures to limit the growth of trade within Western Europe and the EEC are not inconceivable (although this pressure will not yet assume major proportions). But such is the high level of interdependence that national policy-makers have little freedom of manoeuvre: trying to control imports from close trade partners will assuredly lead to retaliation. It therefore seems highly likely that textile employment will continue to fall, either because the high level of trade within Western Europe will assure continued restructuring, or because a collapse in the trade system would cause a domestic slump.

Thus arguments about whether or how to renew the MFA may well not be the central issue in future restructuring, but since they remain an issue in North–South relations, it would make sense to envisage some form of long-term commitment to liberalisation within the MFA.

If the inevitability of falling employment is the bad news, one should try to finish with some good. First, the Western European textile industry probably has a substantial future under any reasonable scenario: other sectors, such as clothing, where Europe's costs are too high, or steel or ships, where demand is far more sensitive to business cycles, are at greater risk. Secondly, the recent decades of restructuring experience have not been entirely wasted: Western Europe's weaker producers are probably now in a better position to compete without protection than they were ten or twenty years ago.

Notes

1. For two recent and more detailed treatments of changes in the textile industries of advanced countries, see OECD (1983) and Toyne *et al.* (1983).
2. For a recent history of barriers to trade in textiles, see Keesing and Wolf (1980).
3. Thormählen (1978) and Breitenacher (1981) provide some of the factual background for the German analysis.
4. See Breitenacher (1978) on outward processing.
5. An analysis of the post-war development of state–industry relations in textiles by Mytelka (1982) provides much of the background to the French analysis.
6. See Lorenzoni (1979).
7. On other cases of productive decentralisation in textiles, see Federtessile (1980) and current research in progress by Francesco Silva and Paolo Ferri at the Bocconi University in Milan.
8. For the illuminating view of an insider on Courtaulds' experience, see Knight (1974).

9. On this relationship, see National Economic Development Office (1982).
10. On the US industry, see Toyne *et al.* (1982).

References

Breitenacher, M. (1978), 'Bekleidungsindustrie lässt zunehmend im Ausland fertigen', *IFO-Schnelldienst*, No. 2/78.

Breitenacher, M. (1981), *Textilindustrie: Strukturwandlungen und Entwicklungsperspektiven für die achtziger Jahren*, Berlin: Duncker & Humblot.

Federtessile (Federazione fra le Associazioni dell Industrie Tessile e Abbigliamento in Italia) (1980), *Il Settore Tessile e Abbigliamento in Italia*, Milan: Franco Angeli Editore.

Keesing, D. B., and Wolf, M. (1980), *Textile Quotas Against Developing Countries*, Thames Essay No. 23, London: Trade Policy Research Centre.

Knight, A. (1974), *Private Enterprise and Public Intervention: The Courtaulds Experience*, London: George Allen & Unwin.

Lorenzoni, G. (1979), *Una politica innovativa nelle Piccole Medie Imprese. L'Analisi del Cambiamento nel Sistema Industriale Pratese*, Milan: Etas Libri.

Mytelka, L. K. (1982), 'In search of a partner: the State and the Textile Industry in France', in S. Cohen and B. P. Gourevitch, eds, *France in a Troubled World Economy*, London: Butterworths.

National Economic Development Office (1982), *Changing Needs and Relationships in the UK Apparel Fabric Market*, London.

OECD (1983), *Textile and Clothing Industries: Structural Problems and Policies in OECD Countries*, Paris.

Shepherd, G. (1981), *Textile-industry Adjustment in Developed Countries*, Thames Essay No. 30, London: Trade Policy Research Centre.

Thormählen, G. (1978), *Die Grossunternehmen der Westdeutschen Textilindustrie im Strukturwandel*, doctoral dissertation, Hamburg: University of Hamburg.

Toyne, B., Arpan, J. S., Barnett, A. H., Ricks, D. A., and Shimp, T. A. (1983), *The US Textile Mill Product Industry: Strategies for the 1980s and Beyond*, Columbia, S.G.: University of South Carolina Press.

3 STEEL: TOO MUCH INVESTMENT TOO LATE

Patrick Messerlin and Christopher Saunders

3.1 From growth to stagnation

In the 1950s and 1960s, Western European steel production grew rapidly (Table 3.1 shows growth in 1960s). From the early 1970s, production stagnated, apart from spasmodic bursts of demand (in 1973/74 and again in 1979), while Western Europe's share of world output began to fall. Production in the Community in 1979, a relatively good year for the 1970s, was hardly greater than in 1970. The further collapse of demand brought output in 1980–2 down to less than two-thirds of theoretical capacity.

Three factors account for the shift in Western European steel output from growth in the 1950s and 1960s to effective stagnation in most of the 1970s. The first factor, of course, is the *slowdown of overall economic growth*—broadly speaking from average growth rates of 4 to 5 per cent a year in GDP until the end of the short-lived boom of 1973 to rates of 2 to 3 per cent a year thereafter.

The second factor is a shift in the relationship between the demand for steel in the industrial economies and their rates of overall growth, which can be described as a declining *demand elasticity for steel*, or as a declining steel content of output (Table 3.2). In the 1960s, domestic consumption of steel was almost keeping pace with the increase in total industrial production, with an elasticity of about 0.9 in the EEC-9, the US and Japan. The fall in steel elasticities in the 1970s, although in part cyclical, also reflects longer-term trends: in part a structural decline in the share of some of the big steel-using industries in the Western industrial economies (shipbuilding, construction and motor vehicles are obvious examples); in part, technological changes resulting in smaller inputs of steel (for example, through the use of higher tensile and better quality steel), and higher value added for given end-products, and the use of alternative materials (cement in construction; plastics and aluminium in vehicles and machinery; paperboard for containers). Thus part of the framework for adjustment strategies, in a period of slower overall economic growth, must be the probability of only very small increases in the consumption of crude steel in the Western industrial countries even when overall economic activity resumes its growth. The

Table 3.1 World crude steel production and capacity, 1960–82 (million tons)

	Production						Estimated capacity (beginning of year)	
	1960	1970	1974*	1979	1981	1982	1966	1982
EEC (9)	*98.1*	*138.0*	*155.3*	*140.1*	*125.1*	*110.6*	*140.6*	*197.6*
Germany	34.1	45.0	53.2	46.0	41.6	35.9	48.0	67.7
France	17.3	23.8	27.0	23.4	21.2	18.4	23.6	29.6
Italy	8.5	17.3	23.8	24.2	24.7	24.0	17.2	39.8
Netherlands	1.9	5.0	5.8	5.8	5.5	4.4	3.7	8.6
Belgium	7.2	12.6	16.2	13.4	12.3	9.9	11.1	19.1‡
Luxembourg	4.1	5.5	6.4	4.9	3.8	3.5	5.2	6.4
UK	24.7	28.3	22.3	21.5	15.4	13.8	31.3	25.2§
Ireland	–	–	0.1	0.1	–	0.1	0.1	0.3‡
Denmark	0.3	0.5	0.5	0.8	0.6	0.6	0.4	0.9‡
Austria	3.1	4.1	4.7	4.9	4.7	4.3	..	5.1‡
Spain	1.9	7.4	11.6	12.3	12.9	..	..	17.5‡
Sweden	3.2	5.5	6.0	4.7	3.8	..	..	6.1‡
US	90.1	119.1	132.0	123.3	111.3	67.7	..	..
Japan	21.5	93.3	117.1	111.7	101.7	99.5	..	159.6‡
Canada	5.2	11.2	13.6	16.1	14.8	..	..	21.2‡
USSR	65.3	115.9	136.2	149.1	148.5	..	..	..
Poland	6.4	11.7	14.6	19.2	15.7	..	..	..
Czechoslovakia	6.8	11.5	13.6	14.8	15.3	..	..	..
Romania	1.7	6.5	8.8	12.9	13.0	..	..	..
P.R. China	9.5†	18.0	25.0	34.5	35.6	..	..	..
Brazil	1.8	5.4	7.5	13.8	13.2	..	..	..
South Korea	0.1†	0.5	1.9	7.6	10.8	..	..	11.6‡
World	*336*	*594*	*708*	*747*	*708*	..	..	..
of which EEC (9) %	*29*	*23*	*22*	*19*	*18*	..	..	..

* Post-war peak in EEC, US and Japan.
† 1961.
‡ 1981.
§ *Manned* capacity of BSC stated as 14.4 million tons a year (*Financial Times*, 14 June 1982).

Sources: 1970–81: UN, Economic Commission for Europe, *The Steel Market in 1981*, New York; 1960: UN, *Growth of World Industry, 1967*, Volume II, New York; 1982: EEC: Eurostat, *Iron and Steel Quarterly Bulletin*, 4/1982, Luxembourg.

competitive struggle among the world's steel industries, with their present overcapacity, is becoming fiercer.

The third factor is the growth of *competition from other parts of the world*. Despite restrictions, the proportion of imports from non-EEC members to total apparent consumption in the EEC, in tonnage, rose from 3 per cent in 1961 to 12 per cent in 1980 (for the Nine).[1] The largest imports came from Eastern Europe,

Table 3.2 EEC, US and Japan: ratios of steel consumption to industrial production, 1960–2 to 1978–80

Annual averages	Domestic steel consumption*			Industrial production† indices		'Elasticity'‡ steel/ind. production	
	Mn. tons	Indices					
	1979–80	1969–71 / 1960–62	1978–80 / 1969–71	1969–71 / 1960–62	1978–80 / 1969–71	1960–62 to 1969–71	1969–71 to 1978–80
EEC (9)	113.60	146.2	97.6	159	126	0.9	0.8
Germany	37.13	141.0	95.2	157	123	0.9	0.8
France	21.18	158.1	95.2	157	132	1.0	0.7
Italy	25.26	178.6	129.1	173	134	1.0	1.0
Netherlands	4.52	164.2	87.9	189	134	0.9	0.7
Belgium–Luxembourg	4.27	169.2	97.0	155	118	1.1	0.8
UK	18.77	119.2	79.6	131	114	0.9	0.7
Ireland	0.57	252.9	132.6	180	151	1.4	0.9
Denmark	1.90	162.0	90.9	..	..	..	..
US	134.31	145.5	102.4	160	136	0.9	0.8
Japan	69.39	277.6	110.0	294	149	0.9	0.7

*Apparent consumption in crude equivalents, including both 'ECSC' and 'non-ECSC' steel products. Apparent consumption is production plus imports less exports adjusted for changes in stocks so far as recorded.
† Based on 1975 = 100. Construction generally excluded.
‡ Index of steel consumption divided by index of industrial production.

Sources: Steel consumption: EEC: Eurostat, *Iron and Steel Yearbook*, Luxembourg, 1976 and 1981, Table 6.2; US and Japan: UN, *Economic Commission for Europe, The Iron and Steel Market in 1980*, New York Table 2, and earlier issues; Industrial production: OECD, *Principal Economic indicators: Historical Statistics 1960–1979*, Paris, 1980; and OECD, *Principal Economic Indicators*, Paris, January 1982.

Austria, Sweden and Spain. Although these Third-country imports were small and were restrained after the mid-1970s by Voluntary Export Agreements, their effects on EEC prices accentuated the weakness of the steel market. At the same time, exports from the EEC to the rest of the world rose only slowly; from 20 per cent of output in 1961 to 27 per cent in 1980 (Table 1.2, page 7). It is in these non-EEC markets that the effect of growing competition from other parts of the world may have been most marked. The growing 'internationalisation' of the world steel market, through both intra-EEC trade and trade with the rest of the world, affected all EEC countries.[2]

3.2 Technological change in a competitive world

Most, though not all, of the major technical improvements in steel-making require for their efficient exploitation a larger scale of production than was common in the past. The steel industry has hitherto been an industry in which economies of scale are particularly prominent. But to realise these economies of scale involves very heavy investments in the erection of up-to-date plants. This enhances the comparative advantage of steel industries in nations where overall economic growth is fast and is expected to remain fast.

Of the chief technical innovations of the post-war period, the most crucial is the *basic oxygen steel process* (OSP) which now dominates crude steel production in most OECD countries. The main advantage of this process is its much faster speed of operation than that of the older processes (labour productivity is two to three times greater than in the older techniques). Modern integrated plants can reach optimal efficiency with outputs of 4 to 5 million tons a year with large oxygen converters. The striking economies of scale explain the rapid spread of the oxygen technique and the great expansion of total steel-making capacity in the EEC from about 141 million tons a year in the mid-1960s to almost 200 million tons in 1981 (Table 3.1). In the 1960s, when demand was on an upward trend, a technology based on scale economies appeared the obvious strategy and brought about a race for scale economies between the steel-makers. The cost began to appear in the 1970s when steel demand ceased to grow, and the rates of capacity utilisation fell to unprofitable levels.

A second major innovation was the *electric arc steel furnace* (ESP). Hitherto, this process has been adopted mainly for relatively small-scale production; thus it was called a 'mini-mill' technology to contrast it with the oxygen process.

By the 1980s, the oxygen process accounted for over 75 per cent of crude steel production in the main steel-producing countries of the Community, except in Italy and the UK. Nearly all the rest of the output comes from electric furnaces.[3] The Japanese proportions are very similar to those in the EEC, but the Japanese industry was modernised earlier.

The third important innovation in steel-making is *continuous casting* which cuts out intermediate steps in processing, reduces waste, and generally brings down costs, particularly of energy. In this respect, Japan takes a clear lead.

One result of the innovations just described, a result even more relevant now than in earlier years, is the *diminishing use of energy* in iron and steel production. Japan, again, is the most energy-efficient in terms of energy use per ton of steel produced, although West Germany and Sweden are not very different. The UK showed (in 1977) a higher consumption than the other countries for which data are available (0.86 tons of coal equivalent per ton of steel against 0.56 tons in Japan).[4]

Innovations in technical processes have brought about a combination of the various stages of steel-making in the shape of integrated units carrying out all stages of production from coke manufacture to finished steel products—another aspect of economies of scale due to the saving of transport of materials from place to place and of energy in repeated processing, and one reason for the concentration of production.

Concentration

The steel industry, if only for its economies of scale, has long been an industry of great firms. About three-quarters of crude steel output in the EEC has been accounted for by thirteen firms (or groups of formerly independent firms) throughout the 1970s (Table 3.3). In the UK (British Steel Corporation) and Italy (the IRI through Finsider), and now in France, nationalised groups control most of the industry; in Belgium (Cockerill), Luxembourg (Arbed) and the Netherlands (Hoogovens) a single firm is dominant. In Germany, four great groups predominate—a similar degree of concentration to that in Japan. It is true that in all EEC countries a competitive fringe remains of smaller firms; but the strength, or weakness, of the European steel industries depends very heavily on the management and strategies of the handful of major enterprises.

Technical progress, in conditions of a quite fast growth of demand until the 1970s, followed by relative stagnation, has been associated first, with waves of investment in expansion and

Table 3.3 Major steel-producing groups in the EEC, US, and Japan: crude steel production, 1979

	million tons *1979*	*% of EEC-9 production* *1971*	*1979*
EEC:			
British Steel Corporation (UK)	17.7	19.6	12.6
Thyssen AG (Germany)	13.5	6.2	9.6
Finsider (Italy)	12.4	7.0§	8.9
Arbed* (Luxembourg-Saar)	10.7	7.2	7.6
Usinor (France)	9.4	6.3	6.7
Sacilor† (France)	6.3	6.2	4.5
Hoesch AG‡ (Germany)	6.0	4.9	4.3
Hoogovens NV‡ (Netherlands)	5.5	3.6	3.9
Krupp-Stahl (Germany)	5.4	2.8	3.8
Klöckner (Germany)	4.7	2.4	3.3
Salzgitter (Germany)	4.4	2.9	3.1
Mannesmann (Germany)	4.3	2.8	3.0
Cockerill (Belgium)	4.2	4.8	3.0
	104.5	76.7	74.2
US:			
US Steel	27.0		
Bethlehem Steel	17.6		
Jones & Laughlin	16.4		
Japan:			
Nippon Steel	33.5		
Nippon Kokan	14.4		
Kawasaki	12.9		
Sumimoto	12.9		

* Including Röchling (Germany) and Sidmar.
† Estimated.
‡ Hoesch and Hoogovens formed a merger (Estel) in 1973, dissolved in 1982.
§ Estimated.

Source: International Iron and Steel Institute, *World Steel in Figures, 1981*, Brussels, and earlier issues.

modernisation aimed at labour-saving, and, second, with declining employment.

Investment

A usual, if not wholly satisfactory, method of comparison between countries is to use the Eurostat data of investment per ton of crude steel produced.[5] So far as it goes, this measure shows a wave of investment in the mid-1970s tailing off from 1976 (even in current prices) following an earlier wave of investment in the early 1960s (at least among the Six). The high level of investment in the mid-1970s was most conspicuous in Britain, but this reflects slow British investment in steel in earlier years. Section 3.3 on the major countries shows how important an element in investment expenditure, especially after the early 1970s, has been the funding provided in various forms by governments, generally for bulk steel production. Most of this government support has been for retrenchment or reconstruction, sometimes in almost last-ditch efforts to preserve a national industry or to stave off bankruptcy of major national firms.

Employment and productivity

Employment in the EEC steel industries has fallen since 1960 by nearly 40 per cent, from 870,000 in 1960 to 536,000 in 1982—a relatively moderate decline until 1975, accelerating fast thereafter when production stagnated (see Table 3.4). But over the whole period 1960–82, production increased by nearly 20 per cent. The fall in employment was steepest in the UK and France. In only two EEC

Table 3.4 Employment in the EEC's iron and steel industry, 1960–82*
(Thousands)

	1960	*1970*	*1975*	*1979*	*1982*
EEC (9)	*870†*	*795†*	*781*	*680*	*536*
Germany	290	244	227	204	182
France	192	160	157	125	97
Italy	65	78	96	98	95
Netherlands	14	21	23	21	21
Belgium	65	60	61	49	43
Luxembourg	24	25	23	17	14
UK	220	205	191	162	83
Ireland	..	..	1	1	1
Denmark	..	..	3	3	2

* Total employed, including manual and non-manual workers and apprentices, EEC definition of the industry. Annual averages for 1975 and 1979 (based on January–November figures for 1982); end-year figures for 1960 and 1970.

† 1960 and 1970: rough estimates, total employed based on figures for manual workers only (assuming 1975 ratio to total employment, for which figures not given in source).

Source: EEC: Eurostat. *Iron and Steel Year Book 1981*, Luxembourg, 1981, Table 2.2; and (for 1982) Eurostat, *Quarterly Bulletin of Iron and Steel Statistics*, 3/1982, Table 2.1.

countries, Italy and the Netherlands, was there any substantial increase. Changes in labour productivity are difficult to measure with any precision because of important changes in product mix. The evidence suggests a good rate of productivity growth in the 1960s, but slowing down in the first half of the 1970s. The stagnation of output after 1975 finally forced drastic cuts in manpower as plants were closed down, put on short-time or reorganised. This led to fast gains in labour productivity, about 5½ per cent in a year in 1975–81, when the level of output hardly changed.

3.3 Policies and adjustment: the EEC and the Member States

The role of ECSC and EEC

The role played in the development of the steel industry by the High Authority of the European Coal and Steel Community (ECSC, established by the Treaty of Paris in 1952), and by the EC Commission when the Executives were merged in 1967, goes back to the origins of the Community. It must not be forgotten that the first aim of the Treaty of Paris was political, to establish as strong as possible a link between Germany and France in industries regarded as basic to defence and economic growth.

At the same time it was understood that to insist upon integration by bringing about a clear-cut specialisation between members' industries would not be acceptable; the aim should rather be a 'balanced' interpenetration between national markets. The Treaty of Paris looked neither to free trade nor to perfect competition, especially in view of the industry's long tradition of agreements and cartelisation at the national and international level. (The International Steel Cartel of 1926, which came to include most of the continental producers except the Soviet Union, operated price controls and production quotas quite effectively until weakened by the slump of 1930.)

The main functions of the High Authority—now the EC Commission—included the regulation of prices, the coordination of investments, international trade policy and competition policy: a wider range of powers than for any sector except agriculture.

The price control system, the 'multiple basing point system', which prevailed until the 'manifest crisis' measures of 1980 brought production quotas and firm prices, defines the limits set on competition between member countries. Each producer chose a basing point (generally a transport terminal) for which a base price for each ECSC product was determined and published. The actual or delivered price to the purchaser within the Community was the base price plus transport charges to the destination. An element of oligopoly was introduced because firms in a given country were able to choose the same basing point, despite considerable differences in production costs. Within each country prices tended therefore to be the same, while higher transport costs meant higher delivered prices to foreign purchasers.[6] Thus the system tended to soften price competition while favouring sales to domestic consumers. However, price competition is not ruled out; firms were entitled to offer (and frequently did) rebates on the set prices, provided that these rebates were openly declared, were justified in principle by special conditions such as bulk orders, and did not discriminate between EEC customers. These conditions were difficult to monitor. That competition did indeed develop is shown by the expansion of intra-EEC trade. In times of stable or rising demand, the system appears to have worked fairly smoothly.

But the price system was insufficient to control the steel market when demand weakened in the mid-1970s, while productive capacity was rising fast as a result of the investments of earlier years. Under the 'Davignon Plan' of 1977, the Commission established minimum prices for some products for which the markets were particularly depressed and 'guidance prices' for all steel products. These measures proved insufficient to stabilise the market and restore profitability. The Commission then turned in 1978 to the introduction of voluntary *production quotas* negotiated with the firms but not fully binding. The production quotas proved a more effective instrument than the price controls for a time, partly because they were less easy to evade and partly because of a revival in demand. But by mid-1980, when production fell again, prices began to collapse. In November 1980, the Commission strengthened its powers, invoking for the first time the 'manifest crisis' clause of the Treaty of Paris (Article 58). This allowed the Commission to impose *compulsory* production quotas (accompanied by inspectors and fines). The Commission's problems in managing a deeply depressed market have been intensified by conflicts over the establishment of 'fair shares' for the individual member countries, in particular by the reluctance of the more competitive German and Italian industries to accept limitations on their output. But despite some reported difficulties in enforcing the quotas, the result was a substantial fall in output and some recovery in prices. The latter was encouraged by the Commission's 'target' price increases (November 1981) promulgated in an effort to restore profitability and reduce the level of national governments' rising emergency subsidies. These anti-crisis measures were renewed in mid-1982 for another twelve months, although the strains of the market collapse in 1982 (particularly in Germany) have led to a spate of 'secret' discounting which has again softened prices.

European steel industries have traditionally been well protected by high tariffs. The abolition of high tariffs in intra-EEC trade helps to explain its growth (see Table 3.5); intra-trade in steel rose from about 20 per cent of EEC consumption in 1960–1 (for the Six) to

Table 3.5 EEC: foreign trade in steel ('ECSC products'), 1960–1 to 1979–80*
(annual average)

Quantity (million tons)	EEC-6		EEC-9	
	1960–1	1973–4	1975–6	1979–80
Intra-EEC trade	9.00	21.85	21.59	25.31
Extra-EEC exports	10.62	20.29	18.64	23.45
Extra-EEC imports	1.92	5.15	7.96	9.20
Extra-EEC export surplus	8.70	15.14	10.68	14.25
Total exports	19.61	42.14	40.22	48.76
Total imports	10.92	27.00	29.54	34.52
Intra-EEC trade as % of total trade				
Exports	45.9	51.9	53.7	51.9
Imports	82.4	80.9	73.1	73.3

*Data relate to ECSC products only, in actual weights (i.e. products covered by the Treaty of Paris establishing the ECSC).

Source: Based on EEC: Eurostat, *Iron and Steel Yearbook 1981*, Luxembourg, 1981, Table 5.5, and earlier issues.

nearly 30 per cent in 1979–80 (for the Nine). Against non-members the nominal Common External Tariff is not high—about 5 to 7 per cent on average for all finished steel products—but the 'effective' tariff (that is, the import duty as a percentage of value added) is probably at least twice as high. More significant in recent years is the Commission's activity in promoting Voluntary Export Restraint Agreements (VERs) to regulate imports from non-EEC members. The first of these, with Japan in 1975, limited Japanese exports to the EEC to 1.6 million tons a year (about 1 per cent of EEC consumption); in fact, imports from Japan have not reached this level. Indeed, it appears that the Japanese industry has accepted since about 1970 a stabilisation of its share in world steel output, despite its cost advantages, as a part of the general Japanese strategy of shifting resources to industries with higher value-added. The agreement with Japan was followed by a series of agreements with eleven other exporters to the EEC (five East European countries, Austria, Finland, Norway, Sweden and Australia).

The other side of the coin is the restriction on EEC exports to the US. These measures began with VERs negotiated with the EEC, and with Japan, in the early 1970s but subsequently abandoned when the US market improved in the mid-1970s. The increasing weakness of the US market from 1977 onwards and fast-rising imports caused US steel producers to press for anti-dumping duties. The Carter Administration endeavoured to stave off the industry's complaints by introducing in 1978 the 'trigger price mechanism', in effect setting minimum prices for imports (based on Japanese costs) and imposing duties on imports below these prices. With the following collapse of the US market in 1980–2, the industry's pressure for anti-dumping measures was resumed. The US threatened punitive duties on a range of European imports, particularly from the UK, France and Belgium, which it claimed were heavily subsidised. A last-minute deal was stitched together in November 1982 which imposed substantially tightened quotas until the end of 1985 across a wide range of products. The negotiations proved doubly difficult because of understandable German resentment at being penalised for what it saw as the faults of its partners.

While activities have recently been concentrated on the short-term problems of market management in circumstances of recession, the Commission's functions in the restructuring process have a longer-term significance. These concern both the preservation of competition and the encouragement of the integration of the industry, two aims difficult to reconcile in an industry where economies of scale and the need for structural reorganisation are both regarded as essential for preserving the industry's competitiveness in world markets.

On the one hand, the Treaty of Rome's rules empower the Commission to prohibit agreements among firms to fix prices, allocate markets or establish other restrictive practices, in so far as such agreements affect trade between Member States. Further, the Treaty of Paris (Article 66) allows the High Authority to take action against mergers which prevent effective competition.

On the other hand, in all the main steel-producing countries, a continuous reconstruction of firms, involving the concentration of production by mergers, has been in progress. Such mergers, as well as large investments in new capacity, require Commission approval and appear to have been generally accepted by the Community authorities as part of the strategy for improving the competitive position of the Community's industry, particularly in relation to the Japanese steel industry. What has not happened on any considerable scale, although it might have been considered an element in European integration, is cross-frontier mergers. Important exceptions are Arbed (the Luxembourg-Saar group) and the uneasy cohabitation, now terminated, of the German Hoesch and the Dutch Hoogovens under the holding company Estel. The steel industry is now an industry of increasingly large national oligopolies.

But while concentration has brought the closure of many old plants, integrated complexes first planned in the early 1970s have come on stream. The result is that installed capacity in the EEC has hardly changed since 1974. Meanwhile, output has fallen from 155 million tons in 1974 to an estimated 117 million tons in 1982. Commissioner Davignon claims that much of this capacity is swelled by obsolete plant that steel-makers have used to argue for higher production quotas. Even so, the EC Commission feels that national governments have so far done little to face the reality of market prospects.

In its efforts to arrive at a lasting European solution, the Commission is reported to take the view that a 30 per cent reduction in EEC capacity, from the current (theoretical) level of almost 200 million tons of crude steel a year to about 140 millions (back to the level of the mid-1960s), would be a realistic target for 1985, when subsidies are to cease.[7] That kind of level, if it could be achieved, might permit the EEC industry as a whole to reach a break-even use of capacity *assuming* some increase in production above the 119 million tons of 1982. The problem, of course, is to secure agreement about who scraps what. The UK, for example, thinks that it has had its full share of cutbacks—but its market has been the weakest. The Commission can exercise some influence on the pattern and dimension of closures and new investment through promises of loans and interest rebates, provided that its recommendations are accepted by the national authorities, which remains uncertain. To encourage rationalisation, the Commission further proposes a Community subsidy for each worker displaced, conditional on restructuring (or reducing working hours).

Germany: a case of national cartelisation

In crude steel capacity (nearly 70 million tons a year in 1981) and in output Germany has fairly consistently accounted for about one-third of the EEC steel industry over the past twenty years—although less than half as large as either the Japanese or the US industry.

The relationships between the industry and the government (both Federal and Regional (*Land*) authorities) have been as complex as in any EEC country, except Italy. Government policy has had both its interventionist and market-oriented elements, intervention becoming increasingly dominant in recent years. Moreover the generally market-oriented policy has been modified in the steel industry by the strong tradition of cartelisation among the steel firms.

Federal aid has hitherto consisted mainly of large subsidies both for R & D and for anti-pollution equipment (for example, the 1979 programme for anti-pollution subsidies, mainly for the Ruhr area). The steel industry has also gained indirectly from large Federal subsidies to coal and shipbuilding, a major supplier and a major customer respectively for steel. More direct Federal financial aid had grown in recent years (for example, the construction of new plants in the Saar and Dortmund). And the Federal government owns Peine-Salzgitter, which accounts for around 10 per cent of steel production. At least equally significant, however, is the important aid derived from Regional (*Land*) governments due to the high geographical concentration of the steel industry, mainly in Lower Saxony, Rhine-Westphalia (Ruhr) and the Saar.

The other aspect of government policy is the effective acceptance of the cartel-like activities of the steel producers, accepted too by the EEC authorities. These activities took two forms: the common sales agencies for pooling and allocating orders, the *Stahlkontore*, set up in the 1960s by steel producers; and the series of agreements between the firms. Four *Kontore* (agencies) covered, in the later 1960s, nearly 90 per cent of sales of rolled steel on the German market. The justifications for authorising this procedure are: the pooling of orders and their allocation among producers encourage specialisation and are not otherwise restrictive; the agreements between producers and the *Kontore* do not give the producers collective control of prices or power to restrict production or marketing. Moreover, the share of the *Kontore* in the ECSC market as a whole, which is relevant to Community policy, is much less dominant than on the German domestic market.

The effectiveness of the *Kontor* system may help to explain why the process of rationalisation in the German steel industry largely took the form of various kinds of agreements for specialisation and the organisation of market shares, rather than of formal mergers. The regional *Kontore* generally quoted identical price lists for their members and thus maintained 'price discipline'. It can be claimed, moreover, that the system allowed greater flexibility and some competition between firms in long-term strategies, whereas mergers imply both high costs and irreversibility. Finally, the avoidance of formal mergers reduced the risk of intervention by the Federal Cartel office.

Nevertheless, a number of mergers occurred: about seven between 1966 and 1977. One significant merger was that between Hoesch and the Dutch Hoogovens in 1973 under the name 'Estel'. The object was that the coastal Hoogovens' plant at Ijmuiden, which was new and highly efficient, should supply crude steel to Hoesch along the Rhine. The recession of the early 1980s has produced more far-reaching schemes of combination. In February 1982 it was announced that Krupp and Estel, both having incurred heavy losses, were to merge their steel-making activities, with mergers of other divisions to follow later. It appeared that the Federal government approved the deal in principle but expressed doubts about the financial assistance expected.[8] One consequence, however, was the dissolution of the Hoesch-Hoogovens union, partly, perhaps, because of German alarm at possible high import penetration of a collapsed domestic market, and partly because of the heavy recent losses of the Estel combine attributed mainly to Hoesch. A different combination of interests was proposed in early 1983 by an expert group commissioned by the government and industry.[9] Their report recommended the formation of two giant groups together embracing most of the German industry: one between Thyssen and Krupp; the other between Hoesch, Klöckner and the state-owned Salzgitter. The scheme is reported to include government aid (about DM 3 billion) to finance the operation—which may not be easily accepted by a market-oriented Federal government.

Over a longer period, the internal strategies of the steel producers have been directed towards diversification, particularly towards shifting production into downsteam activities, to a greater extent than in other steel industries; for Thyssen, Krupp and Mannesmann, steel production and processing now represent only 35 to 40 per cent of total turnover, in contrast to Salzgitter (51 per cent), Hoesch (68 per cent), and Klöckner (93 per cent).[10] This strategy of diversification is long and complex, as can be illustrated by the experience of Thyssen—an example which may be relevant to other European steel firms. Thyssen benefited, indeed, from a long tradition in this respect, having acquired interests both in coal-mining and in engineering as early as the 1880s. However, after the Second World War, as a result of the Allied occupation authorities' policies, Thyssen was reduced to steel production. Until the late 1960s, the strategy adopted was to concentrate on steel, introducing new technologies, notably the oxygen process, and reorganising the product mix with emphasis on rolled products; to keep input costs down, mines were bought in Brazil and Liberia; and among ways of penetrating growth markets, a steel-producing plant was established in Brazil. From the end of the 1960s, the company, seeing poor prospects for crude steel production in Europe, returned to a strategy of diversification downstream, moving again into special steels, engineering and even plastics.

Diversification has been one response to the problem of adjustment in a stagnant European steel market. Another response was a strong push of direct exports into non-EEC markets. A crucial role was played by the *Kontore*, which subsidised such exports on a substantial scale. Since the subsidies were financed by all member firms, all had a certain incentive to take advantage of them. Thus West Germany was the only EEC country where direct net exports of steel to non-EEC markets increased substantially even in the late 1970s.[11]

France: a case of ad hoc planning

The need for reconstruction and rationalisation of the French steel industry was recognised from the end of the war by the government and the industry. But until the mid-1960s, although output was rising, very little progress was made either in reorganisation or in the adoption of new techniques, and the level of new investment in steel was low. One reason was that the steel producers, concentrated in Lorraine and having large interests in the iron ore fields, devoted substantial resources to the development of iron ore mining and iron production with a view both to meeting import competition in ores and strengthening their positions as iron consumers for steel-making. By 1965 there was only one steel works with a capacity exceeding two million tons (Sollac, a non-integrated plant); however, the first part of a large coastal plant at Dunkirk was completed (by Usinor). Other projects, for an oxygen steel works, by Sidelor, and for a second coastal plant at Le Havre or Fos, were shelved. The government, in the early 1960s, was not inclined to commit funds for large steel projects.

The Fifth Plan (1966–70) optimistically envisaged a more definite strategy of expansion, investment and concentration in the steel industry. Negotiations between government and the industry, based on proposals by the newly formed Chambre Syndicale de la Sidérurgie Française (CSSF) which acquired a recognised status as partner of the state, opened the way to an agreement, the Convention Générale Etat-Sidérurgie of 1966. The government announced its willingness to provide investment funds at preferential rates of interest for several years, together with reduced transport costs for steel products and assistance with labour adjustments. For its part the industry, under pressure from the increasingly powerful CSSF, accepted the need for concentration and rationalisation (*regroupement*) involving the construction of new steel plants with state aid (including the doubling, to three million tons, of Usinor's Dunkirk works); at the same time a number of old plants were to be closed. But a crucial feature of the agreement was that the restructuring was to be embodied in separate conventions between the government and each of the firms concerned.

These plans were not realised in full, but the Sixth Plan (1970–5) again displayed an optimistic approach by the government and the CSSF, incorporating an expansion of crude steel capacity from 26 to 36 million tons and a number of new projects including massive introduction of the oxygen process and a major development of rolling mills for sheets and special steels. The financial position of the firms was expected to allow for 60 per cent of the most important projects to be self-financed.

State aid to the industry has taken the form essentially of subsidies to capital investment (low interest loans and loan guarantees) made through the Fonds de Développement Economique et Social (FDES). Such loans amounted in 1968–75 to £430 million representing around one-fifth of the total investment outlays of the steel firms during these years.[12]

Although a substantial part of the proposed reconstruction of the industry was achieved between 1965 and 1975, the plans, again, were not completely realised. Thus by 1982, crude steel capacity had not exceeded 30 million tons and production 23 million tons. Within each planning period, optimistic expectations have been disappointed. Failure of demand and insufficient competitiveness weakened the capacity of the firms to finance the new projects and delayed their progress.

Concentration of the industry has been an essential element in the restructuring. The obstacles were: on the one hand, the traditional separation between producers of crude steel and producers of finished steel products, hindering vertical integration; on the other hand, the unwillingness of large consumers—of whom some, such as the state railways, exercised considerable influence—to see competition reduced among their suppliers. Hence the concept of 'national champions' among crude steel producers proved difficult to realise. One important merger—between Usinor and Lorraine-Escaut—was arranged quite rapidly with state financial support since their outputs were complementary. The completion of the Dunkirk plant increased the firm's capital intensity, in particular raising the proportion of output produced by the oxygen process from 53 per cent in 1970 to 75 per cent in 1974. A second important merger, between De Wendel and Sidelor (now called Sacilor) with a number of other interlinked firms, took over two years to negotiate and came under financial stress in the early 1970s. There followed in 1973 a major rationalisation, including the dismissal of about 11,000 (out of 60,000) workers and a more highly specialised division of output. At the same time, the big project at Fos was completed. Mergers in the special steels and final products sector were arranged more easily, leading, by the 1970s, to the creation of the diversified Creusot-Loire with 60 per cent of French production of special steels. But efforts (in 1974) by Usinor to move into downstream activities by taking control of Creusot-Loire were abortive: the government was hesitant, preferring to keep a balance between Usinor and De Wendel, while the EC Commission was worried on anti-trust grounds. Together with a number of other mergers, the general result was a reduction in the number of steel producers (that is, firms) by about half between 1966 and 1975.

Although concentration among the firms appears substantial, the intended rationalisation and specialisation at the plant level did not always follow. The new firms still consisted of a mix of modern and old plants, resulting in high operating costs. The problem of adjustment within the new firms, especially in Lorraine, remained after 1975.

The labour redundancies implied by the reconstruction brought the workers and unions into the bargaining process. While the government insisted on discussions with the unions, it refused to become directly involved; until 1978, indeed, the official attitude appeared to be that increased capital intensity would not necessarily imply harsh problems of declining employment. The problems of labour force adjustment were allowed to accumulate. Since 1977, a more realistic approach has prevailed. Redundancies and closures have been pushed. Between 1975 and 1982 the total labour force in French steel was reduced by nearly 40 per cent—more than in any EEC country except the UK. The biggest cuts were in Lorraine and precipitated the protest riots of 1979. Such pressures prevented the more complete concentration of the industry in the modernised plants at Fos and Dunkirk intended by Sacilor and Usinor.

The stagnation of output, demand and productivity which began in the mid-1970s, on top of the heavy and increasing debts already incurred by most firms, forced the government into action to avert threatening bankruptcies. A reconstruction—basically financial— was introduced in 1978. The state and quasi-public creditors (FDES, the banks and others) became shareholders in new finance companies which in turn became effective owners of the major steel producers. A special institution (the Caisse d'Amortissement pour l'Acier) was established to manage the privately held debts. The overall cost of the exercise and the redundancies created in Lorraine and other places is estimated at about FF 50 billion (£5 billion), most of it being met by the French exchequer.[13] The result is that the state, directly or indirectly, came to own two-thirds of the steel firms; the nationalisation of Usinor and Sacilor by the Mitterrand Administration formalised a *de facto* relationship (although 4 to 5 per cent of the shares are still privately held). Since nationalisation, the French government has put forward an ambitious reconstruction plan of FF 26 billion (£2.3 billion) aimed at improving the competitive strength of the French industry and eradicating losses.[14] But the outcome is uncertain since the capacity of the economy to maintain a large steel industry is hotly debated within France.

Although the main purpose of the 1978 plan was a financial reorganisation, the new managements have used the opportunity to introduce important structural changes, centralising production and enforcing a greater degree of specialisation within the firms. These implied substantial redundancies and the end of the illusion that continued modernisation and increases in productivity were compatible with long-run maintenance of the level of employment. Yet there is not much evidence that the long-term need for greater geographical concentration and diversification of the major firms has been fully accepted, and the attachment to the historical sites in the Lorraine ore fields remains an obstacle to full modernisation.

Italy: a dynamic industry

The Italian steel industry, quite unlike the other major steel industries discussed here, is a new industry built up since the Second World War. In 1937, crude steel production was a mere two million tons, and was highly protected. Moreover, the Italian industry has throughout been developed without the basis of domestic coal and iron ore resources upon which the other major European industries were originally established. The development of the industry thus resembles in some ways that of the steel industries in Japan or the newly industrialising countries.

Post-war expansion brought Italian steel production and capacity (40 million tons a year by 1982) above the level of France and the UK, surpassed in Western Europe only by West Germany. The rapid rate of growth was based principally on the equally rapid growth of industrial production and of domestic steel demand. Steel consumption more than tripled from 1960 to 1980—three times as fast as in the Community as a whole and not far off the Japanese growth rate. The elasticity of steel consumption to total industrial production in Italy was, exceptionally, about one throughout both the 1960s and 1970s, reflecting particularly the growth of construction in Italy (Table 3.2). Crude steel production tripled and employment rose 50 per cent, Italy being the only major EEC producer except the Netherlands in which steel employment was not reduced in 1960–80. Simultaneously, there was a healthy development of exports, rising to about one-quarter of production by the late 1970s, while import penetration of the home market has remained fairly constant, since 1960, at about one-quarter. While the level of protection, as elsewhere in the EEC, has been greatly reduced, imports into Italy— but also Italian exports—are to some extent limited by relatively high transport costs (less true of imports, however, since the construction of the French steel complex at Fos on the Mediterranean). Thus it is only with difficulty that the Italian industry can be expected to renounce its opportunities for continued growth in the interests of 'fair shares' for all EEC steel industries in a weak market.

The Italian steel industry inherited after the war a structure which was small but rather well adapted for post-war expansion. A large part of the industry had been taken over before the war by the state-owned IRI and was relatively advanced. A quarter of the steel was produced in electric furnaces. The major post-war development was undertaken by Finsider, the holding company for IRI's steel interests, now accounting for 55 to 60 per cent of total crude steel production (the rest of the industry consisting of a number of small private firms). The Finsider group, with its production of nearly 14 million tons (1980), is among the Western world's largest steel-producing groups. Finsider's main operating company is Italsider.

The major element in Italsider's strategy to cope with increasing demand was the creation of the giant Taranto plant (in 1969–73) with a capacity of 10.5 million tons a year, the largest integrated steel plant in Western Europe, representing a quarter of Italy's total crude steel capacity. The plant should thus be able to take full advantage of economies of scale after the Japanese pattern, economies which are particularly marked for the flat products in which it specialises. Its coastal location is designed to compensate for Italy's lack of coal and iron ore. Another purpose of the Taranto location, although not fully realised, was to form the base for a widespread industrial development in the Mezzogiorno. Italsider's other plants are mostly medium sized, with capacities of up to three million tons a year. Italsider has avoided the strategic mistake observed elsewhere: the flexibility allowed by a mix of large and medium-sized plants makes it easier to meet demand fluctuations without incurring the costs of running large plants below capacity.

Italsider did not, however, escape the difficulties of the European steel industries in the late 1970s, although production, including stockpiling to avoid lay-offs, was not actually reduced until 1981. The recession exposed certain weaknesses which had been masked by the earlier fast expansion. First, although the rate of capacity utilisation in crude steel production was quite well maintained, it fell off for a number of intermediate and final steel products. Secondly, unit labour costs rose faster than in most other EEC steel industries in association with Italy's fast rate of inflation. It proved particularly difficult in Italy to organise reductions in the labour force and disturbed industrial relations resulted in a number of labour conflicts; indeed, employment continued to rise through 1980, although it fell by 6 per cent by 1982. Thirdly, losses became heavy: at the end of 1979, Italsider's losses represented over one-third of the firm's assets. By Italian company law, a reduction of capital had to be undertaken to absorb the losses. At the same time, large new loans were made through IRI. In addition, an industrial adjustment programme was developed for the whole Finsider group involving the reconstruction of Italsider into Nuova Italsider, with some changes in the pattern of specialisation.

The quadrupling of the capacity of the Italian steel industry in the past twenty years naturally involved an immense investment, particularly in the construction of the Taranto plant. The feature of Finsider's capital structure is the remarkable dependence on medium and long-term loan capital, which represents two-thirds of its total investment outlays. The financial charges account for a large part of the heavy losses incurred when the crisis struck. Equity investment has been negligible. Finsider appears to have chosen this form of financing because of its access to IRI funding (IRI owns banks), and appears to have some kind of loan guarantees from the state. Also, Finsider has been able to raise loans at quite reasonable rates on the Euro-markets or from international bank consortia and benefits from state-subsidised interest rates but not so far, it seems, from direct state subsidies. In addition, the European Investment Bank was largely involved in the Taranto project.

A new state financial programme for 1981–5 has been planned for the public steel sector, involving something like $5 billion, partly in loans but including $2.5 billion of subsidy (increasing the IRI's equity holding).

The private sector consists of two important producers—Teksid, belonging to the Fiat group, and Falck—together with about one hundred small firms. The sector specialises in long products, for which demands tend to be more volatile than for the flat products which make up most of the public sector, and for which small firms are better adapted.

The best-known of the small private firms are the 'Bresciani', located in the Brescia province in Northern Italy, which specialises in reinforcing bars (representing about 20 per cent of Italian steel production). Their competitiveness (like that of many other small-scale industries in Northern Italy) is based on low costs, ability to adopt new techniques (such as continuous casting), on good industrial relations and full use of commercial skills. The result is a remarkable export performance. Furthermore, financing has been relatively easy, being derived largely from family funds; however, the programme for state aid for 1981–5, mentioned above, provides for loans of $1 billion for the private steel sector in addition to the aid for the public sector.

Belgium–Luxembourg: banks in the leading role

The steel industries of Belgium and Luxembourg (B–L) are old and big industries in small countries, with their production geared mainly to export. Crude steel *production* per head of population is probably greater than in any country in the world, and the economy, especially in Luxembourg, is more dependent upon steel than in any other nation. The combined crude steel capacity of the two steel industries (25 million tons a year) is not much less than that of France and about as large as that in the UK (Table 3.1).

Another crucial characteristic of the B–L industries has been the dominant role of the banks as main, or exclusive shareholders in the principal steel firms. A close connection can be observed between the concentration process among the steel firms and that among the owning banks. Thus the six financial centres of the early 1960s were reduced by 1970 to three major ones (Société Générale, Bruxelles-Lambert and Cobepa-Paribas), with an important financial interest in the steel industry also held by a steel trading firm, A. Frère. The Société Générale was largely responsible for building up Cockerill as the core of the leading steel group in the early 1970s, creating one dominant pole in the industry. A second pole was created by Cobepa together with Bruxelles-Lambert and Frère, a combine of smaller firms known as the Triangle de Charleroi. While the concentration of ownership in the financial centres could have facilitated technical modernisation, it may be that the interests of the banks did not necessarily coincide with the rationalisation of the steel firms themselves. And the difficulties of the steel firms in the 1970s resulted in the accumulation of heavy debts. Thus, even in 1965–74, Cockerill was operating on a very small profit margin, turning into heavy losses thereafter.

Until 1977–8, the Belgian government's aid to the industry was on a relatively small scale and consisted mainly of subsidised interest rates and other state aids available to all industries. In 1977–8, the system of state aids was dramatically expanded. One reason was the disastrous effects of the steel crisis on the finances and debts of some Belgian steel firms, especially Cockerill. A second reason was a reform of the Belgian Constitution with substantial devolution of power to regional authorities—particularly important because the weakest firms are located in Wallonia.

This new intervention by the state (the Belgian financial plan of 1978) made possible a complete financial restructuring of the main Belgian firms. The debt charges—amounting to 8 to 12 per cent of turnover—and some cash requirements were capitalised in public bonds. As a result, a large share of the ownership of the steel firms passed to the Belgian state, involving the setting up of new investment institutions financed through the Budget (*Fonds de Renouvellement Industriel* and the *Sociétés Régionales d'Investissement*). After the operation, the ownership of the firms was generally divided into 30 per cent for the state, 20 per cent for the 'stable' private shareholders (essentially the banks), and 50 per cent for smaller shareholders.[15] An investment programme for 1980–5 was agreed in 1980, establishing programmes for each firm; it appears that approaching half was to be allocated to Cockerill, and nearly a quarter to the Triangle de Charleroi. But realisation of these programmes remains doubtful.

The contrasting experience of two leading firms in the Belgium–Luxembourg steel industry illustrates an essential point in the consideration of industrial strategies.

Cockerill's problems derived from its somewhat heterogeneous collection of rather small plants—mostly in Liège, some new but some obsolete—with low productivity (said to be around half that in Germany while wage levels are about the same), subject to many labour disputes and with heavy inter-plant transport costs. Under pressure from the government, now the dominant shareholder, a reorganisation plan was introduced in 1979 involving: (a) the closure of a number of plants over the following three or four years and massive redundancies, which have already led to riots; (b) the linking of some of Cockerill's activities with other European firms (with Arbed in Luxembourg, Estel and Klöckner in Germany and Usinor in France). The survival of Cockerill as a large producer, requiring in 1981 £1 billion of funding by the government and the EEC,[16] appears to depend rather heavily on the social and political pressures to avoid exacerbating unemployment in depressed Wallonia, and thus suffers from the instability of Belgian politics.

By contrast, the Luxembourg-based Arbed seems now to have developed a well-defined industrial strategy. The firm's position in the early 1970s was not particularly good by European standards. The bulk of the capacity, spread over Luxembourg and the Saar, was old and the product mix not very favourable. The new strategy of the 1970s was essentially one of geographical diversification in three directions. First, links have been tightened with German producers, especially with Röchling with its production in the Saar; the two firms have planned an integrated set of plants benefiting from German aid to the Saar. Also, Arbed entered one of the German selling agencies (*Kontore*). Secondly, Arbed has been the dominant shareholder in the coastal plant of Sidmar. Thirdly, Arbed has diversified to a small extent downstream into engineering in Germany, as well as in Belgium, and into steel merchanting. It has also been developing new high-technology steel products, especially in wires and special steels.

Apart from this international diversification, Arbed has undertaken, and has pursued throughout the 1970s, a large programme of rationalisation and modernisation of its plants in Luxembourg. New plants have been built and older ones, especially rolling mills, closed so that the emphasis has shifted, with trade union cooperation in redeployment of workers to avoid redundancies, to bulk steel production. In these efforts Arbed has been able to get financial support from both the Belgian and German governments and from the EEC.

It is still uncertain whether Arbed's strategy will be successful. It rests on the assumption that a bulk steel producer can still be viable in Europe, at least when combined with some locational diversification to maintain a strong position in EEC markets. But like the other European producers, Arbed has been hit by the market collapse in 1982 and shares their apprehension that recovery will bring scant relief for bulk steel producers.

The UK: modernisation, not so much too little as too late?

Two features characterise the relative development of the UK iron and steel industry. The first is the near stagnation of both steel production and domestic demand, associated with the slow growth of the UK economy and with the decline in the steel export surplus. In 1982 UK crude steel production at about 14 million tons was

40 per cent less than in 1960, while production in the rest of the EEC (9) rose by 40 per cent. UK productive capacity at the beginning of 1982 is put at 25 million tons a year, a rather theoretical figure including many plants at present closed, but a considerable reduction on the 31 million tons of 1966. Over these sixteen years every other EEC steel industry increased its capacity (see Table 3.1). The UK steel industry with 60 per cent fewer employees than in 1960 (twice as large a cut as in the rest of the EEC) can be said to have carried out a quite drastic 'adjustment'.

Secondly, not only has state intervention played a larger role in the UK than elsewhere, but also the forms of intervention have been subject to great and damaging fluctuations in policy. The Labour government's nationalisation of the industry in 1949, followed by Conservative denationalisation in 1953 and then by a second Labour nationalisation of most of the industry in 1967 (with a present prospect of an effort to denationalise, at least in part, when market conditions are more favourable) are a part of the story.

In the period of private ownership, the Iron and Steel Board (the supervisory body established by the government under the Iron and Steel Act 1953) produced Development Reports setting out a medium-term strategy and projections in consultation with the industry, execution and financing being left to the steel firms. But the overhanging threat of renationalisation hindered large-scale risk-taking. The sequence of reports (like the French plans) shows a certain, if declining, optimism about future prospects and projections which failed to be realised.

Under the renationalisation of 1967, the British Steel Corporation (BSC) took over the fourteen biggest steel producers with nearly forty separate plants. It is important to note that a substantial section of the industry remained private: over 100 companies with about a quarter of the output in tonnage, but concentrated in special steels (alloys) and higher value finished steels which, until recently, have proved the stronger sector of the industry. The result is an industry in some respects subject to quite strong internal competition, and also, of course, to the competition of imports; BSC's share of the domestic market by the end of the 1970s was reduced to a half.

A first task of the BSC, although it took four years, was to establish a ten-year development plan.[17] The plan represented a compromise between rosy and less rosy views of future demand for UK steel. Much controversy resulted in a projected target for crude steel capacity in the mid-1980s within the range of 36 to 38 million tons a year, compared with 30 millions when the report was drawn up.

In fact, as optimism receded with time, the theoretical capacity (which includes many plants not now in production) was reduced by 1982 to 25 million tons and actual production to about 14 million tons.

The optimism of the late 1960s was based not only on continuing economic growth but also—and more important—on the recovery of competitive power to be achieved by modernisation and by concentration of output into a handful of up-to-date plants making use wherever possible of economies of scale and new techniques. Five existing and large integrated plants near the coast were planned to be brought up to maximum capacity in order to carry the main weight of future steel output: Scunthorpe (capacity 7 million tons), Lackenby (4.7), Llanwern (3.5), Ravenscraig (3.2), Port Talbot (3.0). Also, a new complex was to be built on Teeside. The emphasis was on modernising liquid steel output in giant plants using the basic oxygen process, with Japanese and continental examples in mind, while the improvement of blast furnaces and rolling mills, and product diversification, were to be postponed. At the same time, substantial progress was made in reallocating production among the BSC plants. In the early 1970s, too, hopes of successful competition in Europe were raised by entry into the Community, particularly since UK steel prices were then below German or French prices.

Depression and inflation hit after 1974, just when BSC could have expected to reap rewards from these modernisations. Euphoria was replaced by the beginnings of a surgical operation which still continues. Stagnating demand at home and abroad—notably for cars, construction and shipbuilding—was one factor. But another has been the failure of the UK industry to maintain its competitive position either in the home market or abroad. The export surpluses of the 1960s (and early 1970s) gave way to import deficits, or at best a rough balance, after 1973, increasing imports coming mainly from the EEC. Thus by 1981 and 1982 output of crude steel in the UK was only about half of its level in 1970.

The major adjustment really began in 1978. Until then the policy had been to hang on in the hope that the market would recover. From 1978 a drastic programme involving closing down old plants and trimming the labour force began. These cuts were carried through in the face of strong resistance from the unions—modified only after an unsuccessful strike—and with the help of an expensive scheme of compensation for redundant workers. Production has had to be spread between plants, partly to lessen the social problems, and the expected cost advantages of economies of scale were largely lost. Even now the future of the five major integrated coastal plants remains in doubt.

The consequent heavy losses of the industry, as well as a large share of the investments carried through under the development plan, were met by public funds (largely in the form of public dividend capital under which the government took an equity interest) and borrowing. By early 1981, the total, long-term debt of the BSC had risen to £1.2 billions.[18] BSC has recently made more use than most countries of the long-term borrowing facilities of the European Investment Bank and the ECSC. About £500 million in the long-term debt figure quoted above came from these sources.

The BSC's and the government's increasing realism (or pessimism) about long-term prospects for the UK steel industry resulted in a new programme, now being executed, for reducing effective BSC capacity in crude steel to 14.4 million tons. The new Corporate Plan was drawn up in 1979–80 by a new chairman of BSC, Ian MacGregor, and approved by the government as a drastic and perhaps final effort to restore BSC to competitiveness.[19] The plan involved a substantial writing off of accumulated debt to the government and of the government-held capital, and held out the prospect— no longer likely to be realised—of returning to profit (before the remaining interest charges) in 1982–3. Agreements with the unions on redundancies and other matter such as the breaking down of job barriers have resulted in major productivity gains, bringing BSC closer to continental productivity levels. For example, employment per 1,000 tons of production fell from 8.7 to 5.7 between 1974 and 1981. (The German level in 1981 was 5.1.)

The private sector in the steel industry accounted by the late 1970s for about one-third of the industry's ouput in value; its share had grown considerably since the establishment of BSC in 1967. Although mainly engaged in special steels, the private firms have also made inroads into bulk steel production by building 'mini-mills', mainly electric furnaces. Six such mills were built in 1972–6. Their total capacity is about 2.2 million tons a year, the largest (the Greek-owned Alpha Steel) having a capacity of 1 million tons. The mills, four of which were built by foreign firms, were built in less than two years, a considerable advantage in an inflationary period, and were cheap in capital costs (in 1972 prices, the capital cost can be put at about £70–75 per ton compared with at least five times as much for an integrated steel works).[20]

Apart from regional subsidies, available to all, the investments in mini-mills were funded by the owners. Until recently, relationships with the government were relatively unimportant (except as regards locations). The private firms, however, have not been able to escape the general recession or the rise in costs. Their ability to maintain a competitive advantage against BSC has been difficult within the EEC cartel arrangements. Private producers of steel castings for example, are jointly halving their capacity with governmental encouragement, and similar programmes, including agreements with BSC for joint operations, are under way in other products.[21] The producers have successfully obtained assistance from the government under Section 8 of the Industry Act to help the process of slimming, but continue nevertheless to find it increasingly tough.

The basic strategic problems of the UK steel industry remain. Continued drastic adjustment by closure and redundancies has been unavoidable. Overmanning is no longer the major cause of uncompetitiveness, but inevitable pressures to keep capacity open limit scale advantages. The question now is whether a thinned-down and reconstructed industry will achieve the economic and technical competitiveness necessary for survival. The outcome is still uncertain.

3.4 Towards a Community steel strategy?

The focus of this chapter has been *national* industries and *national* government policies, because most of the action for long-term reconstruction has been at the national level. Within the Community, the compelling necessities of immediate emergencies have diverted attention away from long-term strategies and towards short-term and cartel-like management of market crises. What are the prospects for an international strategy, at least within the Community?

The obstacle is the present wide disparities in costs and competitive positions among the Community industries, disparities which were apparent well before the recession. Their consequences have been temporarily surmounted, with great difficulty and for no-one knows how long, by the current measures established by the Commission for output and price controls. Such measures hardly form a satisfactory basis for the long-term reshaping of the European industry. There is general recognition by now of the inevitability of retrenchment, that is, of a substantial reduction of steel-producing capacity. The problem is how the burden of retrenchment is to be shared.

One the one hand, the *UK* and *French* steel industries which have undergone the deepest cuts in output and employment, remain heavily dependent on financial support from their governments (with significant contributions from the EEC). The *Belgian* and *Luxembourg* industries undertook a limited measure of reconstruction sooner than the British or the French. The small but technically efficient *Netherlands* industry is vulnerable to the state of the

European steel market, especially since the breakdown of its promising link with Hoesch.

By contrast, the *German* industry has proved its superior efficiency, at least until lately, with relatively little government aid. Hence the German reluctance to accept the EEC crisis measures to restrict output; a reluctance overcome, perhaps, by fears that a renewed collapse of the steel market would further endanger the already difficult finances of the major firms. In a free-for-all, the German producers might gain market shares, but only at considerable expense in profits. It is largely through German insistence that EEC crisis management has been accompanied by acceptance of a code for state subsidies, and for their effective disappearance by 1985. The *Italian* position is more complex. The industry is modern, with high productivity, and has been able to maintain production better than most of its competitors.

It is these disparities which have created highly defensive national approaches in the high-cost industries, and reluctance to yield competitive advantages in the low-cost ones. The defensive approaches are shared by the governments which have become the owners, or at least the major creditors, of the financially weakened steel industries. A nationalistic approach is reinforced both by the social problems of a geographically concentrated industry and by the concept, even if it can be regarded as a form of economic mythology, of the 'strategic' role of the steel industry in a national economy.

What form could a Community strategy for long-term reconstruction and rationalisation take in the face of these obstacles? Such a strategy need not be regarded as a forlorn hope, if improbable in present circumstances.

One possibility for European policy-makers is to promote a much stronger degree of integration and production, even of nationalised industries, across the frontiers (and, for that matter, with non-EEC industries), as is happening increasingly in motor vehicles and electronics. It could be hoped that such an integration would reduce the disparities in costs, in technology, and in working methods.

It may also be necessary (and this is more fundamental) to make the strategic decision about how far the EEC industries should seek to maintain a strong position as producers of bulk steel, and for how long. The question is whether the present technological advantages of at least some European producers will for long offset the labour-cost advantages, as well as the advancing technology, of many outside competitors in European (and world) markets for bulk steel. The experience of the last two decades suggests that the policy of concentration of effort on huge production units for bulk steel, following the Japanese model, has diverted investment away from the higher-value products, especially in the UK and France. The thrust of adjustment strategies may now need to be directed downstream towards the greater diversification of the industry into activities where Europe has comparative advantages.

In broad terms, then, the future holds the possibility of a group of much thinned-down steel industries in Western Europe and North America, capable of meeting world competition, and with a shift away from crude steel into steel products of higher value added. This may come about through a competitive struggle, mainly among the handful of major producing groups which survive. It is unlikely in such circumstances that all national governments will refrain from giving competitive subsidies in one form or another, open or concealed, to their own national champions. But, alternatively, it may be possible, at least within the Community, to arrive at a negotiated programme of reconstruction. Such a programme, if it is to be more than an equal scaling-down of capacity all round—which would only prolong the unstable *status quo ante*—must differentiate between the countries concerned; and that means differentiating between the individual major enterprises. In such a negotiation the Commission will need to play a constructive and vital part, not only as a middleman or arbitrator but also as an initiator.

In neither case can the risks of erroneous expectations of future steel demand, or of technical development, be averted. But the experience of the last few years has finally substituted a measure of realism for the over-optimism which helped to bring about the present crisis.

Notes

1. See Table 1.2, p. 7.
2. For data on individual countries, see OECD (1982).
3. For production by process, see Eurostat (1981), Tables 3.15 and 3.16.
4. Carlsson (1981).
5. See Eurostat (1981), Tables 7.2 and 7.5.
6. However, under the system known as 'alignment', producers could reduce delivered prices, but only to the extent necessary to *equal* the prices charged by a member-country competitor. There was no such restriction on the prices required to meet competition from non-member countries.
7. *Guardian*, 25 January 1983. According to estimates made for 1981 in United Nations, Economic Commission for Europe (1982), however, producers in EEC countries estimated capacity in 1984 and 1985 to remain at about 200 million tons.
8. *The Times*, 27 March 1982.

9. *Guardian*, 2 January 1983.
10. Messerlin (1981).
11. Thus from 1977 to 1980 German net exports to non-EEC countries rose from 3.8 to 6.5 million tons (crude equivalent), while such net exports from other EEC countries fell by 1 million tons (Eurostat (1981), Table 5.1).
12. Messerlin (1981).
13. National Economic Development Office (1981), Annex C, France.
14. *Financial Times*, 10 June 1982.
15. Messerlin (1981).
16. *Financial Times*, 25 February 1982.
17. Department of Trade and Industry (1973).
18. British Steel Corporation (1981).
19. See Statement by Sir Keith Joseph, then Minister of State for Industry (House of Commons, 1981, p. 745) supporting the BSC Corporate Plan.
20. Cottrell (1981), pp. 75–6, and *Guardian*, 1 December 1981.
21. *National Institute Economic Review* (1982), p. 59.

References

British Steel Corporation (1981), *Annual Report and Accounts 1980–81*, London.

Department of Trade and Industry (1973), *British Steel Corporation: Ten Year Development Strategy*, Cmnd 5226, London: HMSO.

Carlsson, B. (1981), 'Structure and performance in the West European steel industry: a historical perspective', in de Jong, H. W., ed., *The Structure of European Industry*, The Hague: Martinus Nijhoff.

Cottrell, E. (1981), *The Giant with Feet of Clay*, London: Centre for Policy Studies.

Eurostat (1981), *Iron and Steel Yearbook 1981*, Luxembourg.

House of Commons (1981), *Parliamentary Debates. Weekly Hansard*, No. 1, 197.

Messerlin, P. (1981), *The European Industrial Adjustment Policies: the Steel Industry Case*, Brighton: Sussex European Research Centre, mimeo.

National Economic Development Office (1981), *Industrial Policies in Europe*, London.

National Institute Economic Review (1982), February, London.

OECD (1982), *The Steel Market in 1981*, Paris.

United Nations, Economic Commission for Europe (1982), *The Steel Market in 1981* (ECE/Steel 39), New York.

4 SHIPBUILDING: ADJUSTMENT-LED INTERVENTION OR INTERVENTION-LED ADJUSTMENT?

Peter Mottershead

4.1 Introduction

This chapter looks at the adjustment problems facing merchant shipbuilding, problems which have led in the past two decades to a great deal of government intervention in many countries as well as to a considerable amount of international activity through the OECD and the EEC aimed to regulate such intervention.

There are two main reasons which might be put forward to explain the strong interest of governments in industrialised countries in the performance of their domestic merchant shipbuilding activities. First, benefits both in terms of export earnings and trade security may be thought to accompany the domestic production of merchant ships. It might be argued also that mature trading economies seem to attach some additional 'psychological' importance to the ability to produce ships domestically, perhaps for self-sufficiency reasons. Secondly, the employment impact of the industry has been considered important in the past, although it is not now so significant. In some countries, this concern is reinforced by the location of the industry in regions with above-average employment. A third possible reason which may have been important in the past—but is surely not so now—is that merchant shipbuilding capacity could act as a supplement to naval building in an emergency.

The shipbuilding industry has grown in the post-war era by substantial amounts. World tonnage completed expanded from 3.3 million gross registered tons (grt) in 1950 to 34.2 million grt in 1975 (Table 4.1), but capacity now significantly exceeds demand: OECD estimates suggest that in 1979 capacity was in the order of twice the output produced.[1] The current crisis is one of greater severity than a normal trough in what is recognised to be a habitually cyclical industry. The main factor leading to the current crisis is the substantial interruption in the growth of world trade associated with the oil price increases of 1973 and 1979. For shipbuilding, the recession has outlasted the 'cushion' normally afforded by a backlog of orders.

Table 4.1 World merchant shipbuilding completions, 1950–81 (000 gross registered tons)

	1950	1960	1970	1975	1976	1977	1978	1979	1980	1981
France	174	174	859	1,150	1,673	1,107	440	720	283	502
Denmark	117	214	518	969	1,034	709	346	263	208	352
Germany (West)	81	1,124	1,317	2,499	1,874	1,595	845	437	376	703
Italy	75	447	546	792	715	778	339	231	248	271
Netherlands	198	682	632	1,028	634	240	315	263	122	173
UK	1,398	1,298	1,327	1,170	1,500	1,020	1,133	691	427	213
Norway	58	254	702	1,052	758	567	325	364	208	310
Sweden	374	710	1,539	2,188	2,515	2,311	1,407	460	348	453
Spain	29	173	649	1,593	1,320	1,813	821	630	395	780
Sub-total: Western Europe	2,495	5,076	8,089	12,441	12,023	10,140	5,971	4,059	2,615	3,757
US	393	379	375	476	815	1,012	1,033	1,352	555	360
Japan	232	1,839	10,100	16,991	15,868	11,708	6,307	4,697	6,094	8,400
Brazil	..	..	100	295	406	380	442	665	729	716
South Korea	..	..	..	410	814	562	604	495	522	929
Eastern Europe*	..	..	1,190	2,120	2,133	1,697	1,933	1,501	1,317	1,267
Other†	134	1,088	2,126	1,470	1,863	2,033	1,904	1,520	1,269	1,503
Total: World	3,254	8,382	21,980	34,203	33,922	27,532	18,194	14,289	13,101	16,932

* Yugoslavia, Poland, East Germany (information incomplete) and USSR (information incomplete).
† Includes small amounts from other Western Europe.

Source: Lloyd's Register of Shipping, *Annual Summary of Merchant Ships completed in the World*, London, annual.

4.2 Current adjustment problems

Current adjustment problems in the industry can be related to a number of factors, of which the most important are:

—the structure of the industry and particularly its links with shipping;
—changes in demand conditions, with important disruptions to the overall growth of world trade and the composition of world cargoes;
—changes in supply conditions, with increased size of productive units together with a shift in comparative advantage to low-labour-cost countries;
—the commercial environment within which both shipping and ship-building operate.

Structure

The shipbuilding industry is a mature industry. It also has few producers, principally because of the scale of production units. It displays the interdependence between producers typical of oligopolistic market structures. With economies of scale perhaps the only significant barrier to entry and no naturally protected market for any individual shipyard, international competition is intense and typically concerned with technical performance, design quality, price and delivery. The importance of credit in the purchase of ships has led to fierce competition on credit terms available to buyers from the shipyards of many countries.

Shipbuilding's important supply industries include the steel industry as well as marine and instrument engineering. It is difficult to be precise about the scale of upstream links, but as an example, the UK government calculates that between one and one and a quarter jobs in the supply sector depend on each job in the main shipbuilding industry. Downstream, the customers of the industry are shipowners, both those providing general shipping services as well as those which maintain their own fleets to transport their goods and commodities. For shipowners, alternative sources of supply are numerous and second-hand vessels provide an alternative to new building. Shipbuilding output can be increased rapidly in response to increased demand through the use of overtime and temporary labour.

The shipbuilding industry in the past was generally best established in those countries which had substantial shipping fleets. But the 1950s saw a decline in the importance of this home demand for the traditional builders as Japan in particular began to establish a growing share of world output. This increase in competitive activity in shipbuilding developed in parallel with an increase in competition in shipping. In particular, the growing use of open registry (flags of convenience) by shipowners of many nationalities has changed the structure of the market within which shipbuilding operates.[2]

Table 4.2 gives an indication of the growth in new fleets, but also shows to what extent certain countries have still been able to 'reserve' their domestic fleet requirements for the domestic ship-builders. The industry structure reflects a general balance in favour of the shipowner, and the industry has continued as a 'contract' and custom-building industry.

But the very factors which produce this balance can at the same time operate to destabilise the shipping market itself. Any tendency to excess capacity in shipbuilding will tend to keep new-building prices down and stimulate demand at any given level of freight rates. But the demand for shipping is a demand derived from the level of world trade and it is unlikely to be affected by conditions in shipbuilding or even those in shipping. Exogenous factors which reduce the demand for maritime transport will therefore confront a shipping industry with a significant surplus of tonnage. Such excess capacity in shipping fleets can be disguised by such practices as part-cargoing, keeping ships in port and slow steaming. Surplus vessels can also be laid up. But the net effect is likely to be a decline in freight rates, a fall in shipping earnings and a reduced demand for new vessels. These fluctuations thus feed back to the shipbuilding sector itself.

Demand

Demand for ships depends on the volume of seaborne trade generated by the overall level of world economic activity. Dry cargo trade increased fivefold between 1950 and 1976, with oil trade increasing nearly eightfold over the same years. In addition to demand for extra ships thus generated, there is a replacement demand for ships lost or scrapped.

The recent downturn in the growth in volume of world trade, both in oil and some bulk commodities, has thus been reflected in a declining demand for new merchant vessels. In addition, the world fleet consists in the main of relatively modern vessels, so replacement demand is limited. The impact of this falling demand is illustrated by Table 4.1 and Figure 4.1, which show how world output has fallen from 34.2 million grt in 1975 to 16.9 million grt in 1981. Even more dramatic, as Figure 4.1 illustrates, has been the impact on new orders.

The biggest impact of falling demand has been felt in the tanker

Table 4.2 Structure of world shipping, 1960, 1970 and 1980

	1960			1970			1980		
	A	B	C	A	B	C	A	B	C
France	4,809	404	96	6,458	809	73	11,925	191	93
Denmark	2,270	159	76	3,314	62	74	5,390	174	98
Germany	4,537	312	99	7,881	1,254	59	8,356	345	78
Italy	5,122	361	100	7,448	512	100	11,096	200	98
Netherlands	4,884	424	78	5,207	266	86	5,724	141	76
UK	21,131	1,651	72	25,825	2,703	39	27,135	502	52
Norway	11,203	887	21	19,347	2,190	17	22,007	522	34
Sweden	3,747	304	84	4,921	367	71	4,234	142	76
Spain	1,801	160	99	3,441	477	100	8,112	281	100
US	24,837	453	94	18,463	381	87	18,464	856	100
Japan	6,931	808	100	27,004	4,117	100	40,960	2,735	100
Greece	4,529	} 2,433	..	10,952	..	..	39,472	} 7,012	..
Liberia	11,282		..	33,297	} 8,522	..	80,285		..
Panama	4,236		..	5,646		..	27,657		..
Other	21,451		..	48,286		..	109,094		..
World	129,770	8,356	60	227,490	21,690	44	419,911	13,101	53

A: Merchant fleets registered in selected countries (000 grt).
B: Additions to fleet completed during the year (000 grt).
C: Percentage of additions domestically-built.

Source: Lloyds Register of Shipping, *Statistical Tables 1981*, London.

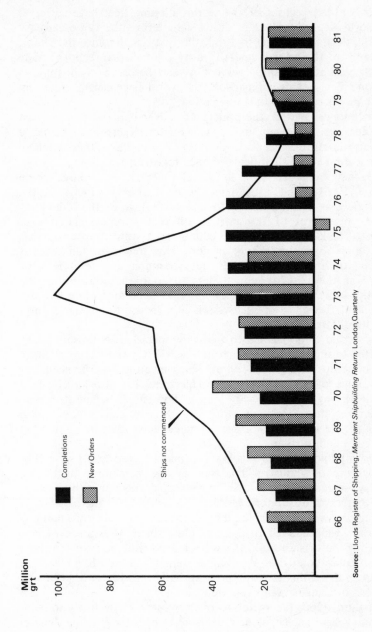

Source: Lloyds Register of Shipping, *Merchant Shipbuilding Return*, London, Quarterly

Figure 4.1 World ship completions, new orders and backlog, 1966–81.

market, but all sectors of the world shipping fleet have suffered. The world fleet measured in deadweight terms, the cargo capacity measure, declined in total in 1982, the first decline since the 1930s. The depth of the crisis is underlined by the fact that seaborne trade in 1982 was at the same level as ten years before, both in tonnage and ton-miles, yet in comparison, the world fleet had increased by almost 75 per cent over the same period.[3]

Over a longer period, the principal trends in demand over the past three decades have been first, a demand for larger ships: second, a demand for more specialised ship types; and third, the switch in shipping from established fleets to open registry.

The first trend has seen the development of very large crude carriers (VLCC) and ultra large crude carriers (ULCC) in the tanker fleet as owners started to take advantage of the reductions in the direct cost of transporting oil that were associated with increased tanker size. Similar reductions in unit transport costs were found to apply to bulk carriers. This trend, for tankers, has reached its limit. This reflects not so much a general lack of ability on the part of shipbuilders to go bigger, but rather the limitations of berthing facilities in ports and, more importantly, the lack of flexibility of such vessels in response to changing world trade conditions.

The second trend has led to a growing specialisation in ship types, with, for example, liquefied natural gas (LNG) and chemical ships, container ships and roll-on-roll-off ships meeting specific needs for the carriage of particular traffic. This trend has also largely been worked through. The world fleet is now more segmented than before, but there are few prospects of significant technological change in the industry, nor special cargo developments to develop this trend much further.

The only exception to this is the demand linked to the growth of the offshore oil industry. The type of vessels required by the oil industry includes jack-ups, submersibles, semi-submersibles, drill-ships, barges and support vessels. Most shipyards are capable of building such vessels provided that, in the case of platforms, building berths are wide enough to accommodate them. The spread of new orders for the offshore oil industry is indeed wide, but concentrated on particular countries. As well as Japan and South Korea, the US emerges as the most important builder, with Singapore and France also receiving significant new orders.

The third trend, the switch to open registry, seems likely to be of continuing significance, as new fleets account for a growing share in the carriage of world trade. Hong Kong shipowners, for example, control a flee⁺ which is now larger than the UK registered fleet, with most vessels under open registry.

Supply

The most important trends on the supply side of shipbuilding concern the growth in size of productive units and the switch in competitive advantage to newly industrialising countries. It was suggested earlier that ships are unlikely to get much bigger, so there is likely to be little pressure for building berths to get bigger, except in so far as offshore oil demand requires large platforms. In any case, with surplus capacity in the industry, not much new investment in capacity can be expected.

In terms of general production techniques, the pace of change, although steady, has not been spectacular. The production process remains essentially one of assembly and the industry has been described as 'medium technology',[4] certainly not beyond the abilities of several developing countries to establish. It is unlikely that future changes in technology will remove this accessibility. The industry is generally labour-intensive in all shipbuilding countries.

The likelihood for the future is that the switch in comparative advantage to low-labour-cost countries will not be reversed. There seems no reason why this cost advantage should be limited to the less sophisticated ship designs, for newly industrialising countries (NICs) could arrange to import any specific technology or skill that they lack and still maintain a cost differential through the use of low-cost labour on the large amount of work in any ship that is necessarily non-advanced.

The extent to which state-trading economies will offer a similar competitive threat to established builders is more difficult to predict, because less is known about the cost stuctures of shipbuilding in these countries.

The impact of new sources of supply is shown in Table 4.3. Losing share largely to Japan in the 1960s, the established European builders generally lost their places in the 'league table' in the 1970s to NICs (including Brazil, South Korea, Taiwan and Singapore) and to Eastern European builders (notably Poland and Yugoslavia). The rise of the South Korean industry is particularly noteworthy.

Commercial environment

The commercial environment within which both shipping and ship-building operate has a major impact on the nature of the industry's adjustment problems. Shipowners normally pay a deposit to the builder at the time of ordering and continue to make progress

Table 4.3 Country shares in world merchant shipbuilding completions, 1950–81 (per cent)

	1950	1960	1970	1975	1976	1977	1978	1979	1980	1981
France	5.3	2.1	3.9	3.4	4.9	4.0	2.4	5.0	2.2	3.0
Denmark	3.6	2.6	2.4	2.8	3.0	2.6	1.9	1.8	1.6	2.1
Germany (West)	2.5	13.4	6.0	7.3	5.5	5.8	4.6	3.1	2.9	4.2
Italy	2.3	5.3	2.5	2.3	2.1	2.8	1.9	1.6	1.9	1.6
Netherlands	6.1	8.1	2.9	3.0	1.9	0.9	1.7	1.8	1.0	1.0
UK	42.7	15.5	6.0	3.4	4.4	3.7	6.2	4.8	3.3	1.3
Norway	1.8	3.0	3.2	3.1	2.2	2.1	1.8	2.5	1.6	1.8
Sweden	11.5	8.5	7.0	6.4	7.4	8.4	7.7	3.2	2.7	2.7
Spain	0.9	2.1	3.0	4.7	3.9	6.6	4.5	4.4	3.0	4.6
Sub-total: Western Europe	76.7	60.6	36.8	36.3	35.4	36.8	32.8	28.4	20.0	22.2
US	12.1	4.5	1.7	1.4	2.4	3.7	5.7	9.5	4.2	2.1
Japan	7.1	22.0	46.0	49.7	46.8	42.5	34.7	32.9	46.5	49.6
Brazil	..	..	0.5	0.9	1.2	1.4	2.4	4.7	5.6	4.2
South Korea	..	..	..	1.2	2.4	2.0	3.3	3.5	4.0	5.5
Eastern Europe*	..	..	5.4	6.2	6.3	6.2	10.6	10.5	10.1	7.5
Other†	4.1	13.0	9.6	4.3	5.5	7.4	10.5	10.6	9.7	8.9
Total: World	100.0	100.0	100.0	100.0	100.0	100.0	100.0	100.0	100.0	100.0

* Yugoslavia, Poland East Germany (information incomplete) and USSR (information incomplete).
† Includes small amounts from other Western Europe countries.

Source: Calculated from Table 4.1

payments to the shipyards during the course of production, with the final payment made on delivery.

Clearly, these payments provide working capital for the shipyard, and one of the most important factors governing a yard's ability to maintain efficient production is success in securing a steady flow of new work. In this way, resources can be kept fully active by new work at design and pre-production stages while existing work is at production and fitting-out stages.

In the past, shipowners were themselves responsible for raising the necessary finance, but in the 1950s Japan led the way in arranging the provision of medium-term export credits for shipowners, covering 80 to 90 per cent of the purchase price and at reduced interest rates. The use of subsidised credit schemes became, and remains, widespread as shipyards of other countries sought to offset the advantage gained by the Japanese.

The shipbuilding market is also strongly affected by movements in relative exchange rates. A significant number of shipbuilding transactions are undertaken in US dollars and the shipyards of a country whose currency depreciates against the dollar relative to other shipbuilding nations will thus have an advantage in securing new orders.

The combination of exchange rate changes and subsidised interest rates, when taken with different rates of domestic inflation, means that commercial factors can play quite a significant role in the generation and destination of new orders. A floor on nominal interest rates means that higher-interest-rate countries will need to provide a bigger subsidy to get rates down to the floor level, but it likewise means that the lower-interest-rate countries will have lost an initial advantage. If higher nominal interest rates are associated with higher domestic inflation, a uniform floor on interest rates means that such countries can operate a lower real interest rate.[5]

Given the importance of credit, effective exchange rates can be somewhat different from nominal rates in such circumstances. Further influences on the effective exchange rate include whether subsidised credit is granted in domestic or foreign currency. Credit granted in the currency of the contract in general means that exchange risk is borne by the lender. Part of the current competitive advantage of Korean yards is credit granted in US dollars.

Korea has also benefited recently from the decline of the Won relative to other currencies. Similarly but earlier, Japan in the 1950s and 1960s had the advantage of a long period of low valuation of the yen. Conversely, Germany in the 1970s suffered competitively in the shipbuilding market as the mark moved upwards relative to the dollar.

4.3 Industry and government responses

Industry responses

During the last three decades, the shipbuilding industry has seen some important developments as companies have reacted to the changes in conditions which faced the industry. The important role of Japan has already been mentioned and Japanese yards were at the forefront of developing improved techniques of production to meet the growing and changing demand.

Japan invested heavily in new and larger shipbuilding berths from the 1950s onwards. Part of its success in making these yards profitable was the concentration on greenfield sites with integrated steel-making facilities. The Japanese at the same time developed more successful design and construction methods, which, when implemented, reduced the time taken in construction. Japan was also at the forefront in the development of high-tensile steel plate, which allowed reductions in thickness, weight and cost. The amount of steel per grt was reduced by as much as 36 per cent between 1958 and 1964.

The Japanese lead in these developments was followed by shipyards in some countries which expanded their berth size. The importance of judging trends correctly, however, is well illustrated by the experience of the Swedish yard Arendal. In 1962, using Volvo production technicians as consultants, the company invested considerable sums in building docks which could utilise modern production methods to build ships backwards in large prefabricated modules. Unfortunately, the designers did not foresee the trend towards the very wide VLCCs and ULCCs, and the yard was too small to build these very large vessels.

More recent developments in production methods have included the introduction of covered berths to reduce interference in production from the weather, and the use of numerical control for cutting and forming the steel plates which are welded together to form the hull. These last two innovations were first introduced in Sweden.

In addition to production techniques, the organisation of work also varies considerably between different countries. The fluctuating level of production activity poses some problems for shipbuilders, and in Japan there is significant use of temporary labour to meet these fluctuations.[6] This widespread use of temporary labour has not been available to shipyards in some other countries, notably those developed economies where the nature of labour relations and employment traditions militates against temporary employment as a permanent feature of work organisation.

One possible production/marketing strategy is the building and sale of standardised ships. It was clear from wartime experience, especially in the US, that sizeable orders for standardised tankers and carriers effected considerable savings in production time. The potential for such a strategy depends as much on the ability to sell the ships as on the ability to produce to a standard design. Yards in the UK, Denmark, Germany, Spain and Japan all have standard ship designs available. The industry, however, remains largely 'custom-built'.

A related production technique, known as series production, has been more widely used. This involves ships of a broadly similar type and size being produced in relatively rapid succession using methods akin to a production line. Certainly Japan and Sweden have yards which can produce a number of oil tankers over a relatively short period of time. But the decline in demand for tankers and the switch in demand to more specific and sophisticated ship types limits the applicability of such techniques at present.

In the light of this, an alternative response by yards in some established shipbuilding countries has been to develop particular specialisations in the more sophisticated types of ship. West Germany, for example, produces a significant proportion of container ships and France has developed a specialisation in LNG carriers.

The most recent developments in product design concern automation in ship control, where labour-saving navigation and control systems are being introduced into vessels, offering shipowners the prospect of lower labour costs. The impact of such savings on total operating costs is, however, likely to be small. The main companies undertaking such developments are Japanese.

The Japanese also have a Nuclear Ship Development Agency, and there has been an experimental West German nuclear vessel, the *Otto Hahn*, although this proved expensive to run. Japanese companies are also experimenting with the possibility of sail-assisted ships. A 1,600 deadweight ton (dwt) tanker (*Shin Aitoku Maru*) has been in service since late 1980, and larger experimental vessels are planned.

The endemic nature of government intervention

While the responses of individual industries and shipyards to changing competitive conditions have been important, government intervention in this industry in many countries has become so widely and so well established that to look at industry responses in isolation is misleading. This intervention has mostly taken the form of subsidy, rather than protection: ships are capital goods, shipping is an internationally mobile industry *par excellence*, and to protect domestic shipbuilders through quotas or tariffs would penalise domestic shippers.

The factors within the control of an individual shipyard have a small impact on competitiveness compared to the powers of governments to subsidise and to protect. And there is a very real sense in which the degree of government intervention has reinforced the conditions which it was designed to alleviate, thus making industry's adjustment problems perhaps more difficult. It certainly is the case that government intervention is not a recent phenomenon and clearly predates the current crisis.

This intervention probably dates from the decision by the Japanese government in the early post-war years to support shipbuilding through state-backed export credits and financial support for builders during construction. Table 4.1 shows that output in Japan expanded more than fortyfold between 1950 and 1970, with its share of world output increasing from less than 10 to almost 50 per cent.

The success of Japan brought forward demands in other countries for, if not protection by name, then at least parallel support to that enjoyed by Japanese yards. The established builders believed that their traditional customers were attracted to Japan as much by the appeal of export credit terms as by the quality of product and speed of delivery.

Other countries thus began to see the use of subsidised export credit as a legitimate means to attract at least some proportion of world demand for home producers. The OECD in 1965 calculated that this form of support was certainly the most widespread measure of assistance provided by Member States to their shipbuilding industries. Not surprisingly, developing countries keen to establish production used the same method to support their infant industries.

Japan

The government has long had a significant involvement in the Japanese shipbuilding industry. The major policy measures to develop the industries were favourable credit terms, enabling the Japanese shipping industry to build up its fleet, and export credits to shipbuilders through the government's Export–Import Bank of Japan. After the collapse of ordering (after 1973) and completions (after 1975), the government assisted the industry in an orderly reduction of activity levels in several ways: it approved the formation of a recession cartel operating in 1979–81 and helped to recommend the targets for restricting output; it organised, and partially funded, a scheme to scrap some capacity by 1980; it revived subsidies to shipping companies in a 'scrap-and-build' scheme. These developments are described in detail in Chapter 10, Section 2.

The earlier measures were undoubtedly an important part of the explanation of Japan's rise to dominance in the 1950s and 1960s. The extent to which its post-1977 adjustment measures have been genuine in trying to stabilise the world market has been questioned by some European builders, notably the Association of Western European shipbuilders, which suggested that Japanese reductions took place only when the market made them inevitable. The more recent increases in output, they believe, confirm this view.

Germany[7]

Shipbuilding was always a relatively important industry within Germany's manufacturing base, although there was considerable destruction of capacity during the 1939–45 war. During the 1950s, the industry again built up output and by the 1960s was among the group of Western European countries which vied for second place in the world after Japan. Indeed, throughout the latter half of the 1960s and after the first half of the 1970s, Germany maintained a steady share of growing world output and was never below fourth place in world production.

Germany's ability to develop shipbuilding despite a number of potentially hostile factors, including a high value of the mark, high labour costs and lack of a substantial home fleet to provide any basis for demand, reflects the industry's ability to specialise in technologically advanced ship types and to develop more efficient production techniques. It is noticeable that, although Germany produces tankers, she has never been so reliant on this type of vessel as most of her competitors.

In developing and maintaining its position, the German shipbuilding industry has had considerable support both from Federal and State governments. The Federal government is involved directly through Salzgitter, a government-owned steel conglomerate which has a 75 per cent share of the largest German yard HDW. The remaining 25 per cent is owned by the Regional (*Land*) government of Schleswig-Holstein. The Regional government of Bremen owns 39 per cent of shares in another medium-sized yard.

State assistance reflects a desire to help the shipping industry as well as the shipbuilding industry directly. West Germany has a relatively small merchant fleet and government policy is to encourage the fleet to become more efficient and competitive and to increase the proportion of trade carried in German ships.

The programmes of support for each industry have had spillover effects on the other and it is not always easy to identify the prime motive for any specific scheme. The most important support has come from subsidised credit for export buyers, although it is likely that the OECD Understanding which established minimum rates of interest (see page 102) may have limited the assistance offered in Germany more than that of her competitors because of the generally lower rates of interest prevailing in Germany. In addition to subsidised credit, there has also been a scheme to help less developed countries buy ships from German yards. Shipyards have also been able to take advantage of loans to modernise their production facilities.

Aid for shipowners has also had an effect on the demand for German yards. The most important of these has been the provision of construction subsidies to German shipowners to cover a proportion of the cost of new vessels. Although such grants were available for foreign-built as well as domestically-built ships, a substantial proportion of home shipowners bought from domestic yards. The grants were set at 10 per cent of contract price from 1965 to 1974, but were increased to 17.5 per cent by 1978. However, in 1979 the Federal budget provided DM 175 million for grants to shipowners for modernisation of the German fleet, while reducing the maximum grant to 12.5 per cent of contract price. In order to qualify, ships had to be engaged on international voyages, be German registered and fly the German flag. This budget also provided for interest-free loans to German shipowners to reduce their interest burden, thereby encouraging new building.

Apart from these Federal aids, the Regional governments in the main shipbuilding areas have all offered additional support to their local shipbuilding companies. In some cases, the Regional government provides credit guarantees for buyers where these have not been forthcoming commercially. Since the later 1970s there has been some attempt to link the Federal and Regional support programmes.

A scheme for specific grants for technically sophisticated vessels was introduced in January 1979. The value of the subsidy was set at 10 per cent for 1979 and 1980 and at 7.5 per cent for 1981. Some repayment of the subsidy may be required.

Since 1975, Germany has closed about twenty of the existing 81 building docks, although some closures may be temporary rather than permanent. Employment in merchant shipbuilding declined by 40 per cent between 1975 and 1979, with most of the decline occurring during the earlier years. Increased use of short-time working, involving probably one-third of the workforce, limited further redundancies, and by the end of 1979, increased Federal and Regional aid schemes had reduced the proportion affected by short-time working to some 10 per cent.

The UK

The poor performance of the UK shipbuilding industry in the post-war years, when it failed to respond to a rapid expansion of world demand, led to increasing government concern, partly for balance-of-payments reasons and partly because of the concentration of shipbuilding in areas of high unemployment. There was also concern over the possible link between the poor performance and the industry's industrial relations record. The industry experienced a high strike rate and demarcation disputes seemed to figure prominently as a major cause of disruption.

Various reports published in the early 1960s examined the industry's problems and identified the causes of low productivity as poor labour relations and poor management. They also stressed the inability to match credit terms offered by competitors. In response, the government in 1962 persuaded banks to provide medium-term credit for exports, including ships, at fixed rates of interest. This scheme, however, created an anomaly for home buyers, who could not get such favourable terms. In order to prevent such buyers being attracted abroad, the government introduced a scheme in 1963 to provide cheap credit for home ship owners buying from UK yards. The original £30 million scheme was quickly subscribed and the limit was soon doubled to £60 million.

The incoming Labour government in 1964 established an enquiry into the industry. The Geddes Report[8] advocated a rationalisation of the industry to create larger units and a 1966 Act established the Shipbuilding Industry Board to effect such a reorganisation. The Act also extended credit provision for home buyers through a new £200 million loan-guarantee scheme. By 1969, of the 27 yards covered by the Geddes inquiry, 21 had merged into seven groups and two were no longer building ships. Further regrouping was prevented by geographical isolation for yards in Belfast and on Merseyside.

Further support for the industry came through the introduction in 1966 of 'shipbuilder's relief', a refund of 2 per cent of the gross value of ships completed in respect of indirect taxes paid by the industry. The ship credit scheme was also extended in stages, to £400 million in 1968, £700 million in 1971, £1,000 million then £1,400 million in 1972. Specific support was also given in 1969 and 1970 to problem yards in Scotland and on Merseyside and to the

Harland & Wolff yard in Northern Ireland, which was eventually taken over by the Northern Ireland government.

In 1971 the Conservative government attempted to reduce the level of support for certain 'lame duck' yards, but was forced to reverse this policy, and support for the industry continued through a scheme of construction grants introduced in 1972. These were set at 10 per cent of contract value for that year, reducing to 4 per cent, then 3 per cent in the following two years. The cost to the government of the home credit scheme also increased at this time with rising interest rates. The government was obliged to refinance loans that the banks had made to shipowners and thus had to pay the interest differential between the subsidised fixed rate and the refinanced market rate.

The minority Labour government of 1974 produced plans to nationalise the industry. The legislation was introduced in 1975, but not enacted until 1977 following parliamentary delays. In the interim, with a worsening situation in world markets, the government introduced a number of supportive schemes. The first of these, in 1976, was cost escalation insurance to give UK shipbuilders a measure of support against exceptional and unpredictable increases in costs. At the same time a refund-guarantee scheme was set up to encourage owners to place orders with yards scheduled for nationalisation. In 1977, a Shipbuilding Intervention Fund of £65 million was established to enable yards to obtain orders. This was renewed in 1978 at an annual rate of £85 million.

One particular order for the UK industry, which received assistance over and above an Intervention Fund contribution of £28 million, was for the Polish Steamship Company (PZM) in 1977. This involved the nationalised British Shipbuilders (BS) establishing a joint venture company APSV, to buy the ships from BS and charter them to PZM for thirteen and a half to fifteen years, after which they would become the property of PZM on payment of a nominal sum. BS was responsible for raising the finance for APSV. Estimates suggest that the losses on the contract will be of the order of £40 million in addition to the £28 million Fund contribution.[9]

In 1979 the Conservative government planned to return the industry to the private sector, along with other publicly owned candidates for 'privatisation'; but for shipbuilding the plans have been postponed. The government has continued to fund the losses of BS and has extended the Intervention Fund.

The impact of current conditions has been substantial. Employment has fallen in merchant building by some 43 per cent between 1975 and 1979, which represents both a shedding of labour and a shift of personnel to the naval building operations of the Corporation. Three yards were closed, with a further seven scheduled to cease merchant building.

Other countries

Among other established builders the pattern of heavy government support is similar (see Table 4.4 which provides details of major policies in OECD countries). In Western Europe export-credit subsidies are general (most of them conforming to the OECD Understanding), there are various incentives for domestic sales of ships (the inevitable consequence of generalised export subsidies), and public ownership is widespread.

Since 1977 *France* has provided grants to shipyards in conjunction with ceilings on orders for individual yards, in a programme to cut capacity. Shipbuilding capacity in *Italy* is 90 per cent government-owned (IRI-Fincantieri). The government has in the recent past operated a scheme providing a grant for tonnage scrapped, provided at least 75 per cent is replaced by new building. In general, however, intervention has suffered from a lack of continuity as a result of frequent government changes. *Spain* has operated a system of direct production subsidies which are at a higher rate for export orders. *Sweden*, like the UK, has nationalised its shipyards (Swedyards), with the last private yard, Kockums, transferred to state ownership at the end of 1978.

The *US*, apart from offshore oil vessels, is not a major builder, yet clearly places much emphasis on supporting some home production. It offers substantial direct subsidies on production, backed up by flag discrimination which requires coastal trade to use only US-built ships. The US is not party to any of the OECD schemes.

Among the non-European NICs, both South Korea and Brazil have emerged as significant producers. *South Korea* doubled its capacity in 1976–81 while world shipbuilding demand collapsed. It has emerged as a major competitor, now occupying second place to Japan in completions and new orders. The industry has benefited from state loans and direct equity capital holdings through the Korea Development Bank. Planning a capacity of 8 million grt by the early 1990s, it clearly plans to follow Japan's footsteps. *Brazil* requires national shipowners to buy through a state body, SUNAMAM, which subsidises Brazilian prices to match European levels. Both countries provide credit at more favourable rates than those set out in the OECD Understanding.

Table 4.4 Measures of assistance to OECD shipbuilders

	State ownership	Tariff protection	Exemption from or rebates of taxes and duties	R & D support	Direct production subsidies	Home credit and assistance to shipowners	Export credit schemes
Denmark			imported materials duty free: ships exempt from VAT	$ 0.5 m p.a.		80% over 14 years at 8% interest: 4 year moratorium	Danish Ship Credit Fund, at agreed OECD rates
France			imported materials duty free: ships exempt from VAT	very small	15–25% depending on size of yard, type of vessel	interest rate subsidies at OECD export rates: grant of equity capital to owners	Commercial Banks, at OECD rates, plus Bank of France
Italy	c. 90% of capacity		imported materials duty free: ships exempt from VAT	3 m lire p.a.	up to 30% (E. Commission to investigate)	70% of contract price loaned by state: state also pays half interest costs	in line with OECD rates
Japan		6% duty on ships less than 100 grt		1.8 b yen 1979 Ship Research Institute, also J. Nuclear Ship Dev. Agency		JDB loans for 65–75% cost over 13 yrs, 3 yr moratorium: 2½–3½% subsidy for modern vessels	Export-Import Bank plus commercial banks, at OECD rates
Netherlands	partial state ownership in a number of yards		imported materials duty free: ships exempt from VAT	small grants	funding of losses in connection with restructuring, up to 75%	interest subsidies to a maximum of 2% below OECD export rates	transitional interest benefits allow rates not more than 2% below OECD agreed levels

Country	Capacity	Trade restrictions	Materials / tax	Amount	Subsidy	Loans	Export finance
Norway	one yard c. 5% of capacity		customs rebate of 6% for new ships, 4% for repairs: ships exempt from VAT	15 m N Kr 1980	up to 18%	loans up to 80% over 12 yrs with 3 yr grace period	Export finance A/S OECD agreed rates
Spain	three yards c. 60% of capacity	14% tariff (10½% with EEC) plus hard to obtain licence	5½% customs rebate for domestic ships (less for exports), 12½% indirect tax rebate prior to VAT		up to 9.5%	loans up to 80% at 8% with up to 2 yrs moratorium	commercial banks and Banco Exterior of Spain
Sweden	Swedyard own most capacity c. 90%		imported materials duty free: ships exempt from VAT	12 m Sw Kr 1979/80	Swedyards funding of losses	loans up to 70% over 12 yrs plus depreciation loans up to 25%	Swedish Export Credit Board OECD agreed rates
UK	British Shipbuilders own all capacity		imported materials duty free, 2% tax relief for indirect taxes: ships exempt from VAT	£0.5 m 1978/79	Shipbuilding Intervention Fund up to 30% plus funding of BS losses	loans at OECD export terms plus interest moratorium up to 3 yrs	commercial banks plus Dept. of Industry OECD agreed rates
US		foreign built ships cannot engage in coastwise trade		$19 m 1978	Construction Differential Subsidy up to 50% of domestic cost	up to 87½% over 25 yrs 6–8%	
W. Germany	partial interest with c. 20% capacity		imported materials duty free: ships exempt from VAT	DM 5.1 m 1977 DM 8.0 m 1978	10% subsidy for technically sophisticated vessels	grants up to 12% plus interest subsidies leaving a minimum of 4% on loans	govt. loans to meet OECD agreed rates

Source: Compiled from OECD (Working Party No. 6 of the Council on Shipbuilding): *Measures of Assistance to Shipbuilding in the Member Countries* (C/WP6 (79) S3 [Final]), Paris, 1980.

Action by the OECD

The potential value of international regulation of the shipbuilding market has long been acknowledged by the established Western builders. In part this is because the subsidy race in the early 1960s was both costly and ineffective, as subsidies cancelled each other and possibly destabilised the market.

The OECD in 1963 set up a Working Party to examine the industry's problems and the responses by individual governments. Its first investigation, published in 1965, found a great degree of support for domestic shipbuilding.[10] The most widespread measure was subsidised credit for shipowners, although many countries had additional support schemes.

The OECD found that the effect of such measures was to shift the focus of competition away from consideration of price, delivery, design quality and technical performance. Their first subsequent action was to try to achieve some regulation of export credit terms, and the first Understanding on Export Credit for Ships was reached in 1969. This established minimum interest rates of 7½ per cent, a maximum repayment period of 8 years and maximum loans of 80 per cent of ship contract price. The members of the OECD Working Party,[11] which excludes the US, all agreed to participate in the Understanding.

The terms of the Understanding have been revised periodically, most recently in December 1979, which established an interest rate of 8 per cent, a repayment period of 8½ years and a maximum loan of 80 per cent of purchase price. General adherence was quite good up to 1976, but the crisis of the later 1970s has led to increasing breaches of the spirit, if not the letter, of the Understanding.

The second main initiative undertaken by the OECD has been a General Arrangement for the progressive removal of obstacles to normal competitive conditions in the shipbuilding industry. This agreement was achieved in 1972 by the European members of the OECD and Japan (the US again not being a party). The Arrangement was intended to lead to a balanced reduction of aids to shipbuilding. These reductions were to be negotiated through the Working Party, and there was some success up to 1975. But since then, there has been increasing use of Clause 7 of the Arrangement, which allowed participating governments to introduce new measures and increase existing aid in particular cases for 'unforeseen and imperative reasons'. Currently, the member countries of the OECD Working Party have decided that further progress on the Arrangement is not practicable in the industry's current state.

The OECD have also brought forward General Guidelines for government policies in the industry. This 'code of conduct', prepared in 1975 and agreed at ministerial level in 1978, was designed to assist governments in adapting the industry, particularly to encourage an even spread of the necessary reductions in capacity.

The OECD is, however, keenly aware of the political constraints that limit the ability of the Working Party to achieve significant progress in reducing aids to shipbuilding. The Working Party commented that the agreements already made 'still remain adequate for this task. But what is essential is the will to give them effect and also the political feasibility.'[12]

Action by the EEC

The European Economic Community has been a party to the OECD Understanding on Export Credit for Ships since its inception in 1969. It has also been concerned to develop a Community initiative to harmonise and reduce other subsidies in line with the Treaty of Rome. Its aims have been to reduce distortions to intra-Community trade, while retaining some matching degree of protection to that of non-Community competitors.

The first attempt to introduce some Community control over subsidies was a draft Directive in 1965, which proposed a 10 per cent ceiling on aid. This Directive was not formally adopted by the Council until 1969, but the general buoyancy of the shipbuilding market at this time provided some scope for Member States to reduce subsidies. In this context, a Second Directive, approved in 1971, reduced the aid ceiling progressively, from 5 per cent in 1972, to 4 per cent in 1973, and 3 per cent in 1974. Italy was temporarily excluded from compliance with the Directive.

In 1973, plans for a Third Directive were introduced, but political and economic conditions at the time were such that the provisions of the Second Directive were three times extended. The Third Directive was approved in 1975 and called for an end to aids, except for Ireland, Italy and France. The Directive was to run to 1977, but was breached in 1976 when the Commission agreed to a UK scheme for cost-escalation insurance.

This relaxation of the Third Directive led the way to a fourth, agreed by the Council in April 1978, to run until the end of 1980. This recognised that the gravity of the crisis in Community shipbuilding justified state aid to the industry, provided three conditions were met: aid should be temporary and progressively reduced; aid should not distort intra-Community trade; aid should be linked to restructuring. The types of aid broadly acceptable included subsidised credit in line with the OECD Understanding, specific aid to rescue an undertaking (subject to Commission approval), and general crisis aid in line with the three conditions set out. The Commission further required Member States to supply information on the level and form of subsidies so that monitoring could take place.

In the light of this information, the Commission proposed a Fifth Directive to run for a further two years, from the beginning of 1982. The broad policy continued, but concern was expressed that the different forms of assistance would cumulatively create subsidies at a level above that permitted by the Commission. As an example, credit schemes for owners which were meant to be available for orders placed in any EEC yards seemed to go exclusively to domestic yards. They were thus equivalent to an additional production subsidy to the domestic yard. Similarly, funding of shipyard losses, especially significant for state-owned enterprise, could likewise act as an additional production subsidy. The Fifth Directive sought explicitly to prohibit the cumulation of such different aids where together they exceeded the approved limit.

The Fifth Directive was proposed in the context of other Community-wide support schemes to encourage the orderly reduction of capacity across the Community. The first of these was a scrap-and-build scheme proposed by the Commission in 1979. In addition, the Commission hoped that non-quota funds from the European Regional Fund could be used to maintain the incomes of older workers who left shipbuilding as a result of industrial restructuring.

The scrap-and-build scheme has encountered problems which have prevented its adoption. It was agreed in principle by the Council, with the Commission to work on specific details, but had still not been implemented by the beginning of 1983. The Fifth Directive was also delayed in its adoption and the Fourth was extended for the first three months of 1981, until the new Directive was agreed in April.

The Commission continues to receive regular reports on the state of the industry and those discussed throughout 1982 saw no prospect of improvement for the industry in the coming years. Partly as a consequence of this analysis, the Commission adopted for presentation to the Council a proposal that the Fifth Directive be extended for three years from its expiry at the end of 1982.

4.4 Assessments and options

It has been argued that the problem facing established builders is an exceptionally deep recession in the industry coincident with the significant growth in the capacity of Third World suppliers. This suggests that government assistance will need to be geared to a permanent reduction in capacity rather than traditional aid to help industry through a bad patch. The evidence from Section 4.3 suggests that government aid is now being structured to achieve such reductions in capacity.

This represents a change in the nature of government support from earlier years. When world shipbuilding prospects were bright, assistance to domestic shipbuilding aimed to secure competitive positions within the world market. But few commentators now see much improvement for world shipbuilding, even into the medium term.

The picture which emerges from the past is of an industry where government intervention has become endemic. For the majority of industries in trouble, the government's role has been seen as the provision of temporary assistance to ease the process of adjustment to changed economic and technological conditions. With shipbuilding, the temporary support schemes have been extended and renewed and, perhaps more significantly, the provision of subsidised credit has achieved apparent permanence.

So any assessment of government policy options in the future has to address two questions about the past: why did governments *start* to intervene in the industry, and how did this intervention become permanent? The answer to the first question turns on three factors: employment in shipbuilding was quite substantial for a number of European countries in the post-war period; the prospects for the industry generally were favourable as the world economy and world trade expanded; and governments generally attached a degree of strategic significance to their shipbuilding industries.

As has been outlined, Japan's rapid expansion of its shipbuilding output in the post-war years was achieved partly through active government support, and when Japan as early as 1956 became the world's largest producer there was a growing demand for state support in other shipbuilding countries. By 1965, the OECD reported that support was already widespread.

The answer to the second question, about the permanence of intervention, depends to a large extent on the way in which widespread government support is self-cancelling, yet adds to the instability and cyclicity of the total market. The self-cancelling nature of various countries' support for shipbuilding has long been recognised, but in general, efforts through the OECD and EEC collectively to limit such support have met with very little success. Latterly, this is largely because a significant proportion of productive capacity is now in the NICs which have different interests and are outside the influence of the international organisations representing the developed countries. But even before this competition became significant, there were differences of interest within the developed countries themselves which highlighted the problems of enforcing collective limitation of subsidies.

These problems can be expressed in terms of a 'prisoner's dilemma' for individual countries: if a country cannot be sure that others will follow the rules of collective limitation, its response may well be to break the rules itself, even though adherence by *all* countries would be best for them all individually.[13]

The impact of widespread subsidisation on the general stability of the shipbuilding market has been outlined earlier. Briefly, sub-sidisation of shipbuilding will lead to a larger world fleet than other-wise, but the level of world trade is exogenously determined, so that the effects on the shipping industry of any fluctuations in trade will be amplified, and these in turn will feed through to the new-building market itself.

The role of government assistance as a destabilising factor in its own right confuses the distinctions between short-run and long-run strategies, and reinforces the generally chaotic picture of the relationship between governments and the industry.

The choice of future strategies for governments will depend both on the objectives they wish to pursue and the state of the industry now and in the future. Although shipbuilding has been used to a cyclical pattern of activity, the current crisis is much deeper and likely to be more prolonged than anything so far experienced since 1945. It is probable that the severity of the industry's longer-run position has become impressed on governments only in the last four or five years.

That both national governments and international bodies now recognise this is clear: the OECD is not alone in talking of the shipbuilding crisis growing to 'dramatic, political dimensions'.[14] It is also clear that individual government policies are now geared more to the rationalisation of their industries and to the reduction of capacity.

Such a rundown of the industry in the developed economies is now more thinkable partly because employment in the industry is not nearly so important as formerly for any of the Western European builders, nor even for Japan. That said, however, it does appear that most of the European countries are unwilling to see the total cessa-tion of shipbuilding activity, whether for regional-employment, balance-of-payments or strategic reasons.

There would be benefits for individual countries in managing any reduction of capacity through international cooperation, because they would then hope to maintain a stable share of world production relative to their competitors whilst reducing the actual level of subsidy provided. It is noticeable, however, that any success that has been achieved in this direction, both by OECD and by the EEC, occurred when the industry was experiencing expansion during the early 1970s. After 1973, individual countries once again reverted to subsidies of varying natures and strengths in an attempt to secure some work for their shipbuilding industries. In the process, they paid scant regard to the terms of international agreements.

In the light of these comments, what policy strategies for European governments can be identified? The growth of new competition from the NICs is clear. One answer to this problem in other industries is to advocate that developed countries should move up-market into more technologically sophisticated products with a higher level of value-added. France has tried to adopt such a strategy in respect of LNG carriers. The potential for success of such a strategy is, however, limited. The low-cost producers such as Korea or a highly efficient producer such as Japan can, without a great deal of trouble, switch production to more sophisticated vessels. Korean yards have, for example, signed technical licensing agreements with both French and American companies to produce LNG carriers, while Japan has started building LNG carriers and is rapidly diversifying into offshore rigs.[15]

Another alternative is to switch away from merchant shipbuilding into naval work, which the UK has done to a certain extent. It is in general not practical to produce both types of work in the same yards so that such a decision would involve reducing merchant capacity and would also, presumably, be based on some assessment of reasonable export demand for naval vessels. Here, the developed countries may still have some competitive advantage, but there may also be constraints on the sale of sensitive defence items to certain countries, which could limit the possibilities for trade.

Apart from these two possibilities, governments could decide to carry on the existing level of subsidy in order to maintain a role as a marginal producer on the world scene. Here, the view of future demand becomes important because to be marginal to a buoyant world market may be a reasonable strategy, whereas to be marginal to a depressed world market may not.

A final possibility is that governments could withdraw state support. It does seem likely that any such decision in isolation would lead to a rapid decline in the country's shipbuilding industry. Here, the issue of whether governments think it appropriate to match the subsidies offered by their competitors becomes important. The arguments in favour of taking advantage of other countries' subsidised products clearly turn on the ability to find alternative uses for the resources released at home. It is perhaps too often the case that those economies with problem industries will not be those with the ability to respond well to new demands and new technologies. This is especially the case when the industrial economies are in recession.

Summing up, it is hard to imagine governments deciding to alter their basic strategies. Subsidy is likely to continue, although restructuring and slimming of the industry will occur. There could clearly be a role for international action to achieve adjustment but it remains to be seen whether individual countries will attempt such cooperation when the past record shows the predominance of short-run national interests. The paradox is that, although subsidy levels per worker are very high in this industry, the relatively small size of the industry within each country's manufacturing base means that the absolute level of support in relation to national budgets is not sufficiently large to create pressure for its elimination.

Notes

1. Shipbuilding output is commonly measured at two stages: launch when the finished hull has been floated; completion when the fitting out has been concluded and the ship handed over. The most common measure of output has traditionally been gross registered tonnage (grt), a measure of total cubic capacity. Sometimes deadweight tonnage (dwt), a measure of cargo capacity, is used. Neither measure, however, bears a fixed relationship to the value of a ship, because the volume of work that a shipyard can produce is dependent on and inversely related to the sophistication of the vessels it produces. In recent years the measure of compensated tonnage (cgrt) has been introduced which adjusts the basic grt by a factor calculated to reflect the actual work content in a ship. Because of the non-standard nature of merchant ships, precise measures of capacity are impossible to provide. The pace of work, sophistication of design, amount of overtime working and use of subcontract labour can all be expected to affect the rate of output. OECD estimates suggest, however, that world capacity in 1975 was some 39 million grt, or about 25 million cgrt (although this retrospective estimation of the compensating factor has technical drawbacks). World output in 1979 was some 11.5 million cgrt, so overcapacity is substantial, even allowing for some capacity scrapped since 1975.
2. The six countries traditionally regarded as open registers are Liberia, Panama, Singapore, Cyprus, Bahamas and Lebanon.
3. *Fearnley's Review 1982* (1983).
4. See Albu (1980).

5. For a discussion of similar issues in process plant contracting, see Chapter 7, Section 4.
6. See Nomura Research Institute (1979), p. 174.
7. See Grant and Shaw (1979).
8. See UK government (1966).
9. See House of Commons (1980).
10. See OECD (1965).
11. Belgium, Denmark, West Germany, Finland, France, Greece, Ireland, Italy, Japan, Netherlands, Norway, Spain, Sweden, the UK and the EEC. Canada and Australia are also parties to the Understanding.
12. See OECD (1980).
13. Grant and Shaw (1979), p. 216, make this point.
14. See OECD (1980).
15. See Japan Economic Journal (1983).

References

Albu, A. (1980), 'Merchant Shipbuilding and Marine Engineering', in Pavitt, K., ed., *Technical Innovation and British Economic Performance*, London and Basingstoke: Macmillan.

Fearnley's Review 1982 (1983), Oslo.

Grant, R., and Shaw, K. (1979). 'Structural policies toward the Shipbuilding and Shipping Industries of the BRD and UK', in Economists Advisory Group, *Structural Economic Policies in the BRD and the UK*, London: Anglo German Foundation.

House of Commons (1980), *Nineteenth Report from the Committee of Public Accounts: Assistance to the Shipbuilding Industry* (1979/80 HC 737), London: HMSO.

Japan Economic Journal (1983), *Industrial Review of Japan/1982*, Tokyo.

Nomura Research Institute (1979), *Prospects for Japanese Industry to 1985*, London: Financial Times.

OECD (1965), *The Situation in the Shipbuilding Industry*, Paris.

OECD (1980), *The Crisis in the Shipbuilding Industry and International Cooperation Efforts Geared Towards Positive Adjustment in the Industry* (Special Group of the Economic Policy Committee on Positive Adjustment Policies CPE/PAP (80) 29), Paris.

UK Government (1966), *Shipbuilding Inquiry Committee 1965-1966. Report* (Geddes Report), Cmnd 2937, London: HMSO.

5 MOTOR CARS: A MATURING INDUSTRY?*

Daniel T. Jones

5.1 Introduction

This chapter has three main purposes: to outline the major changes taking place in the Western European car industry; to assess the strategies and performance of the main companies with special reference to the effects of government intervention; and to discuss the issues and options facing European companies and industrial policy-makers in the next few years.

Until a decade or so ago, the motor car industries could be regarded as playing a 'locomotive' role in Western European economies, their output increasing faster than total GDP (Table 5.1). But this leading role in growth came to an end in the 1970s (even earlier in the UK) and is unlikely to be restored. Western European governments have become increasingly concerned with managing the transition of the industry to slower growth—much as they have long since done in the 'problem' sectors of agriculture, shipbuilding, textiles and railways. On the other hand, technology and market conditions are beginning to push the car industry in new directions in the 1980s, questioning some of the assumptions about scale and the nature of world market integration that are the inherited collective wisdom of the 1970s.

The way in which slower growth, combined with these possibilities of rejuvenation, is managed, is bound to influence the overall pattern of growth in the European economies, if only because of the size of the industry. In the early 1970s the motor industry accounted for 5 to 8 per cent of manufacturing output, investment and employment in Western Germany, the UK, France and Italy, and for over 10 per cent of their manufactured exports. Including employment in the production of materials, components and capital goods, about 3.1 million employees, or about 10 per cent of total manufacturing employment in the EEC, depended on the car industry, and another 1.6 million were engaged in selling and repairing cars.

Moreover, cars have been among the most dynamic elements in world trade. Exports from the eight major producing countries increased fourfold from 1958 to 1978. The prospects are poor for

*This chapter is a shortened and updated version of Jones (1981).

Table 5.1 Western Europe: growth rates of GDP and motor industry indicators, 1960–79 (annual average % change)

	1960–4	*1964–9*	*1969–73*	*1973–9*
GDP				
Germany	5.1	4.6	4.5	2.4
France	6.0	5.9	6.1	3.1
UK	3.1	2.5	3.0	1.4
Italy	3.5	5.6	4.1	2.6
Motor car industry output by value (at constant prices)				
Germany	8.1	6.5	4.8	2.5
France	5.5†	9.1	7.4	5.4
UK	5.6	2.2	0.4	−2.3
Italy*	..	..	3.6§	1.8
Motor car industry employment				
Germany	6.2	2.3	2.3	0.9
France	2.5	2.6	5.1	1.0
UK	2.4	0.9	1.3	−1.7
Italy	4.9‡	6.8	1.5	−0.6
Motor car industry labour productivity				
Germany	1.9	4.2	2.5	1.6
France	3.7	6.5	2.3	4.4
UK	3.2	1.3	−0.9	−0.6
Italy*	..	..	..	1.2

* Relates to transport equipment, not just the motor vehicle industry.
† 1962–4.
‡ 1961–4.
§ 1970–3.

Sources: National statistical sources; Society of Motor Manufacturers and Traders (1980); OECD (1980b); and OECD (1981).

a similar rate of expansion in the 1980s for complete units, although perhaps better for engines and components. With the development of a particularly competitive car industry in Japan, trade in automotive products has become increasingly important in international commercial diplomacy.

Car production is characterised by important economies of scale (in production and in distribution), by organisational complexity (a car is assembled from many hundreds of individual components), and by the long gestation period for major investment decisions (models can last up to eight years, engines up to twenty). These characteristics have imposed significant barriers to entry and production is highly concentrated in the hands of a few producers. The eight largest producers (General Motors, Toyota, Nissan, Ford,

Table 5.2 Structure of the world car industry, 1980[a] (thousands of units)

Country of production	GM[h]	Ford[i]	Peugeot[j]	Renault[k]	Volkswagen[l]	Fiat[m]	Others	Total
US	4,065	1,307		(165)	197		642[n]	6,376
Canada	512	250		(13)	*		72[n]	847
Brazil	180	120		22	433	162	3	898
Mexico[b]	17	38	27	58	113	34	113	303
Argentina[b]	*	72	*	*	28	*	–	219
Andean Pact[c]	*	*			*		–	–
Germany	787	420			1,517		797[o]	3,521
France	*	*	1,446	1,492				2,938
Italy			*			1,185	260[p]	1,445
UK/Ireland	55	343	125	*		*	401[q]	924
Spain/Portugal[b]	*	260	151	325	*	(293)[l]		1,029
Benelux		191	*	(81)	*			272
Sweden/Finland				(192)			65[s]	257
Austria	*						8	8
Japan	(107)	(737)					6,194[t]	7,038
Australia/New Zealand	98	80	*	*		*	4	182
South Africa[bd]	20	52	15	10	53	13	114	277
Poland[b]						(328)	25	353
Yugoslavia[b]			(8)	(40)	(13)	(194)		255
Romania			*	(77)	*			77
Other countries[e]	*	*		*	*	*	1,895	1,895
Total A[f]	5,734	3,133	1,764	1,907	2,341	1,394		
Total B[g]	5,841	3,870	1,772	2,475	2,354	2,209	10,593	29,114

a Car production, ownership and cooperation links of 1983. * denotes an engine, component or assembly plant. ( ) denotes a minority share-holding, joint venture or collaboration and licence production in the CMEA countries, usually involving buyback.

b Includes some assembly; possibly some double counting.

c Colombia, Chile, Ecuador, Peru and Venezuela.

d Data partially estimated.

e USSR (1,327), East Germany (180), Czechoslovakia (185), China (100), South Korea (57) and India (46).

f Total A excludes minority interests and licence production.

g Total B includes minority interests and licence production.

h General Motors owns 34 per cent of Isuzu (Japan) and will import Isuzu and Suzuki cars from Japan and has a joint venture with Toyota in California. European production capacity increased by 300,000 from 1982 with new plants in Spain and Austria.

i Ford owns 25 per cent of Toyo Kogyo (Japan) and sources exports to South-East Asia from Japan. It has cancelled plans to expand capacity in Portugal.

j Peugeot (including Talbot and Citröen) has joint ventures in engines, components and light vans with Renault, Volvo and Fiat. Citröen has designed a car for Oltcit in Romania, and has built a constant-velocity-joint plant in East Germany. Peugeot and Citröen license production in Yugoslavia. Chrysler still owns 15 per cent of Peugeot.

k Renault owns 46 per cent of American Motors Corporation and started US production in 1982. It has acquired 20 per cent of Volvo cars (who produce cars in Sweden, Canada and the Netherlands) and Mack trucks. Renault has joint ventures in engine production with Volvo and Peugeot. It will expand its capacity in Portugal from 1985. It has licensed production by Dacia in Romania.

l Volkswagen now owns Chrysler's operations in Brazil and Argentina.

m Fiat has withdrawn from taking over Seat (Spain). Its ten-year agreement with Poland involves exchanging engines from Poland for CKD kits. Lancia (Fiat) is cooperating with Saab in marketing and joint development of a new model. Fiat has joint ventures with Renault, Peugeot and Alfa Romeo and is cooperating with Alfa Romeo in the development of components.

n Chrysler, US (639), Canada (72), has recently withdrawn from all major overseas markets except Mexico. It has a 20 per cent stake in Mitsubishi and 15 per cent stake in Peugeot.

o Daimler-Benz (439) and BMW (330).

p Alfa Romeo (220) will begin a joint venture with Nissan in 1984.

q British Leyland (396) assembles a Honda car in the UK and is jointly developing another model.

r Seat makes Fiat cars under licence, but will begin assembly of Volkswagen models in 1985.

s Saab (65) is jointly developing a new model with Fiat-Lancia and jointly marketing one model.

t Toyota (2,459), Nissan (2,143), Honda (846), and Mitsubishi (660). Toyota has a joint venture with GM in the US. Nissan has joint ventures with Alfa Romeo, Motor Iberica (Spain) and Volkswagen and a plant in the US. Mitsubishi took over Chrysler Australia. Honda has a plant in the US and a joint venture with BL.

Sources: Society of Motor Manufacturers and Traders (1980); Verband der Automobilindustrie e.V. (1981); *L'Argus de l'Automobile* (1981); Motor Vehicle Manufacturers Association (1980); company sources and press cuttings.

Volkswagen, Renault, Peugeot and Fiat) based in five countries (Japan, US, Germany, France and Italy), accounted for 72 per cent of world production in 1980 (with minority ownership or licensing interests in a further 7 per cent (see Table 5.2). Only four Western-European-owned firms make more than one million cars a year. When the European production of Ford and General Motors is added, these six producers accounted in 1980 for 80 per cent of the total Western European production of 10.4 million cars. The dominance of a few firms, and the geographical concentration of their output in a few large plants, means also that the industry plays a key role in the national management of industrial relations and pay negotiations. For many reasons, therefore, governments can hardly escape a measure of involvement in the affairs of the industry.

This chapter is mainly concerned with the adjustment and intervention experience as it affects the major car-producing firms. For reasons of space it does not treat specialised component manufactures whose fortunes are so closely related, nor producers of commercial vehicles (although many car firms also produce commercial vehicles).

5.2 The changing car industry

Historical background

The progress of the industry has been marked, since the era of the pioneers, by changes in product technology, process technology, and the nature of markets.

In a first phase, from just before the First World War to around 1930, the basic design of the mass production car was defined in the US by Henry Ford with the Model T.[1] Flow-line production was introduced and huge initial gains were made in productivity. The real price per pound of cars in the US has hardly changed since the mid-1920s. Ford's refusal to change the design of the Model T allowed General Motors and Chrysler to enter the market, as they saw the scope for product differentiation. Meanwhile, Ford diffused the technology world-wide, setting up production and assembly in major markets and also giving a lead to the major manufacturers in Europe established at that time.[2]

In a second phase, up to the mid-1960s, different tendencies emerged in Europe and the US. In the US, the trend was towards standardised automobile design and refinement of the organisation of mass production, taking advantage of economies of scale. By contrast, in Europe the mass market was restricted by lower incomes, higher costs and higher taxes. It is estimated that around 1970, by which time European tariffs were not significantly higher than the US level (Table 5.3), the purchase costs of similar cars was from 30 to 60 per cent higher in Western Europe than in the US.[3] In addition,

Table 5.3 Western Europe: tariff levels on motor vehicles, 1913–72 (per cent)

Year	Germany	UK	France[†]	Italy[‡]
1913	3	–	9/14	4/6
1924	13	33	45/180	6/11
1929	20	33	45	6/11
1932	25	33	45/70	18/123
1937	40	33	47/74	101/111
1956	17	30	30	35/45
1962*	10/19	28	15/28	27/38
1968	0/18	18	0/18	0/18
1972[§]	0/11	11	0/11	0/11

* After 1962 differential rates for EEC members and non-Member States.
† France maintained quotas on car imports until 1959.
‡ Italy still has a quota on Japanese cars, agreed pre-EEC entry.
§ Tariff rates unchanged until after the implementation of the Tokyo Round cuts after 1980.

Source: Jones (1981), Table 17.

the trend towards standardisation was undermined by a number of successful product innovations in Europe, such as front-wheel drive and transverse-mounted engines. The American Standard—the large car with its six or eight cylinder engine—was not, it became clear, to be the dominant design in world markets. The locus of innovation shifted from the US to Europe, and has since begun shifting to Japan. The 1960s saw the beginning of the concentration of the industry at European level. European integration, GATT tariff reductions and rising exports of smaller cars to the US all contributed to breaking down the frontiers between the world's national and regional markets.

In the 1970s, demand growth slowed down and became more unstable as markets approached maturity; the Japanese emerged as strong competitors; pressures for technical change arose from higher fuel prices and consumer demands for reduced pollution and improved safety standards; and finally, new opportunities for technical change in both product and methods of production were presented by advances in electronic technology. All these pressures persist into the 1980s and the structure of the industry is again being redefined, but this time on a world level (see Section 5.4).

The pressures for adjustment

The continued slowing down of the rate of growth in demand in the major domestic markets is bound to affect the development of the car industry in Western Europe. In almost all Europe's high-income countries, the car market appears to be approaching saturation (that is, replacement demand—which, being postponable, tends to be unstable—dominates). Because of greater population density and urbanisation, higher motoring costs and more extensive public transport, saturation is likely to be reached in Western Europe at a lower level of car density than in North America. Slower economic growth will also continue to depress demand, as it has done since 1973.

The second major factor is the integration of world markets. For the first time in many decades, the main world markets are buying similar types of cars, converging on the small and medium models. In the US in particular the demand for the former American standard models has fallen dramatically (Table 5.4). An obvious reason for this convergence lies in the oil price shocks of 1973 and

Table 5.4 Western Europe and the US: car sales by market segment, 1960–85 (per cent)

	US				Western Europe			
	1960	1970	1978	1985 (forecast)	1960	1970	1978	1985 (forecast)
Extra small	–	–	–	–	10	7	5	6
Small	–	1	1	5	29	21	24	23
Light subcompact	7	10	24	41	30	28	23	23
Medium/large compact	24	21	25	30	31	44	48	48
US Intermediate	–	24	26	15	–	–	–	–
US Standard	69	44	24	9	–	–	–	–

Source: Jones (1981), Table 5.

1979 and the subsequent introduction of government regulations for greater fuel efficiency. Thus US regulations of 1975 called for progressive increases in average miles per gallon from 18 to 27.5 between 1978 and 1985. The necessary investments by US companies are enormous: about $80 billion over the seven years for the big three producers. At the same time, imports of small cars, mainly from Japan, increased to 28 per cent of the US market in 1980.

The American producers reacted late in the day. One response was to build on their long-established presence in Europe to gain economies of scale by designing cars for world-wide production. General Motors and Ford are the most multinational producers in the world (see Table 5.2 and its footnotes, giving extensive information on the international links of the major companies). General Motors leads the other US producers in down-sizing its fleet and now has a competitive range of models in Europe. It has led the way in developing the 'world car', the Chevette having been produced in seven countries. It is also integrating its production of engines and components world-wide. Ford followed in 1980 with its new Escort, produced across the world. While it has a strong model range and has been very profitable in Europe, it is in difficulties in the US. Chrysler on the other hand, failed to react to the changes in the US market and was obliged to sell its foreign operations. It can no longer be considered a world-ranking multinational producer. In 1980 the company was obliged to call for a financial rescue by the US government and its future remains uncertain. Since 1979, there has been something of a collapse in the US industry. Employment has fallen substantially and it has become clear that high wages and insufficient productivity have made the industry uncompetitive with Japanese imports. Much less has been heard about the 'world car'.

The third pressure for adjustment has come from changing foreign competitiveness, especially, now, from Japan. Japan's climb to the front rank among car producers is the most significant structural shift in the industry in the last decade. By 1980 the industry had achieved a 20 to 30 per cent landed-cost advantage over North American and European firms.[4] This was due mainly to low labour costs, harmonious labour relations, a well-educated workforce, a high level of process automation; advanced quality control, and a flexible relationship between car firms and component suppliers (helping, for instance, to reduce stocks to a minimum). Japanese firms have now established a new standard of best practice in the organisation of automobile production. Their advantage is less to do with greater automation than with the deliberate elimination of intermediate buffer stocks. This then highlights bottlenecks in the system which are in turn tackled, resulting over time in a smooth continuous flow system from the steel roll to final assembly (and eliminating costly stocks). To this must be added the full integration of component suppliers into the production schedule, a zero defects policy doing away with expensive testing and rectification, a well-educated labour force, harmonious labour relations and, until recently, lower labour costs. These strengths are the outcome of an historical process of intense competition among a number of firms and the industrial groups supporting them. (See also Mototada Kikkawa's description of the development of the Japanese car industry in Chapter 10, Section 3. This stresses the reduced role that MITI was able to play in the development of the industry after the 1950s.)

Europe's share of the US market fell from 11 to 7 per cent between 1970 and 1980, while Japan's share rose from 4 to 21 per cent; European exports of cars to the US in 1980 were less than half as many as in 1970, and close to the 1960 level (Table 5.5). European

Table 5.5 World production, consumption and trade in cars, 1960, 1970, 1978 and 1985 (millions of units)

	1960	*1970*	*1978*[†]	*1985*[†] (forecast)
Western Europe				
Production	4.8	10.2	11.3	11.7
Imports*	–	0.2	0.8	1.6
Exports*	1.1	1.8	1.8	1.3
Consumption	3.7	8.4	10.3	12.0
Imports from Japan	–	0.1	0.6	1.2
North America				
Production	6.1	9.2	10.3	9.3
Imports*	0.6	1.6	2.2	3.3
Exports*	0.1	0.1	0.2	0.5
Consumption	6.6	10.7	12.3	12.1
Imports from W. Europe	0.6	1.4	0.7	0.8
Imports from Japan	–	0.2	1.5	2.4
Japan				
Production	0.1	3.1	6.0	7.6
Imports	–	–	–	0.1
Exports	–	0.8	3.1	4.3
Consumption	0.1	2.3	2.9	3.4
Rest of world				
Production	0.6	1.8	4.2	8.9
Imports	0.6	1.0	2.4	1.6
Exports	–	0.1	0.3	0.5
Consumption	1.2	2.7	6.3	10.0
Imports from W. Europe	0.5	0.4	1.1	0.4
Imports from Japan	–	0.5	1.0	0.7

* Excluding intra-regional trade.
† Years chosen to represent cyclical peaks.

Sources: Calculated from Jones (1981), Table 3, and, for 1985, author's estimates.

exports to developing countries as a whole, even in 1980, were roughly matched by those of Japan, although France still maintained a significant presence in Africa, and the UK in Asia (Table 5.6: most of the European exports were kits for local assembly while Japanese

Table 5.6 Car exports by area, 1980 (thousands of units)

Importing areas*	Germany	France	Italy	UK	Japan	North America
N.W. Europe	1,338	1,062	367	133	978	26
North America	365	64	39	34	2,045	— ¶
Japan/SANZA	50	29	17	48	194§	7
S. and E. Europe	43	140†	18	10	25	—
Latin America	20	82†	16	9	144§	64
Africa	22	111†	31	20	81	3
Asia	25	25	22	105‡	480§	71
Developed	1,753	1,155	423	215	3,217	33
Developing	110	358	87	144	730	138
Total	1,863	1,513	510	359	3,947	171

* N. W. Europe = EEC plus EFTA less Portugal; SANZA = South Africa, New Zealand and Australia; S. and E. Europe = Spain, Portugal, Greece, Turkey, Yugoslavia and the CMEA countries; Africa less South Africa; Asia = Asia plus Oceania but excluding Japan, Australia and New Zealand.
  † Main CKD kit exports to: Spain (101), Argentina (72), Nigeria (61), and the UK (35).
  ‡ Main CKD kit exports to Iran (69).
  § Main CKD exports to: Australia (105), South Africa (103), Mexico (43) and Taiwan (38).
  ¶ Intra-North American trade: US to Canada (510), Canada to US (550).

Sources: Society of Motor Manufacturers and Traders (1981); Japan Automobile Manufacturers Association (1981); Verband der Automobilindustrie e.V. (1981); *L' Argus de l'Automobile* (1981).

exports were largely assembled). Western Europe has also lost its share in non-European markets as a result of the establishment of local car industries in many developing countries, generally behind high tariff walls and with stringent local content rules, or with imports tied to exports.

European producers were also increasingly being challenged on their home ground. Japan's share of the Western European market reached 10 per cent by 1980, the share rising to 20 to 40 per cent in most countries without substantial car production of their own (Table 5.7). The share was lowest in Spain and Italy, where Japanese imports are tightly limited by quotas, and in France, where strong government action was successfully threatened as long ago as 1977

Table 5.7 Share of Japanese imports in the domestic markets of Western European countries and the US, 1967–80 (per cent)

Country	1967	1972	1977	1980
Italy	–	0.1	0.1	0.1
Spain	–	–	–	–
France	0.2	0.4	2.7	2.9
Germany	–	0.4	2.5	10.4
UK	0.2	3.1	10.9	11.8
Portugal	0.1	23.6	13.0	7.6
Sweden	0.1	2.8	10.3	14.2
Austria	–	7.5	6.4	20.9
Switzerland	0.6	14.0	12.1	23.1
Belgium	1.9	10.0	19.1	24.5
Netherlands	0.8	9.6	20.0	26.4
Denmark	0.6	7.2	17.4	30.8
Ireland	–	–	15.1	30.9
Finland	14.3	19.6	22.5	35.5
Norway	2.7	15.9	23.6	39.2
Western Europe	0.4	2.7	6.5	9.8
US	–	6.0	12.1	21.3

Source: For 1967, 1972 and 1977: Jones (1981), Table 10; for 1980: industry sources.

if any attempt was made by the Japanese to capture more than 3 per cent of the market. In the UK, imports have been limited since 1966 to their current level by 'voluntary' Japanese export control. The growth of protectionist pressures led to the US securing a similar voluntary restraint in 1981, followed in short order by Canada, Germany and the Benelux countries. Thus Japan found itself restricted in every major producing country on both sides of the Atlantic. In the light of these restrictions the strategies of the Japanese producers have shifted in the short run to exporting a more up-market model mix and greater exports of kits for overseas assembly. For the longer term Japanese producers have reluctantly begun the process of establishing production facilities abroad, both independently and in joint ventures with local producers.

The fourth adjustment pressure comes from technical change. This has been accelerated by intensified international competition, the rising price of oil and the new opportunities for process automation offered by the microelectronics revolution. All the major producers are increasing the level of automation, and the most visible and direct consequences are substantial job losses. The full potential of automation has been realised most easily where managements have been able to secure agreement to lower manning levels or to redeploy labour. To some extent, however, the loss of jobs is mitigated by the growing complexity of car design.

Innovations in product technology, to meet higher standards of quality, energy consumption and pollution, have been as marked in the Western European companies as in the US or Japan. In particular, most major car producers have forged links with electronics companies for the supply of microelectronics to control and monitor car functions.

5.3 Public and private responses to change in France, Germany, Italy and the UK

Corporate survival in the car industry depends upon the capacity to make the right long-term, or 'strategic', decisions about new models in the light of rapidly changing market conditions, to keep pace in technology and marketing with competitors, and to generate sufficient profits to finance these expensive activities. The market test of short-term profitability is inappropriate: mistakes may only become evident after a long time and take years and large sums of money to correct. Thus governments inevitably become deeply involved in the affairs of the industry.

Such involvement requires a massive exercise of judgment: its success depends on the capacity of officials and advisers to make independent assessments of the firms concerned, their managerial competence, and the resources available to carry through strategic decisions. Intervention may take two forms: changing the environment in which companies operate, for instance by protection and R & D support; or participating directly in the decision-making process by supporting, financially or otherwise, the strategies of particular companies or encouraging or impeding the entry of foreign firms into the domestic industry.

France

So far, the French car industry has gone from strength to strength in a buoyant domestic market. The industry's response to the pressures for adjustment has been an aggressive, perhaps risky, policy of expansion and internationalisation, accompanied by a close dialogue and a series of bargains between the firms and the government. This cooperation has been facilitated by a consistent and clear set of objectives on the part of the Ministry of Industry, and by government willingness and ability to underwrite strategic objectives. The high status of the Ministry of Industry within government has enabled it to recruit the best talent and to offer rapid promotion to senior positions and later to a career in senior management in industry. The common backgrounds and inter-change of senior personnel greatly facilitate developing a consensus on the appropriate strategy for the industry.

One major government objective has been to preserve wholly domestically owned industry and thus to ensure the survival of at least one, if not two, French firms in the world car league. Although high protective tariffs had to go after the establishment of the EEC (Table 5.3), the government, in perhaps its most significant inter-vention, has severely restricted imports from Japan since 1977. Its reluctance to agree to common EEC standards for cars provides a potential non-tariff barrier to imports from other European countries. In addition, the government has retained its power to control foreign investment, helping the French producers to maintain their share of the domestic market. Thus the proposals of General Motors and Ford to establish assembly plants in 1964 and the Fiat attempt to take over Citröen in 1969 were rejected. The restric-tions were relaxed in 1980, but only for firms from other EEC Member States.

Within this favourable national environment, the French industry has become concentrated into two dominant firms, the Peugeot Group and Renault. The growth of the privately owned Peugeot Group is the result of three strategic decisions. The first was to move away from being a single-model producer, despite high profits and full-capacity operation. The second was the 1974 take-over and rehabilitation of Citröen's car production (with the encouragement of a government loan of £150 million, repaid in two years) and the 1978 purchase of Talbot from the European operations of the ailing Chrysler Corporation. The third stage was expansion outside France, assisted by the 1977 transfer from the Ministry of Industry of a senior official to head Peugeot—an indication of the close relation-ship between the firm and the government. Peugeot now produces cars in France, the UK and Spain, and has licence and cooperation agreements for production of its cars and components in East Germany, Romania and Yugoslavia (see Table 5.2).

Peugeot faces the considerable problem of absorbing and integrat-ing its three constituent, and so far largely separate, parts: Peugeot itself, Citröen and Talbot. The Talbot dealer chain is now being merged with that of Peugeot, and with the integration of engines, floor pans and components throughout the group, Talbot may eventually disappear. More cutbacks and redundancies are almost certainly necessary in the process of rationalisation. Were Peugeot to encounter difficulties, it is almost certain that the French government would provide aid (although the management, with its strong private-enterprise philosophy, is likely to resist any proposed merger with Renault).

Renault, now producing similar volumes of cars to Peugeot, emerged after its nationalisation in 1946 as the government's own 'national champion'. Renault's success has given it an important degree of independence from day-to-day intervention. Top company posts are appointed in close consultation with the government. The government approves the basic strategies, having, for instance, given strong support for the development of smaller cars and for the expansion of exports. Moreover, the government has injected considerable amounts of capital, it does not require dividends on its equity and it has allowed Renault favourable tax treatment and alleviated the burden of social security payments.

Renault has thus been able to restrain price increases and to become an increasingly strong competitor with rising shares in domestic and foreign markets. Partly because of government support, low profitability in the 1970s has not prevented Renault from raising capital on the market. There is no doubt that, if financial difficulties arose in the future, the government would provide the necessary further support.

Renault is belatedly beginning to establish itself as a multinational. In 1978, it gained a foothold in the US market by taking a controlling interest in the American Motors Corporation, where it now produces a Renault car for the US market. Renault also took a 20 per cent interest in Volvo in 1980. It is, moreover, integrating its operations in Spain with its French facilities and plans to do the same in Portugal, anticipating the opening up of the Iberian market with the enlargement of the European Community. Renault models are produced under licence in Romania and in Yugoslavia.

Close links have been established between Renault and Peugeot through exchanges of technology and joint production of engines and components, but official encouragement failed to bring about a common effort by the two firms to develop electronic components: Peugeot linked with the French electrical firm Thomson while Renault (less to the liking of the government) formed a joint company with the US firm Bendix. The French government has also taken an active part in the structuring of the weak components industry and has resisted the incursion of foreign investment. Finally, the one major area where the state has taken the initiative is in establishing a programme to stimulate new fuel-saving technologies.

Germany

Pre-war government efforts to promote a strong domestic car industry in Germany were insubstantial. Tariffs were not high (Table 5.3) and foreign companies, including General Motors (which took over Opel) and Ford, were welcomed; the smaller firms, either individually or after their 1932 merger into Auto Union, failed to emerge as strong domestic producers. It was only in the Nazi period that the government had an impact on the industry through protection, controls and standardisation programmes. But no 'national champion' appeared until Volkswagen, created by the state in 1937 to produce a small car for the masses, entered civilian production after the war with its successful 'Beetle'. The company was partly denationalised in 1961 (the Federal government and the Niedersachsen government each retaining 20 per cent of the shares).

The most critical time for VW came in the early 1970s, when the painful transition had to be made from a successful but increasingly risky one-model producer (compare Peugeot's experience) to a major force in the world motor industry. This was not easy. It required consensus on a complete change of direction among the different parts of an elaborate management structure. In particular, it took a number of changes in the top management to get the new strategy through the Supervisory Board on which the Federal and Regional (*Land*) governments, the metalworkers' union and the trade-union-owned bank formed a strong and resistant majority in a debate that had to be conducted largely in public. Moreover, the first attempts to broaden the model range failed and later efforts, although ultimately successful, were impeded by difficulties in containing costs. There was resistance, too, to the management's proposals to build a VW plant in the US to replace declining exports. When deadlock threatened the viability of the company, the Federal Chancellor became involved in replacing top management and establishing better relations in the Supervisory Board. With this backing, the future of the company was secured; in the mid-1970s the model changes were carried through, the US plant was established, and the workforce in Germany reduced by 25,000. Currently, VW accounts for about 40 per cent of car production in Germany.

VW's present world strategy is based on plants in the US supplying North America, plants in Brazil and Argentina supplying Latin America and the rest of the Third World, and plants in Germany supplying the home market and the rest of Western Europe. VW now also has an arrangement for Nissan to assemble one of its models for the Japanese and Asian markets from 1983. The shift of emphasis away from high-cost Germany is further promoted by the planned supply of engines from the Mexican plants to the US, by engines and gearboxes from Brazil to Germany, and by the licence production of small VW models in Spain by Seat.

VW now has a strong model range and its competitive strength lies in its design philosophy of constant improvement in the product, notably in fuel economy. The company is also collaborating with MAN to produce a full range of commercial vehicles, while its other attempt at diversification through the purchase of the office equipment firm Triumph-Adler has proved a failure. An attempt to take over the Nixdorf computer firm was also unsuccessful. VW is now cooperating with Bosch in developing the use of microprocessors.

Two other smaller German-owned car producers, Daimler-Benz and BMW, specialise in up-market luxury cars. They are both vulnerable to the declining market for cars with high petrol consumption. Despite high labour costs and the appreciation of the DM, export performance has so far been impressive (see Table 5.8), particularly in the quality market (average unit values of German car exports are nearly 40 per cent above those of French or UK exports). The preference of the home market for high quality and performance should continue to favour domestic cars. The increasing Japanese penetration of the German market initially hit imports from France and Italy and more recently affected Ford and Opel (General Motors) more than the German-owned producers.

Apart from the intervention in the affairs of Volkswagen in the early 1970s and the securing of Japanese export restraints in 1981, Federal government involvement in the German car industry has been limited. The German government, unlike the French, does not have a particular set of strategic objectives for the motor industry, nor does it devote resources to day-to-day monitoring.

There are three reasons why German government intervention has generally been less necessary than in France, the UK or Italy — reasons which apply not only to the car industry. The first is the successful performance of the economy as a whole and of the car firms in particular. The second is the generally favourable social bargain which involves the unions in managerial decision-making and helps create positive attitudes to technical change and the relocation of production. The centralised union structure, with its substantial professional and research staff at union headquarters has on the whole facilitated cooperative working relationships. The third reason is the traditionally close involvement of the banks in industrial decision-making through shareholdings and board membership. Consensus building among the main actors has thus created a

Table 5.8 EEC and Japan: trade in cars, parts and engines, 1973 and 1980*
($ billion)

	1973			1980		
	Exports	*Imports*	*Balance*	*Exports*	*Imports*	*Balance*
Germany						
Cars	5.6	1.7	3.9	14.6	4.8	9.8
Parts	2.1	0.6	1.5	6.6	2.1	4.5
Engines	0.9	0.2	0.7	2.9	0.8	2.1
France						
Cars	2.6	0.9	1.7	6.7	3.2	3.5
Parts	0.8	0.5	0.3	3.7	1.9	1.8
Engines	0.3	0.3	—	1.2	1.0	0.2
Italy						
Cars	1.2	0.9	0.3	2.4	4.6	− 2.2
Parts	0.4	0.3	0.1	1.9	1.0	0.9
Engines	0.2	0.2	—	0.7	0.7	—
UK						
Cars	0.9	1.1	−0.2	1.9	4.9	− 3.0
Parts	1.2	0.3	0.9	3.6	1.5	2.1
Engines	0.5	0.1	0.4	1.8	0.6	1.2
EEC†						
Cars	5.8	0.8	5.0	12.3	6.0	6.3
Parts	2.6	0.5	2.1	9.2	2.0	7.2
Engines	1.2	0.3	0.9	4.2	1.3	2.9
Japan						
Cars	2.6	0.2	2.4	16.1	0.5	15.6
Parts	0.3	—	0.3	2.2	0.1	2.1
Engines	0.3	—	0.3	1.8	0.1	1.7

* New SITC headings (old in brackets): 781 (7321)—passenger motor vehicles; 784 (7328)—parts and accessories; and 713 (7115)—internal combustion engines and parts. The latter two include parts and engines for commercial vehicles, tractors, etc.

† Excludes intra-EEC trade.

Source: OECD (1973 and 1980a).

framework conducive to the taking of long-term decisions. The government may from time to time influence the consensus but it is rarely able to take a direct initiative.

However, there are two ways in which outside influences have affected the structure of the car industry. First, the banks—not the government—succeeded in frustrating the efforts of General Motors to take over Daimler-Benz; in another case, the Federal Cartel Office successfully opposed a merger between Guest, Keen & Nettleford (UK) and the German component group Sachs. Secondly, a form of intervention peculiar to Germany is the involvement of some Regional governments in the rescue of firms in trouble. The Bremen government attempted, in 1961, to arrange the rescue of Borgward, but gave up the attempt in the face of opposition from the banks and industrial experts. In another case, the Bavarian government was able in 1967 to mobilise bank support for credit guarantees for BMW, despite the firm's rather shaky financial condition; in that case, optimism about the firm's prospects was more generally shared.

Italy

The Italian motor industry, unlike the French, German and British, is dominated by one firm, Fiat. Fiat, too, is in the peculiar position of being one of the few large corporations in Italy still in private hands (controlled by the Agnelli family). Attempts by the American majors to establish themselves in Italy have been actively resisted, both before the Second World War and since (for instance, Ford's proposal to acquire Lancia was prevented when Fiat acquired it in 1979).

Most of Fiat's traditional strengths, its leadership in small cars, its price competitiveness and design skills, have now disappeared or are no longer unique to Fiat. Its main weakness lies in severe problems of industrial relations, which it has tried to alleviate by greater automation and diversification into commercial vehicles, construction equipment, machine tools and automated production systems. For electronic development, Fiat has its own subsidiary (which may collaborate in future with the electronics specialist SGS-Ates). Fiat has, indeed, been able to develop a strong position in process technology, especially in automation equipment. Diversification has, however, involved a sacrifice of market share: the costs had to be met by raising car prices and restricting investment on the development of new models. Fiat's share of the home market—highly protected by tariffs before the operation of the EEC's Common External Tariff and by other taxes favouring small cars—has been eroded from 88 per cent in 1971 to 52 per cent in 1980 (Table 5.9).

Imports from Japan have been virtually excluded by quotas (through a trade agreement made before entry into the EEC), but Germany and France have taken large shares of the Italian market and Japanese exports to Germany have severely hit Italian exports there.

Fiat at one time appeared to be building up a network of integrated facilities abroad. It proposed to take over Seat in Spain, which was already producing Fiat cars under licence, but this fell through

Table 5.9 Shares of EEC car markets, 1980

	Markets					
	Germany	France	Italy	UK	Benelux	EEC-9
By country of production (%)						
Germany*	72.0	10.9	13.5	18.2	35.5	33.2
France†	8.9	72.5	21.5	10.9	22.5	27.2
Italy‡	4.3	5.0	56.3	4.1	5.9	14.2
UK	0.5	1.4	1.4	45.4	2.2	9.4
Spain§	2.2	5.9	6.0	4.6	0.8	4.1
CMEA	0.4	0.9	0.3	1.8	1.5	0.9
Japan	10.4	2.9	0.1	11.9	25.5	9.1
Other countries	1.3	0.5	0.9	3.1	6.1	1.9
Total	100.0	100.0	100.0	100.0	100.0	100.0
Of which by major firm (%):						
Peugeot	4.7	36.6	11.6	9.4	14.5	15.0
Renault	4.7	40.5	10.5	5.8	8.7	14.4
Volkswagen	30.3	11.2	5.2	4.5	10.1	14.2
Fiat¶	3.5	3.3	51.7	3.4	4.7	12.4
Ford	10.3	3.6	5.0	30.7	8.6	11.5
General Motors	16.7	1.8	3.5	8.7	11.8	8.9
British Leyland	0.3	1.1	0.7	18.2	1.5	4.0
Total ('000)	2,426	1,873	1,530	1,514	875	8,386

* Including Ford and General Motors in Belgium.
† Including Renault and Peugeot in Belgium and some Spanish-built cars sold in Europe.
‡ Includes Seat cars sold as Fiats in Europe and some Polish-built Fiats.
§ Excludes some Renault, Peugeot and Seat cars sold as French or Italian in Europe.
¶ Including Seat-built Fiats.

Sources: Society of Motor Manufacturers and Traders (1981); Verband der Automobil-industrie e.V. (1981); *L'Argus de l'Automobile* (1981); and author's estimates.

because of lack of resources and an unwillingness to tackle the social problems of reducing overmanning in Seat. Fiat was refused permission by the French to gain control of Citröen and subsequently sold its shares. Fiat also proposed to increase integration with its Polish and Yugoslav licensees and to establish plants in Latin America. It is still an open question whether the company will in fact be able to develop an international network of production centres and it recently withdrew from the US market completely. On the other hand, the export of car-making *plant* has been a strong point in Fiat's internationalisation strategy ever since, in the mid-1960s, it won the contract to design and build the Togliatti complex in the Soviet Union.

Alfa Romeo, accounting for about 15 per cent of Italian car production, is now the only other car producer of any consequence. The company was taken over by the state in 1933, becoming part of the IRI group. Alfa Romeo became an important instrument of regional policy when it set up an assembly plant in the South in 1968. But the firm is increasingly costly to support and it needs to develop wider links if it is to survive. A joint venture was agreed with Nissan in 1980 to produce a new model in a new plant near Naples. This could lead to more substantial cooperation in future, which might help both to expand employment in the South and to increase Alfa Romeo's inadequate scale of production; but it might also increase the difficulties of Fiat.

The most important element in government policy towards the motor industry has probably been the quota on imports from Japan. Until recent years Fiat has neither sought nor received substantial government support. Hitherto relations between the Agnelli family and governments have often been strained. However, three factors may signal a change. First, the Agnelli family has withdrawn from day-to-day management of the firm. Secondly, the parliament recently approved the establishment of an innovation fund for certain industries, including the car industry. As in France this is seen as a way of giving the industry a stronger technological base in the future, although unlike in France the government has not been involved in defining the technological objectives of the programme. Thirdly, since a critical strike was broken in 1979, the labour relations deadlock in Fiat has given way to strong management efforts to eliminate serious over-manning and the introduction of automated production equipment.

The complexity of political bargains between the Communists and the various factions within the Christian-Democratic party forms the background to all government intervention in Italy. The importance of the political bargaining process can be illustrated by the long arguments over the agreement between Alfa Romeo and Nissan. A genuine division of views over the wisdom of allowing the first entry of a foreign firm—especially a Japanese firm—into the industry as a solution for the increasingly unviable situation of Alfa Romeo was the main issue, but it was complicated by personal and factional interests.

The UK

The high protection enjoyed by the UK car industry from 1919 until the GATT tariff cuts of the 1960s (Table 5.3) was not accompanied by hostility to the entry of foreign producers. Both Ford and General Motors (Vauxhall) established a strong presence in the 1920s, and Ford became a leader in production efficiency with the opening of its Dagenham plant in 1931. UK producers were slow to react to the challenge from Ford until Austin and Morris merged to form the British Motor Corporation (BMC) in 1952. However, earlier antagonisms between the two resulted in a failure to integrate the two parts. BMC expanded within the buoyant markets of the 1950s and 1960s, maintaining the two separate model lines and distributive networks and concentrating on the Mini and 1100 (which were technically successful but never profitable) while lacking a really effective middle-market model. At the same time, the commercial vehicle producer, Leyland, had taken over Standard-Triumph and, like BMC, was expanding by buying up a number of smaller companies (BMC taking over Jaguar, and Leyland taking over Rover). But neither combine seems to have been able to rationalise its acquisitions —weaknesses which became apparent when the market sagged in 1967. The major weaknesses lay both in management, especially in production and design management, and in industrial relations.

The Labour government entering office in 1964 began to pursue an active policy of direct intervention in industry, among other things establishing the Industrial Reorganisation Corporation (IRC) to promote industrial restructuring. The common underlying assumption of the time was that production units in many sections of UK industry were too small to compete internationally. In this context, and in the face of a threatened collapse of BMC, ministers took a leading part in bringing about the 1968 merger between BMC and Leyland into the British Leyland Motor Corporation (BL) with the help of an IRC loan of £25 million.

The merged BL proved profitable in the boom years of 1971 and 1973, but the problems of running so large and diverse a company, and internal conflicts which led to postponement of rationalisation and cancellation of new models, became critical again in 1974. Lord Ryder (the head of the National Enterprise Board (NEB) which took over the functions of the IRC) prepared a plan for the rescue of BL based on very optimistic forecasts of increased production and market shares and recommending the injection of substantial funds. Lord Ryder's report led to the nationalisation of the company in 1975.

The underlying problems, far from being resolved, were compounded by a new centralisation of decision-making and by the creation of a single car division employing over 100,000 people and based on the continuation of earlier convictions of the merits of economies of scale *per se* rather than on practical ways of increasing productivity. This proved to be a fundamental mistake, for management was already dangerously overstretched. Moreover, it was not clear where ultimate accountability lay between the firm itself and the NEB, which became increasingly involved in management. Delays in decision-making and a breakdown in communication led to a worsening both in management morale and in relations with the unions. British Leyland's share of the domestic market continued to fall, from 30 per cent to 24 per cent between 1975 and 1977.

It was not until 1977, when Michael Edwardes took over as Chief Executive, that the situation at BL began to come under control. With political backing, Edwardes was able to close all but two of the main plants and introduce new work practices, reducing the workforce by over 85,000 between 1978 and 1982. This new strategy of radical rationalisation was carried through despite initial hostility, followed by grudging acceptance, from the workforce. Losses continued but were still made up, despite misgivings, by the Conservative government elected in 1979—a government pledged to take a tougher line with the deficits of nationalised industries. Through the NEB, about £1,200 million was provided in 1975–80 and further government funding of £990 million has been agreed for 1981–3. The government's firm refusal to grant more, together with a growing appreciation by the workforce and unions of the severity of BL's problems, gave Edwardes the necessary support to carry through his programme. An important element in the programme was the successful introduction in 1981 of the Mini Metro, built in a new, and highly automated factory and accompanied by substantial increases in productivity. It was followed by BL's assembly under licence, from 1981, of a Honda car, the Acclaim, for sale in the EEC and by an agreement, later in 1981, for the joint development, with BL as a more equal partner of Honda this time, of a new up-market model for both the UK and Japanese markets. In 1983, a new model for the middle segment of the market, the Maestro, was succcessfully launched.

As the smallest and weakest of the full-range European car producers, British Leyland remains very exposed. Besides losing its share of the home market (down to around 20 per cent in 1980), the company has sold off its production facilities abroad (in Australia, Belgium, Italy, Spain· and elsewhere), and its exports, particularly to Western Europe, have fallen off. Nevertheless, if overall productivity can be raised through rationalisation and if the new models are successful, British Leyland stands a reasonable chance of surviving, or at the very least of becoming an attractive asset for a larger grouping.

British Leyland has not been the only UK car firm calling for government rescue by injection of taxpayers' money. Rootes was taken over in 1967 by the Chrysler Corporation, which was by 1975 making heavy losses both in the US and in the UK. Chrysler faced the British government with the alternative of taking over Chrysler UK, or taking an 80 per cent shareholding, or seeing the subsidiary close down with consequent loss of 55,000 jobs (largely in Scotland). Despite much resistance from the Department of Industry and its advisers, and despite doubts about the long-run viability of Chrysler UK, the government finally agreed to underwrite its losses in the UK for a limited period at a cost of £72.5 million, a sum reckoned to cost the taxpayer less than half the cost of a complete closure.

The prospects for the British car industry are brighter since the major questions of a fragmented structure and low productivity began to be tackled after 1979 (see Table 5.10).[5] The UK's traditionally strong components industry has maintained a healthy balance of trade (Table 5.8) and the UK now has certain attractions as a low-wage location for production for the European market. There is

Table 5.10 Motor vehicles produced per employee, 1955–78*

	UK	Germany	France	Italy	US	Japan
1955	4.1	3.9	3.6	3.0	19.3	2.2
1965	5.8	6.4	6.2	6.3	23.2	5.9
1973	5.8	7.7	6.9	7.1	21.6	13.1
1978	4.7	8.6	6.6	6.2	20.9	16.3

* Equivalent motor vehicles weighted by size of car (see original source). Growth of productivity should be interpreted with caution as no allowance is made for quality changes over time or between countries.

Source: Jones (1981), Table 14.

still a long way to go to reach European levels of productivity and much depends on the success of BL's new model range. BL's cooperation with Honda may prove the initial step in an emerging UK strategy of closer cooperation with Japan. Nissan has been examining, with much UK government encouragement, the feasibility of investing in an assembly plant in the UK. As of early 1983, this prospect seemed doubtful.

British governments have had to face the most difficult adjustment problems among the countries examined here. They were called upon, at a critical period, to support financially, and ultimately to take over, the fundamentally weak 'national champion'; in France, on the other hand, the government was continuously reinforcing companies which were basically strong and aggressive. The situation in the UK is marked by the absence of both close involvement of labour and finance in strategic decision-making that exists in Germany and by the substitute of close government–industry cooperation that exists in France. Until recent years UK policies towards the car industry have been responsive to crisis situations and *ad hoc* in nature. But governments have gradually come to terms with the growing divergence between the performance of the UK industry and its main competitors and are in the process of a painful learning process in discriminatory intervention.

5.4 Issues for the future

Medium-term prospects

The ability to compete internationally, substantial overcapacity, and low profitability will continue to pose large problems for the Western European car industry in the medium-term. On the other hand, the industry has, since the 1970s, responded energetically to pressure for change. It has had to resort to protection from imports from Japan, but it is nevertheless beginning to learn from the Japanese challenge. Some of the weaker firms, notably BL, appear to have improved their prospects of survival, if at great cost.

A number of forecasts of prospects for the trend rate of growth in Western European demand (by number of cars) tends to converge on a figure of 1 to 1½ per cent per annum, though, as the market becomes increasingly saturated, this demand will become increasingly unstable. With most Japanese imports controlled and no prospects of dramatic rises in imports from Eastern Europe or the NICs, demand growth of this magnitude could mean growth in Western European output (by numbers of cars) of up to 1 per cent per annum. Much of this growth will take place in Spain and Portugal where substantial capacity expansion is underway. If, for instance, labour productivity were to continue to rise at about 2 per cent per annum, as in the past decade, this could mean that employment in the EEC would fall by 1 per cent or more per annum—by about 175,000 between 1981 and 1986, or perhaps 300,000 if employment in the supplying industries is included (out of the 2½ million or so at present engaged). Higher rates of growth of productivity would increase this job loss by a proportionate amount.

These medium-term prospects, by no means the most dismal among Western Europe's industries, are predicated on assumptions about developments in policies (particularly the maintenance of Japanese export restraint), the impact of technology, and Western Europe's competitive capacity. Many of the conditions of the 1970s have been inherited by the 1980s, notably the trend to product innovation as a result of intense global competition, the high price of energy, and the impact of regulation and microelectronics. However, new trends are now apparently emerging which might offer brighter prospects for Western Europe's producers than was evident a few years ago.

A 'dematuring' car industry?

The 'world car' view, propounded in the main by the US companies, was that cars were an increasingly mature industry.[6] Convergent consumer tastes were allowing the production of identical, standardised models in multiple locations. Substantial design and production economies would result in a high level of concentration, greater vertical integration and a dedicated and less flexible production technology, requiring little skilled labour (hence readily transferable to low-cost locations).

This view of the future has recently come to be questioned.[7] The first reason is that the elimination of a number of medium-sized producers has been resisted and frustrated. In Western Europe governments have supported ailing firms through subsidy, protection against Japanese imports, the use of national standards as potential or actual non-tariff barriers, and—at times—the blocking of foreign investment. This intervention has had several other effects. It has encouraged Japanese firms to move up-market in their export product mix. They have also begun to invest in Western Europe. The defence of existing firms by governments has also been one of the major reasons for the extraordinary mushrooming of inter-firm cooperation agreements—in some cases as an alternative to business failure or merger—within Western Europe and more globally.

The second problem with the 'world car' concept is that many of its claimed advantages have not materialised. Despite a convergence in the size of cars bought, national conditions and government regulations have in some cases offset the benefits of common design. Indeed, European markets still have quite different patterns of demand, which continue to allow local producers to benefit from a certain specialisation: for instance, Germany in up-market cars (where Japan continues to be weak) and Italy in small cars (which producers in the US still cannot compete in).

Thirdly, and following the heavy investments undertaken by car firms over the last decade, car industry technology, far from becoming more standardised, is able to offer a growing number of different solutions to market demands and production needs. Innovatory activity and product design have become much more important than hitherto and the industry is busy exploiting the possibilities of increasing fuel efficiency—for instance, through the application of plastics, ceramics and electronic controls in engines. Many new design concepts will also potentially have a significant impact on the way cars are built, making some existing facilities obsolete before they are fully written down. Hand-in-hand with these changes, advances in production technology, through robotics and automated production and control, promise fundamental changes in the economies of scale in production by offering greater flexibility—for instance, to vary the mix of models to follow changes in the pattern of demand. Because of these changes in the technological outlook of the industry, the view has been put forward that it is potentially going through a process of 'dematurity' where technology is diverging rather than converging.[8] This results in a less vertically integrated industry where medium-sized producers stand a much greater chance of survival through the skilful exploitation of particular technologies and market niches. The chance of survival is enhanced by the opportunities for inter-firm cooperation that have developed.

Western Europe's competitiveness can be defined in terms of product technology, process efficiency (incorporating both production technology and the efficient organisation of the entire production chain), and marketing placement (the positioning of the firm in different market segments and locations to maximise the benefits from the international division of labour). The Japanese advantage in process efficiency is widely acknowledged and the US producers have at least a potential advantage, if difficult to realise, in their market placement. It is arguable that the Europeans are second in each of these but currently still have the lead in product technology, with world leadership in small car design and high performance cars with sophisticated handling. This lead is currently under threat from the Japanese who may have caught up, in some cases, by the mid-1980s.[9]

Policy issues

There is little doubt that the main issue facing Western Europe's car industry in the short and medium term is that of the appropriate structure of trade relations. The danger is that the uncoordinated slide into restrictions on imports from Japan becomes a permanent state of affairs. Not only would this be a significant blow to the continuing functioning of the international trading system, but it would exacerbate existing tensions within the industry and within the EEC. The tensions within the EEC derive most notably from the differences in levels of national protection against Japanese imports. But there is also a particular divergence in attitudes to inward Japanese investment and to the issue of local content that arises should such investment lead to exports in the EEC. At the two extremes, a clear strategy of forging links with Japanese producers has emerged in the UK, while the French government and car firms currently favour a more exclusively European strategy and the exclusion of both Japanese imports and investment. This divergence of approaches would have the consequence of creating a threat to free trade within the Community (in contravention of the rules of the Customs Union, it should be noted) if member countries were perceived to be exporting locally assembled Japanese cars not deemed to have sufficient European content.

The only way to begin the process of removing restrictions on Japanese imports is through establishing a collective international agreement (that is, between the EEC and the US) that, when an upturn comes, restrictions are simultaneously lifted in all markets. There are other concerns that have to be addressed collectively if confidence in a relatively free trading system is to be rebuilt. Change in the car industry is complex and does not follow the inevitable logic of the product cycle. Appropriate domestic policies and institutional arrangements may usefully be directed towards both encouraging resources to move out of the industry in advanced countries and stimulating technological change that promises to rejuvenate the industry. The previous section of this chapter emphasised the importance of strong firms, the banks and labour in facilitating such adjustments. Government policies are in many cases a last-best in this context.

A major issue for Europe concerns the mechanisms whereby the burden of adjustment does not only fall on the losers, but can also be shared by the winners. One avenue, at least for the larger markets, is the channelling of the more dynamic technological and managerial characteristics of the more successful producers towards the less sucessful economies via foreign direct investment, either through joint venture or on a green-field site. This process is beginning to get under way in Western Europe, partly through intra-European cooperation, partly through investment and cooperative links with Japan (which have been a positive consequence of protection). The growth of Japanese car investment in Western Europe is probably inevitable and should be welcomed. It will be threatened to the extent that minimum-local-content rules become an issue in intra-EEC trade. It should also be clear that Japanese inward investment undermines the potential for a more specifically European strategy, say of 'European champions' behind high protective walls. I believe that, in any case, the 'dematurity' process will serve to undermine the vision of a high degree of oligopoly that lies behind a 'European champions' strategy.

A subsidiary issue is the dismantling of trade protection for industries in the leading NICs that can no longer be considered infant industries. Spain, which has recently helped create trade tensions with the EEC through its high tariffs on cars, can be considered as a particular regional problem in this category. Participation in a Western European division of labour must eventually be assured by a more liberal treatment of car imports in the future.

Another issue that may become increasingly important is how competitive subsidy wars can be avoided or constrained. Whenever a major producer announces its intention to open a new plant, it is able to bid one government against the other in the level of discretionary subsidies each can offer. Similarly, the state promotion of R & D in Germany set off demands for similar support in France and Italy. The situation is the same in regard to automated production technology and robots. There is a clear task here to be tackled by the EEC's competition policy rules.

Some measure of agreement on the above issues could form a basis for a return to a new, more open trading system in cars, once the current recession ends. However, the basis for such a trading system has to be built in the intervening period in order to take advantage of the situation when it does arise.

Notes

1. The best history of the technology and economics of the US car industry is found in Abernathy (1978).
2. See Wilkins and Hill (1961).
3. See Kravis *et al.* (1978).
4. US:Japanese estimates in Abernathy *et al.* (1981) and estimates by J. E. Harbour quoted in Burck (1982). European estimates summarised in Commission of the European Communities (1981).
5. See Jones (1983).
6. For an example of the 'world car' view, see Bhaskar (1980).
7. By, among others, Abernathy *et al.* (1981), Jones (1983), and Hayes and Abernathy (1980).
8. Clark (1982) and Jones (1983). On developments in the machine tool industry, which have played a large role in this technological change, see Chapter 8.
9. See Jones (1982).

References

Abernathy, W. J. (1978), *The Productivity Dilemma*, Baltimore: John Hopkins University Press.

L'Argus de l'Automobile (1981), June, Paris.

Abernathy, W. J., Clark, K. C., Kantrow, A. M. (1981), 'The new Industrial Competition', *Harvard Business Review*, September–October.

Bhaskar, K. (1980), *The Future of the World Motor Industry*, London: Kogan Page.

Burck, G. C. (1982), 'Can Detroit catch up?', *Fortune*, 8 February.

Clark, K. C. (1982), *Competition, Technical Diversity and Radical Innovation in the US Auto Industry*, Boston: Harvard Business School Working Paper HBS 82-5.

Commission of the European Communities (1981), *The European Automobile Industry: Commission Statement*, COM(81)317, Brussels.

Hayes, R. H., and Abernathy, W. J. (1980), 'Managing our way to industrial decline', *Harvard Business Review*, July–August.

Japan Automobile Manufacturers' Association Inc. (1981), *Motor Vehicles Statistics of Japan*, Tokyo.

Jones, D. T. (1981), *Maturity and Crisis in the European Car Industry: Structural Change and Public Policy*, Sussex European Papers No. 8, Brighton: Sussex European Research Centre.

Jones, D. T. (1982), *Technology and Competitiveness in the Automobile Industry*, paper presented to the second International Policy Forum on the Future of the Automobile, Hakone, Japan.

Jones, D. T. (1983), 'Technology and the UK automobile industry', *Lloyds Bank Review*, April.

Kravis, I. B., Heston, A., and Summers, R. (1978), *International Comparisons of Real Product and Purchasing Power*, Baltimore: Johns Hopkins University Press.

Motor Vehicle Manufacturers' Association (1980), *World Motor Vehicle Data 1980 Edition*, Detroit.

OECD (1973), *Statistics of Foreign Trade, Series C*, Paris.

OECD (1980a), *Statistics of Foreign Trade, Series C*, Paris.

OECD (1980b), *National Accounts of OECD Countries, 1960–1978*, Paris.

OECD (1981), *National Accounts of OECD Countries, 1961–1979*, Paris.

Society of Motor Manufacturers and Traders (1980), *The Motor Industry of Great Britain 1980*, London.

Society of Motor Manufacturers and Traders (1981), *The Motor Industry of Great Britain 1981*, London.

Verband der Automobilindustrie e.V. (1981), *Tatsachen und Zahlen aus der Kraftverkehrwirtschaft. 44 Folge 1981*, Frankfurt.

Wilkins, M., and Hill, F. E. (1961), *American Business Abroad: Ford on Six Continents*, Detroit: Wayne State University Press.

6 ELECTRICAL POWER PLANT: MARKET COLLAPSE AND STRUCTURAL STRAINS*

John Surrey and William Walker

6.1 Introduction

Against the background of a widespread slump in power station ordering since the mid-1970s and intensified export competition, this chapter examines the evolving relationships between governments, utilities and power plant suppliers in Western Europe and the possibilities for further structural adjustment. Given the global outlook of the industry, Western Europe is in some respects too narrow a focus for study. Nevertheless, European suppliers face many common problems which have led to attempts at common action, including the historical interest in market sharing through the International Electrical Association (a cartel) and various technical collaborations, especially in the nuclear field.

A number of industry characteristics help to explain the general problems facing the power plant industry. On the demand side, the variability and 'lumpiness' of ordering are due to the large size and value of individual power plant and long construction lead-times (typically five to ten years). This is an area in which the principles of free trade find few adherents. The foundations of nationalistic procurement lie in perceived national benefits in terms of the balance of payments, skilled employment, security of supply and technological chauvinism. The industry's special status is reflected in close relationships between governments, utilities and plant suppliers.

On the supply side, there are also a number of distinguishing features. First, the costs and risks of developing new technical systems are exceptionally high and development lead-times extend over years or even decades. Secondly, power plants are assemblies of a wide variety of equipment. Thirdly, the industry relies heavily on a developed industrial infrastructure, including, in the case of nuclear power, external R & D institutions. Finally, equipment failure imposes very high costs and utilities therefore attach a high premium to quality, reliability, and the suppliers' ability to service the plant throughout its operating life (twenty to forty years).

Long time horizons, high costs, and the complexities of managing

* This chapter is mainly a condensed version of Surrey and Walker (1981).

large, sophisticated projects have created stiff barriers to new entrants, production being concentrated among ever fewer producers in the advanced countries. Most of the surviving 'core' producers are among the largest, most diversified and dynamic corporations. They are 'electro-technical' firms for whom power plant manufacture is only one, not necessarily the major, area in a broad range of electrical, electronic and science-based activities.

There are two elements to production capacity in this industry: highly skilled labour in development and design engineering, project management, planning, and on the shop floor; and specialised physical assets used in the manufacture of turbine generators, steam supply systems and other sophisticated hardware. The measure of capacity mostly used in this chapter, gigawatts (GW) per annum, is but a proxy for capacity which, in this industry, is somewhat elastic in that it depends among other things on the size and types of generating units ordered.

The focus of this chapter is on the main contractors for conventional and nuclear generating plants in France, the Federal Republic of Germany, Switzerland, the UK and Italy, which constitute the core of the European industry. Considerable discussion of the leading suppliers outside Europe, the US and Japan is, however, unavoidable. The chapter further concentrates on nuclear steam systems (NSSS) and turbine generators (driven by steam from nuclear reaction or fossil fuels, or by water) for public electric utilities—the key aspects of power plant supply.

The next part of this chapter concentrates on the historical development of the European industry, followed by an examination of the fundamental market changes since the mid-1970s which have interrupted this historical development 'trajectory'. The final part looks at the prospects for future structural change.

6.2 The development of the European industry

The oligopoly established

Capital goods for generating and distributing electricity came to form a new industrial sector which was firmly established by 1914 in Europe and the US. Throughout the inter-war period two major US groups, General Electric (GE) and Westinghouse, strengthened their positions in their comparatively large domestic market and obtained a flow of licence income from numerous overseas sources. Since European home markets were generally small, the numerous European suppliers then in existence had strong interests in extending their 'base markets' beyond national frontiers. The hold of core

European firms (in Germany, Switzerland, and to an extent the UK) over domestic and 'premium' export markets was accompanied by extensive collaboration on technology and markets. There were particularly close ties between US and German corporations, notably Westinghouse with Siemens and GE with AEG. The core groups also licensed technology to, and in some cases invested directly in, newer entrants to the industry in the UK, France, Italy and Japan. These international patterns of technical collaboration were to prove remarkably long lasting.

Technical progress in generation, transmission and distribution made electricity cheaper and consumption grew rapidly, even in the slump of the 1930s. The emphasis placed by utilities on technical progress for further cost reduction reinforced the market power of the core groups. Competition was controlled domestically and internationally by price and technical exchange arrangements. The International Electrical Association (IEA), formed in the early 1930s, has survived as a cartel to the present day (albeit without US membership during the post-war period because of US anti-trust laws). Suppliers could not have exercised such control without the tacit approval of governments, but, outside the USSR, these were only indirectly involved in the affairs of the electricity supply and power plant industries before the Second World War. Electricity supply became a strategic concern during the war and an important factor in post-war reconstruction. In countries with decentralised political systems (for example the US, Canada and Germany) the structure of electricity supply evolved on a regional basis; but in more centralised countries, authority gradually passed to the state (for example, in the UK and France), culminating in nationalisation into centralised undertakings in the late 1940s. These structural disparities were to affect both the use of procurement as a policy instrument and the acceptability of domestic monopoly-supply arrangements for power plant.

The three decades after 1945 were marked by sustained growth in electricity demand. This was the result of economic growth, the development of major new markets (such as the substitution of electricity for steam power in industry), and falling costs (due to continued technical advance and cheaper fossil fuels).

Extensive rationalisation of the European industry was necessitated by structural strains which first arose in the mid-1960s as a result of three related factors. The first was the increased size and sophistication of new generating units. The second was the intensification of foreign competition, allied with European fears of US technological domination. By the early 1960s, with domestic reconstruction completed, German and Japanese suppliers had become highly competitive with the US, UK and Swiss suppliers. At the same time, European governments were becoming increasingly apprehensive about the perceived threat of US technological domination in various advanced industries, including electrical power plant. Westinghouse, for instance, had attempted (unsuccessfully except in Belgium) to create a large manufacturing base in Europe through a series of take-overs of smaller firms. The third factor was the commercialisation of nuclear power.

Nuclear power

From a manufacturing viewpoint, the main difference between nuclear and conventional plant lies in the nuclear steam supply system (NSSS), in which the boiler in a conventional steam plant is replaced by a nuclear reactor and associated contaminant, heat transfer and safety systems. The electro-mechanical parts are not dissimilar, except that in the nuclear plant they tend to be larger and more sophisticated. There are several major NSSS configurations: *light-water reactors* (LWRs), originally scaled up by US manufacturers from submarine propulsion reactors, which now account for 90 per cent of all nuclear generating capacity in operation and under construction, and which come in two types, the pressurised water reactor (PWR) and the boiling water reactor (BWR); the *heavy-water reactor* (HWR), developed mainly in Canada; *gas-cooled reactors*, independently developed by the UK and France in the 1950s and 1960s; the as yet experimental *fast-breeder reactor* (FBR); and the *high-temperature reactor* (HTR).

For leading European firms the manufacturing difficulties in nuclear technology were not insuperable, although significant organisational changes were required. High costs and long lead-times made it inevitable that governments, would become involved in initial development work, especially where there was also interest in military applications. Where this involvement extended into the commercialisation stage, it raised questions of how the costs and risks should be apportioned between the state, utilities and plant suppliers; which technology should be adopted and who should assume responsibility for design and engineering; and whether a monopoly NSSS supply structure was more suitable than one with several firms. In addition, internationally agreed rules were necessary to prevent exports increasing the likelihood of weapons proliferation, and to prevent such issues as safeguards from being sucked into the competition for markets.

Because of their military programmes, the US, UK and France had a head start with nuclear technologies. In the UK and France, natural uranium fuelled gas-cooled reactors were originally developed to produce plutonium for weapons. In contrast, LWRs were fuelled with enriched uranium. This early technological division sprang from the US's carefully protected monopoly of large-scale uranium enrichment capacity as a result of its nuclear weapons programme in the 1940s and 1950s.

In the US, responsibility for commercialisation was assumed by the four leading firms, GE and Westinghouse in particular (see Table 6.1). Lacking the large domestic market and the strength and innovative drive of the US firms, UK and French plant suppliers were unable to assume leadership in reactor development. In both countries, consortia were created to bring together the necessary skills, but technical leadership rested with the large agencies: the Atomic Energy Authority (AEA) in the UK and the Commissariat à l'Energie Atomique (CEA) in France—which had been created by government to undertake military and civil nuclear R & D and to organise the fuel-cycle. The consortium approach was not very successful.

With the international adoption of American LWRs during the 1960s (based, as it turned out, on optimistically costed contracts), France and the UK found themselves isolated from the mainstream of thermal-reactor development. In both countries there were strong scientific, industrial and bureaucratic interests in maintaining independent nuclear capabilities. These interests were increasingly at odds with those of the utilities which, on cost grounds, favoured US technology. France finally switched to American LWR technology in 1969, while a coherent nuclear strategy evaded UK policy-makers throughout the 1970s.

In many countries without weapons capabilities, there were strong motives for adopting LWRs under US licences. In particular, Germany, Italy and Japan wanted to avoid suspicion of military intentions and therefore proceeded cautiously in developing their own fuel-cycle capabilities. The alliances which formed in the nuclear field generally followed existing links between the main 'core' groups (see Table 6.1). However, the German industry terminated its US licences once it had passed the prototype stage and was ready to compete internationally. (At the same time it launched an attack on the US turbine generator market.) Canada has been the exception, having succeeded through consistent efforts since the 1950s in developing its CANDU reactor design—so far, the only heavy-water design which has been developed and proven on a commercial scale. However, despite excellent performance in Canada, CANDU exports have been few.

	Owner	Component manufacture (licensing firms in brackets)				Nuclear contractor by type of reactor (licensing firms in brackets)
		ST	GEN	LB	HNC	
France						
Framatome	70% Creusot-Loire, 30% CEA[c]				HNC	PWR (West)
Alsthom-Atlantique (AA)		ST (BBC)	GEN	LB		
Germany						
Kraftwerk Union (KWU)	Siemens	ST	GEN			PWR,[f] BWR,[g] HWR
Brown-Boveri (Mannheim)	Brown-Boveri & Cie	ST	GEN			
MAN	{ Gutehoffnungshütte Aktienverein	ST (AA)				
GHH-Sterkrade						
Deutsche Babcock				LB	HNC	
Steinmüller				LB	HNC	
Italy						
Finmeccanica[a]	IRI	ST	GEN	LB (CE)	HNC	PWR (West), BWR (GE), HWR (AECL)[h]
Franco Tosi		ST (West)				
Marelli	Brown-Boveri		GEN (West)			
TIBB			GEN			
Switzerland						
Brown-Boveri & Cie (BBC)	Brown-Boveri	ST	GEN			PWR (BW)
UK						
National Nuclear Corporation (NNC)	30% GEC, 35% AEA,[d] 35% BNA[e]					AGR, Prospective PWR (West)
General Electrical Company (GEC)		ST	GEN		HNC	
Northern Engineering Industries (NEI)[b]	88% NEI, 12% CE	ST	GEN	LB (CE)	HNC	
Babcock Power				LB	HNC	
US						
General Electric (GE)		ST	GEN		HNC	BWR (own technology)
Westinghouse (West)		ST	GEN		HNC	PWR (own technology)
Babcock & Wilcox (BW)	Ray McDermott			LB	HNC	PWR (own technology)
Combustion Engineering (CE)				LB	HNC	PWR (own technology)
Japan						
Hitachi		ST	GEN (GE)	LB (BW)	HNC	BWR (GE)
Mitsubishi		ST	GEN (West)	LB (CE)	HNC	PWR (West)
Toshiba/IHI		ST	GEN (GE)	LB	HNC	BWR (GE)

[Notes and source opposite]

The degree of government involvement in establishing nuclear plant industries varied widely between the US and Germany, where the industry took the lead, and France and the UK, where the lead was taken by the state and nationalised utilities. In all cases, however, governments were involved in setting up regulatory institutions, financing reactor development, supporting large nuclear R & D establishments, establishing the fuel cycle as a separate new industry, and sometimes organising international collaboration. In all the relevant countries there was a strong community of interests among governments, utilities, power plant manufacturers and R & D institutions in promoting nuclear power. This engendered intense rivalry as each nation sought to appropriate the maximum benefît from the new technology.

France

The French government and the state-owned utility Electricité de France (EdF) were centrally involved in the bold restructuring of the French industry in the late 1960s and particularly in the mid-1970s. Using the carrot of substantial nuclear ordering and the stick of public procurement, they transformed the fragmented industry into one with two monopoly suppliers: the nuclear plant contractor, Framatome, and the heavy electrical manufacturer, Alsthom-Atlantique.

By the late 1960s, the French industry was widely considered to be too fragmented to hold its own against foreign competition or to build nuclear power stations efficiently. The sense of urgency over rationalisation was heightened by Westinghouse's bid for control over a generator producer, which was anathema to the government. The 1969 decision, after several years of conflict, to abandon the indigenous gas-cooled reactor technology in favour of the LWR represented a victory for the EdF and industrial concerns of the CEA and the Gaullist preference for technological independence at all costs. The CEA saw its thermal reactor interests reduced, but was

Notes and Source to Table 6.1

[a] Includes Ansaldo and Breda.
[b] Includes Parsons and Clarke Chapman.
[c] Commissariat à l'Energie Atomique.
[d] UK Atomic Energy Authority.
[e] British Nuclear Associates.
[f] Formerly Westinghouse.
[g] Formerly General Electric.
[h] AECL is Canadian.

Key to component manufacture: ST: Steam Turbines, GEN: Generators, LB: Large Boilers, HNC: Heavy Nuclear Components.

Source: Surrey and Walker (1981) Table 20.

compensated through the expansion of the FBR programme and of its fuel-enrichment and reprocessing interests.

After the 1969 decision, two groups competed for LWR orders. One was a consortium centred around Alsthom which offered BWR designs under licence from GE. The other was Framatome, a subsidiary of the metallurgical conglomerate Creusot-Loire (part of the Belgian Schneider group). In 1970 EdF placed orders with Framatome for six PWRs. This encouraged Framatome to invest heavily in PWR component manufacture and assembly and to gain a share in a PWR fuel fabrication company.

Alarmed at France's vulnerability after the oil crisis, the government launched a major nuclear programme in 1974 (the Messmer Plan). Given Framatome's production facilities and production experience, it was decided to standardise on 900 MW PWRs to be built by Framatome under licence to Westinghouse. The BWR option was abandoned and Framatome, as sole NSSS supplier, expanded its production capacity.

In 1976, Alsthom merged with Chantiers de l'Atlantique, an engineering group, which gave the new company, Alsthom-Atlantique, a turnkey capability for conventional power plant export contracts. At the same time, the government engineered a series of asset exchanges giving Alsthom-Atlantique a monopoly over domestic turbine-generator production, as some compensation for excluding it from nuclear contracting. The firm subsequently expanded capacity, rationalising production throughout the group.

Under pressure from the French government, Brown-Boveri (Switzerland) ceded control over its French subsidiary, CEM, to Alsthom-Atlantique while Westinghouse's shareholding in Framatome was bought out in two stages, in the mid-1970s by the CEA (in exchange for uranium which was much needed by Westinghouse) and in 1981 by Creusot-Loire. Framatome also terminated its PWR licence with Westinghouse in 1981, although technical collaboration has continued at a lower level. Again in 1981, the French part of the Schneider Group was sold to the financial and industrial concern Paribas, which was subsequently nationalised, giving the French government total control over the nuclear industry.

France, therefore, having opted for dependence on foreign technology in launching its ambitious nuclear programme, gradually assumed control over both production and technology, with the aim of maximising domestic benefits and gaining freedom of action in export markets.

Germany

The core of the German industry comprises Kraftwerk Union (KWU), a subsidiary of Siemens, and the Mannheim subsidiary of Brown-Boveri. Both companies supply steam turbine generators and nuclear design and contracting services. There are several other major equipment producers (see Table 6.1). AEG and Siemens gained experience of BWR and PWR technology respectively in the 1960s through licences from GE and Westinghouse. Anticipating the high investment costs of larger turbine generators for nuclear power stations, the two companies combined their turbine-generator interests in 1969 by setting up KWU as a jointly owned subsidiary and built the first factory in Europe specifically designed for series production of very large units. The German utilities did not oppose the merger— they still had Brown-Boveri and MAN (producing steam turbines) as alternative domestic suppliers.

Heavy investment by Siemens and AEG in nuclear R & D enabled them to establish independent nuclear design and construction capabilities. Both companies terminated their US licences and in 1972 transferred their nuclear contracting divisions to KWU. AEG subsequently ran into serious difficulties over the fixed-price BWRs it was building for German utilities. This, more than anything else, brought it to the verge of bankruptcy. It relinquished its interest in large power plant manufacture and Siemens, acquiring full control over KWU in 1976, was left as the dominant German producer.

Unlike nuclear contractors in the US and France, which manufacture major NSSS components, KWU has limited its role in the nuclear field to reactor design, engineering, project management and fuel fabrication. Its manufacturing interests are centred on turbine generators. The subcontracting of the associated heavy nuclear component work (inside and outside Germany) has enabled it to offer inducements when bidding for foreign contracts. Thus KWU sought to establish itself as a major independent nuclear contractor and turbine generator producer, able to compete on equal terms with US firms in export markets and eager to gain supremacy in Europe.

Switzerland

To all intents and purposes, the Swiss industry is Brown-Boveri & Cie (BBC). With a tiny home market and multinational manufacturing facilities, it is something of an anomaly in the world industry. BBC produces steam-turbine generators in Switzerland and Germany, and generators in Italy. Each of its main works manufactures for the home market and export. In a number of other countries it has subsidiaries which make small items and components and enable

BBC to compete for power plant contracts in the guise of a domestic supplier. In heavy electricals, it is technologically independent of other suppliers. It has gained appreciable licensing income from closed markets such as Sweden, Hungary and Poland.

The loss of its French subsidiary, CEM, was a heavy blow, excluding BBC from France's large ordering programme in the latter half of the 1970s (although 1300 MW turbines were produced under licence from BBC). As the only foreign supplier to have obtained a flow of turbine generator orders from the US in the 1960s, BBC's position there was threatened by KWU's entry onto the market in the early 1970s, the appreciating Swiss and German currencies, and the slump in US ordering after 1974. In 1979 BBC acquired a shareholding in Howden, a Canadian engineering company producing turbine generators for the Canadian market.

In the nuclear field, BBC was a late entrant—perhaps advisedly so in view of Sulzer's heavy losses in trying to develop an indigenous Swiss heavy-water reactor design. BBC's first nuclear ventures were in collaboration with GE and Westinghouse in the Swiss market. But, in bidding for a German nuclear contract, BBC felt unable to license from them because KWU already manufactured to their design. It therefore had little alternative but to license from one of the other US vendors, Babcock & Wilcox, without conspicuous success (it only served one firm contract, in Germany).

Italy

The Italian power plant industry is small by the standards of the largest producers and remains dependent on foreign technology. It falls into two parts: first Finmeccanica and its member company Ansaldo, which belong to the huge IRI state-holding group, can supply virtually the complete range of power plant equipment and services. The other part comprises specialist firms in the private sector (see Table 6.1).

When ENEL, the nationalised utility, launched an ambitious nuclear plan after the oil crisis in 1973, there were three Italian consortia offering PWR or BWR designs under US licences. In addition, political and R & D interests were advocating the adoption of indigenous HWR technology. As the nuclear plan foundered over siting and other difficulties, it became clear that there would be insufficient work for these consortia. Rationalisation was therefore set in motion by the government involving, among other things, the exchange of Finmeccanica's aeroengine and Fiat's nuclear interests. Finmeccanica was designated as the sole nuclear contractor and heavy component supplier. However, the private sector was not to be barred from tendering for the non-nuclear part of plant in future nuclear ordering, and the public and private sectors of the industry were to cooperate in exporting.

De facto, the PWR design has now become the sole contestant as Italy tries to launch a more substantial nuclear programme. In Italy, as in France, initiatives to reorganise the power plant industry had been taken by the state—in this case, via the IRI. With less political influence, ENEL played a lesser role in restructuring than EdF.

The UK

UK turbine-generator production is split between GEC and Parsons, and boiler-making between Babcock and Clarke Chapman. Parsons and Clarke Chapman merged with other heavy engineering firms in 1977 to form Northern Engineering Industries (NEI). Each group has interests in nuclear-component supply, but fuel fabrication is undertaken by the state-owned company British Nuclear Fuels Limited.

Under a holding company, the National Nuclear Corporation (NNC), the Nuclear Power Company (NPC) was set up in 1973 with sole responsibility for nuclear design and construction. NNC's shareholders were the AEA and the major nuclear component suppliers. NPC had no manufacturing assets and its low capital value (£10 million) meant, in effect, that the financial risks in nuclear plant contracts fell largely on the utilities, the Central Electricity Generating Board (CEGB) and the South of Scotland Electricity Board.

Efforts to restructure the electrical industry began earlier in the UK than in most other countries, partly because investment in electricity supply peaked earlier. With the aid of the Industrial Reorganisation Corporation, GEC took on its present form in 1968 after its mergers with AEI and English Electric. Rationalisation of electro-technical manufacturing in general was the main objective, but GEC's turbine generator work remained spread between the four separate plants that it inherited.

By 1968–9, it was evident that domestic ordering would continue to fall, but the government was unwilling to force a merger on GEC and Parsons, believing that the trough would be only temporary, and fearing dependence on a monopoly supplier. By 1972–3, it was recognised that there would be no early revival, that the Advanced Gas-cooled Reactor (AGR) programme, decided on in 1965, was beset with problems, and that there was no future for the two remaining nuclear consortia.

It was against this unpromising background that the government created NPC. From the outset, NPC had difficulty in reconciling its disparate constituent interests. After much debate (including a four-year-period in which government and industry were at least nominally committed to commercialising the Steam Generating HWR), it was decided in 1978–9 to order two further AGRs and prepare the way for installing a PWR.

As the industry's position worsened, any intention the government might have had of merging the two heavy electrical producers (as recommended in an official 'think tank' report of 1976) was thwarted by political, management and trade-union resistance. The creation of NEI virtually closed the door on further attempts at nationalisation.

Consequently, against the background of low ordering since 1970 and of political controversy, the UK industry remained technologically independent but had too much capacity in relation to the limited demand for its products. In 1979, the new Conservative government announced a plan to build 15 GWe of PWRs by 2000, under licence to Westinghouse. The size of this commitment was apparently intended to reduce dependence on coal (and the political power of the miners' union) and to encourage UK industry to invest in the specialised facilities to build large PWR components.

Under parliamentary and public scrutiny the government and CEGB stated that this was not a commitment to a whole programme and that each plant would be decided on its own merits. The NNC was reorganised in 1980, but efforts to restructure manufacturing had reached an impasse. The two AGR orders were placed in 1980 to provide immediate work and as insurance against failure to establish the PWR option. After the CEGB had rejected the first PWR design, a revised version was drawn up. The Sizewell PWR Enquiry began in January 1983, with even the official supporting evidence indicating that the Sizewell PWR would show only marginal net benefits.

Faced with a depressed domestic market in the 1970s, GEC increasingly concentrated its attentions on the export market. Its success in winning large contracts in Hong Kong, South Africa and South Korea means that NEI can no longer claim to be on an equal footing with GEC in the turbine generator business.

Other European suppliers

Outside the countries discussed above, the most significant European power plant producer is the Swedish group, ASEA, which is a BWR contractor, a turbine-generator producer, and a leading supplier of high voltage transmission equipment. Elsewhere in Europe there are a number of other, usually smaller, producers which tend to be relatively specialised and dependent on foreign technology. Historically, they have been courted by the large producers eager to gain licence income and entry to their domestic markets. Prominent in the conventional and nuclear fields are Belgian, Dutch and—increasingly —Spanish firms. There are also a number of specialists in water turbines, notably in Austria, Switzerland and Norway.

Main features of the 1960s and 1970s

After successive reorganisations in the 1960s and 1970s, the European power plant industry is now highly concentrated behind national frontiers. However, in terms of manufacturing capacity, it remains fragmented compared with the US and Japanese industries (see Table 6.2). In turbine-generator manufacture, two US firms have the

Table 6.2 Turbine generator and reactor suppliers in international markets, 1980

	Number of manufacturers (capacity in GW per year)						
	France	*Germany**	*Italy*	*Switzerland*	*UK*	*Japan*	*US*
Turbine generators	1(9)	3(14)	2(7)	1(6)	2(8)	3(15)	2(41)
Nuclear plant	1(7)	2(8)	1(3)	1(2)	1(2)	2(8)	4(25)

* BBC-Mannheim is included here under Germany and excluded from Switzerland.

Source: Surrey and Walker (1981), Table 4.

capacity of nine European firms: in nuclear-plant contracting, the two largest US firms have the capacity of all six European firms.

During the 1960s and 1970s, several European firms passed through a phase of dependence on US firms in nuclear-reactor technology. Outside Italy (and possibly the UK if the PWR programme moves ahead) dependence on the US has been much reduced. Among the major European suppliers, there has historically been little interdependence in nuclear plant manufacture or technology: only in the nuclear fuel cycle and advanced nuclear R & D is there significant cooperation.

The extent and means by which governments have influenced the structure of the industry have varied widely. In France, Italy and the UK, state and utility involvement in industrial restructuring has been substantial, although variable in its form and effectiveness. In Germany it has been limited or at least indirect. These differences of approach are likely to be important in determining the extent to which governments, individually or collectively, can shape the future structure of the European industry. Government involvement on the nuclear side has, however, been extensive in all countries, but governments have been increasingly constrained since the early 1970s by public concern over safety.

6.3 The transformation of markets in the 1970s

Domestic market conditions

A widespread boom in plant-ordering in the late 1960s and early 1970s boosted confidence in the future of the power plant industry. Particularly in the wake of the 1973–4 oil crisis, the era of commercial nuclear power seemed to have begun, based mainly on LWR technology. The next technological objective—at least, the one favoured by government R & D agencies if not by the plant manufacturers—appeared to be to commercialise the FBR.

The industry's hopes were dashed, especially for nuclear plant, when demand in the OECD region all but dried up after 1974. Except for firms in France and Japan, the second half of the 1970s was a period of deepening crisis as electricity demand forecasts were heavily cut back as the result of economic recession. The large amount of plant under construction cushioned the plant suppliers, but it reduced new plant requirements even further.

Coinciding with this, the economic and political environment in which electric utilities operate deteriorated. Having invested heavily in oil-fired capacity in the 1960s, many utilities then met financial problems as oil prices rose in the 1970s and governments or regulatory authorites resisted electricity price rises. Political controversy worsened the investment climate in many OECD countries, even where, as in Italy and Austria, there was a shortage of generating capacity.

Nuclear power became a particular focus of political discontent, disrupting construction programmes and even threatening the stability of governments. By the late 1970s, controversies had virtually halted nuclear expansion in the US, Germany, Sweden, Italy, Austria and Switzerland and had deterred other countries, for instance, Holland, Denmark and Norway from launching nuclear programmes. The roots of these political disturbances are debatable. Some believe that they stem from a dissipation of political authority coupled with pressure on the environment and disenchantment with industrialisation. Others believe them to have been at least partly self-inflicted by utilities, governments and industries which sought to launch a new technology before it had been adequately developed, with the premature goal of an all-electric future.

These changes in the economic and political environment not only mean an uncertain future for nuclear power, but have also changed the innovative climate for the plant-supply industry, eroded the degree of government commitment to electrification and led to greater regulatory activity. Severe escalation of capital costs and heightened perceptions of risk have made utilities more interested in building to time and cost, as well as in operating reliability and incremental improvements, as opposed to step-jumps in technology. Increasing emphasis is being placed on improved coal-based technologies and to some extent upon energy conservation and renewable energy resources.

As a result, the plant suppliers are facing more uncertainty in allocating R & D resources among the various technological possibilities. In the US, especially after the Three Mile Island accident, and in Germany, concern over safety in the environment has led to greater regulatory activity over nuclear power. In consequence NSSS suppliers have generally been unable to reap the advantages from series production, and authority over the technology has tended to pass from utilities and plant suppliers to regulatory bodies. Plant suppliers and utilities have tended to feel that governments have abdicated their political responsibility for providing a stable framework for planning in the industry.

France is the one major exception. By 1985, all French base-load power capacity will be nuclear. The great momentum of the French nuclear programme has stemmed from the authority and determination of the state and EdF in circumventing the difficulties on which the ambitions of other countries have foundered. This has involved financial, technical and market risk-taking on a scale that has been possible only because of France's centralised and relatively closed political system. Should the gamble succeed, it will bring large benefits to the French economy. Should it fail, the economic and political consequences could be dire. By the time the Mitterrand government entered office the final *tranche* of the massive PWR programme had been decided. Whether or not Mitterrand attempts to fulfil his election pledge of reducing the nuclear programme, the reduction in French electricity demand suggests that by the late 1980s little scope will remain for nuclear expansion; that a number of French PWRs will be working either at low load factors or mainly for the export of power to adjacent countries, and that the French reactor industry faces a sudden transition from fast to famine.

International market conditions.

Whereas the US has exported less than 10 per cent of its large annual output since the mid-1950s, in Europe and Japan the proportion exported has typically been between a third and a half. Significant changes in export market shares have occurred over the past three decades. For electrical power equipment as a whole, Table 6.3 shows large falls in trade shares for the US and the UK, some increases for continental European countries and a pronounced Japanese advance into export markets.

Table 6.3 Shares of world exports of electric power equipment, 1955–79*
           (per cent)

	1955	1959	1964	1969	1972	1975	1979
UK	22.2	19.0	13.2	9.4	8.9	8.8	7.8
France	6.0	6.1	9.1	9.3	10.3	11.6	11.4
Germany	18.5	22.8	22.6	23.7	21.9	21.6	22.4
Italy	1.9	1.8	4.6	5.4	4.9	4.3	4.5
Sweden	2.5	2.5	4.7	2.7	3.3	3.4	2.3
Switzerland	..	..	5.1	5.3	4.8	4.9	5.7
US	31.9	26.2	22.8	20.3	17.2	18.0	14.0
Japan	1.3	5.8	3.8	8.5	10.2	8.5	13.0
Total	84.3	84.2	85.9	84.6	81.5	81.1	81.1
Others	15.7	15.8	14.1	15.4	18.5	18.9	18.9

* SITC 722

Source: United Nations, *Yearbook of International Trade Statistics*, New York, annual.

Deliveries to export markets (hydro and steam-turbine generators) between 1975 and 1987 can be seen in Table 6.4. These figures approximate to export orders placed during the 1970s. Around one-quarter of plant exports is hydro-based, the remainder being steam-based.

During the boom in US ordering from 1966 to 1970, the US became a leading export market for BBC and KWU who both recognised that major US utilities might welcome bids from reliable, technologically advanced foreign suppliers. With the contraction of the US market (and German and Swiss currency appreciation relative to the US dollar), BBC and KWU gained few orders after 1974.

Import penetration of European supplier countries—and now Japan—is even less than import penetration of the US market (see Table 6.4). The remaining available export markets outside the Third World fall into two categories: the first comprises the small 'peripheral' markets in Europe which, since 1974, have been hit by

Table 6.4 Expected deliveries of steam turbine and hydro generators to Western countries, 1975–87*

	Home market (GW)	Imports as % of home market	Imports by source (GW)										
			Total	France	Germany	Italy	Sweden	Switzerland	UK	US	Japan	Comecon‡	Others§
Western Europe	206.6	20	41.2	6.8	11.2	1.2	2.0	10.0	0.1	2.1	4.0	3.3	0.5
Suppliers†	152.9	3	5.0	–	1.0	1.2	–	2.3	–	–	–	–	0.5
Others	53.7	67	36.2	6.8	10.2	–	2.0	7.7	0.1	2.1	4.0	3.3	–
North America	313.0	13	41.8	0.4	6.0	–	0.8	14.5	11.6	0.2	8.3	–	–
US	278.1	10	27.5	0.4	5.5	–	0.8	14.5	3.3	–	3.0	–	–
Canada	34.9	41	14.3	–	0.5	–	–	–	8.3	0.2	5.3	–	–
Latin America and Caribbean	56.6	89	49.9	3.5	8.8	2.5	3.1	1.6	–	1.7	17.2	7.9	3.6
Far East and Australia	117.2	45	52.5	1.0	4.5	0.6	–	2.3	10.7	11.3	19.6	1.4	1.1
Japan	46.3	7	3.2	–	–	–	–	–	–	3.2	–	–	–
Others	70.9	70	49.3	1.0	4.5	0.6	–	2.3	10.7	8.1	19.6	1.4	1.1
Near East and Africa	37.6	100	37.5	6.2	7.9	2.5	–	1.1	7.2	2.3	6.5	3.8	–
Total (Western world)	731.0	31	222.9	17.9	38.4	6.8	5.9	29.5	29.6	17.6	55.6	16.4	5.2
Of which:													
Steam turbine	619.3	27	169.3	12.9	31.3	6.5	1.8	27.8	29.2	17.3	35.2	7.3	–
Hydro	111.7	48	53.6	5.0	7.1	0.3	4.1	1.7	0.4	0.3	20.4	9.1	5.2

* This table covers at least 90 per cent of steam turbine and 66 per cent of hydro deliveries.
† UK, France, Germany, Italy, Switzerland and Sweden.
‡ Poland, Czechoslovakia and USSR.
§ Austria, Canada and India.

Source: Science Policy Research Unit (University of Sussex), Turbine Generator Data Bank, June 1980.

recession and controversy in much the same way as the domestic markets of the main suppliers. The second category comprises the former British dominions which have been more buoyant. They were formerly the natural preserve of the UK industry, but the Japanese have made considerable inroads.

Plant suppliers have turned increasingly to Third World markets, particularly the newly industrialising countries (NICs) which have sizeable electrical power programmes and have been more receptive to nuclear power. There has been a clear pattern behind the historical spread of power plant capabilities. Newer producers, with some variations and exceptions, have generally progressed from dependence on imports of equipment or know-how towards being able to supply a large part of their needs from their own manufacturing bases, and finally towards being independent suppliers—first supplying a domestic market from behind protectionist barriers and eventually competing with established producers in world markets.

Since the 1950s, many European countries, as we have seen, have followed this path in relation to nuclear technology, while Japan has followed it in relation to both heavy-electrical and nuclear plant. Behind them are a large number of countries, the smaller industrial countries in the OECD and the NICs, that either have small specialised industries and depend partly on imports, or are in the process of building up their power plant industries with foreign help.

The bulk of export ordering in the late 1970s came from countries in the latter category, mainly Australia, Canada, South Africa and the NICs. However, the NICs are also the main location of export displacement through their import-substitution programmes. In some cases, export orders are conditional upon providing industrial assistance to, and increasing domestic content in, the recipient country; such exports are part of an apparently self-defeating process of helping others add yet more production capacity (for example, German nuclear assistance to Argentina and Brazil).

Some of the NICs are beginning to compete in less sophisticated exports, for instance in transformers, switch-gear and small water turbines, but are unlikely to win significant orders for nuclear plant and large steam-turbine generators before the 1990s. Import substitution in the Third World is more of a threat to European than to US exporters. Indeed, the expansion of foreign manufacturing has brought a large technological rent to GE and Westinghouse through licensing, without the financial risks that are normally attached to direct exports.

Owing to world overcapacity and the conditions attached to trade by importing countries, exporting to developing countries has become increasingly 'imperfect', often comprising a complicated package of hardware, finance, access to technological know-how, and assistance with training. Competitive advantage has therefore also come to depend on who can arrange the most attractive package.

Two developments have been particularly damaging to European interests in Third World markets. First, the process of technology transfer has run into difficulty, particularly in relation to nuclear power. Secondly, the Europeans are having to contend with formidable competition from Japanese firms in price, quality, delivery, after-sales service, and attractive trade packages.

In the mid-1970s, a series of events led to a breakdown of confidence in existing non-proliferation measures, particularly on the part of Canada and the US. In consequence, Third World countries have been denied full access to nuclear power capability, while suppliers risk incurring the wrath of other countries if they negotiate trade deals that do not fully conform to strict rules.

Despite their sensitivity, nuclear exports are seen as vital by beleaguered European suppliers. It is questionable, for instance, whether the German nuclear industry could have survived the prolonged recession in its present form without the Argentinian, Brazilian and Iranian orders.

Many Third World countries have shifted attention away from nuclear power, some towards large hydro-electric schemes. It is here that the Japanese industry is particularly strong. In spite of the recent success of some European firms in gaining export orders for conventional plant, Europe as a whole has continued to lose market share to the Japanese.

6.4 Prospects for the European industry

In this final section, we shall look at market prospects to the early 1990s, the shorter-term prospects of individual supplier countries, and the longer-term prospects for the European industry as a whole.

Market prospects

Table 6.5 estimates annual plant ordering rates for 1980–92 under scenarios of: replacement demand only; low demand growth; and high demand growth. Rather than forecasts, the figures are illustrative estimates derived from a number of assumptions, notably that the growth in electricity demand between 1980 and 2000 will be in the range of: 2 to 4 per cent a year in the high-income, mature industrialised countries; 3 to 6 per cent a year in countries where

Table 6.5 Scenarios of power plant ordering, 1980–92

	Assumed rates of demand growth to 2000 (% p.a.)*	Est. annual plant ordering rates 1980–92 (GW per annum)§			Approximate steam turbine generator production capacity (GW p.a.)
		Replacement demand only	Low scenario	High scenario	
Europe		1.6	18.7	45.6	47
Germany	2–4	0.2	2.9	6.7	14
France	3–6	− 1.2	2.0	7.5	9
UK	1–2	3.3	4.5	6.0	8
Italy	3–6	0.5	2.9	7.2	7
Sweden	2–4	− 0.4	0.5	1.8	3
Switzerland	2–4	− 0.2	0.4	1.2	6
Suppliers (Total)		2.2	13.2	30.4	47
Developed European export markets†	2–4	0.7	3.3	7.0	
Developing European export markets‡	3–6	− 1.3	2.2	8.2	
North America		− 1.1	25.8	65.0	44
US	2–4	0.0	24.2	59.5	41
Canada	2–4	− 1.1	1.6	5.5	3
Japan	3–6	4.4	12.7	27.1	15
Developing regions		− 11.7	17.9	53.7	..
Latin America and Caribbean	5–8	− 5.6	4.6	16.9	
Africa	5–8	− 0.7	4.3	10.3	
Middle East	5–8	− 1.5	0.9	3.9	
Far East and Pacific	5–8	− 3.9	8.1	22.6	
Total		− 6.8	75.1	191.4	106

(Notes and source opposite.)

consumption is low relative to income levels and where electrification is designed to reduce oil imports; 5 to 8 per cent a year for the Third World.[1]

The estimates in Table 6.5 carry a number of implications:

(a) The higher-demand case would necessitate capacity expansion but the lower case could be met easily with the present level of world plant-supply capacity.
(b) Replacement demand will be rising in the 1990s, but it will generally be small in the 1980s—indeed, it will be zero in some regions (once allowance is made for the large amount of plant under construction).
(c) Under both the high and low demand cases, the less developed countries will account for a considerably higher proportion of potential world ordering in the future. However, even if the constraints on economic growth and project financing allow electricity demand to grow rapidly, an increasing proportion of Third World plant contracts is likely to be manufactured domestically.
(d) The bulk of existing excess capacity is in Europe. In the high-demand case, the European industry would have a good chance of obtaining sufficient exports to fill its present level of capacity. Under the low case, however, it would be left with spare capacity, even if it obtained *all* the potential export business.
(e) Given its present overcapacity and low share of direct exports, the US industry is unlikely to create new capacity principally for exporting. However, that assumption cannot confidently be made about the Japanese industry which could constitute an increasing threat to the European industry.
(f) European suppliers will need to redirect their efforts from their traditional export markets to new markets.
(g) Since nuclear ordering shows no sign of recovery, ordering

---

Notes to Table 6.5

* This refers to demand for public electricity supplies.
† Austria, Belgium, Denmark, Luxembourg, Netherlands, Finland, Norway.
‡ Greece, Ireland, Portugal, Spain, Yugoslavia.
§ These ordering rates represent demand net of plant under construction. Low and high scenarios include replacement demand.

The demand figures set out above relate to both steam (i.e. nuclear and fossil fuel) and hydro plant, while capacity figures in the last column relate to steam turbine generators only. Over the period 1975–87, total identified hydro deliveries amounted to 19 per cent of steam deliveries. On this basis, hydro manufacturing capacity may be estimated at 20 GW/a. Note also that the relatively small, but growing, capacity in developing countries is excluded.

Source: Science Policy Research Unit (University of Sussex), Turbine Generator Data Bank, June 1980 and authors' estimates.

throughout the 1980s will consist mainly of: coal-fired plant, chiefly in the industrial countries; hydro-electric plant, in developing countries; and gas turbines for base load in the oil-producing countries and for peak load elsewhere.

As to the prospect for East–West trade, China could offer some opportunities to Western suppliers, but not on the scale widely expected in the immediate post-Mao years, and nuclear trade will in any case depend on geopolitical considerations. Comecon is not likely to become a major importer of Western hardware or technology, nor, as long as production capacity is filled with domestic orders, to mount a major export offensive to the Third World.

Prospects by country:

The US

During the 1970s, the three pillars of US supremacy, the large base market, geopolitical influence, and technical leadership, began to be eroded. The prospect is that US plant ordering will remain low throughout the 1980s and that utilities will tend to invest in coal-fired, rather than nuclear, plant and will continue to promote conservation and other measures in order to limit the need for new supply capacity.

With low capacity utilisation, US producers now need export orders and they are stepping up their efforts accordingly. But mounting an export offensive will not be easy. The traditional export markets of US suppliers are being eroded, and neither they nor the government are well geared to an export offensive. However, the innovative ability of the industry remains considerable. In recent years, its R & D effort has become more diversified into alternative energy technologies, an area where it may gain international leadership.

Japan

The non-nuclear side of Japan's industry is well loaded, but the nuclear side has suffered setbacks due to public opposition, regulatory activity, and disappointing plant performance. It also continues to depend on foreign technology and fuel cycle services. Overall, the Japanese industry appears to be in a comparatively strong position due to a still buoyant economy, but it faces the strategic choice between (a) remaining dependent on US technology and concentrating exports on other OECD and other Third World markets, and (b) loosening ties with the Americans and launching an offensive to carry it firmly into North American and other markets. Especially if it relinquishes its links with the Americans, the Japanese industry may wish to strike up new links with the leaders of the European nuclear industry, for example KWU and Framatome, possibly as a means of developing the next generation of thermal reactors. In so far as it strengthens its efforts in European markets, which are largely closed to direct foreign competition, the Japanese industry may have to make alliances with some of the smaller European firms which, because of small base markets, may be in danger of falling behind technologically.

France

Mitterrand's nuclear policy is to proceed more cautiously with the domestic programme than did Giscard's government. In any event, domestic ordering will plummet when nuclear capacity exceeds the base load requirement. The need for exports will become more pressing. The downturn in nuclear ordering could put at risk considerable resources in France's heavy-engineering sector. The short construction times achieved so far and the absence of the need for design changes and retrofitting, due to regulatory intervention, suggest that Framatome would have little backlog to sustain it. In nuclear export markets the French industry has significant advantages: it is now experienced and technologically independent, with powerful allies in EdF and the French government which are prepared to use their resources to negotiate foreign business on its behalf. Export success depends heavily on opportunities for nuclear exports, but these are likely to be relatively small and fraught with difficulties. As far as new technologies are concerned, there is a strong lobby in France for a national effort to build a series of fast breeder reactors to capitalise on the expertise gained in building the Superphénix commercial demonstration plant. But as the commercial prospects for fast breeder reactors have receded further into the 21st century, and as other claims for public expenditure have increased, it is less likely that building successors to Superphénix will command priority. Like the British, Germans and Italians, the French may have considerable interest in international collaboration to share the costs and sustain a combined fast breeder effort, even if the grandiose nationalistic plans of the 1970s no longer look politically and economically feasible.

Germany

Although the industry is technically strong, its efforts to achieve international pre-eminence have been thwarted by recession and nuclear controversies at home and by misfortunes overseas. German utilities had been planning to order a series of coal-fired plants in the early 1980s and to resume nuclear ordering, but the necessary political consensus has not existed for a strong revival of the nuclear programme. Even the most optimistic level of domestic plant ordering in the 1980s would leave the German industry's three turbine-generator suppliers with substantial spare capacity. Under these circumstances the cost to German utilities of retaining several domestic suppliers might rise to the extent that a monopoly supply structure (coupled with importing as a necessary discipline) might then have considerable appeal.

The German industry has a high technical reputation. It has maintained a strong, broad-based R & D programme on nuclear and other technologies, but new technologies will first have to be proved in the domestic market. Whether KWU retains a strong position internationally, therefore, depends considerably on the political climate at home.

Switzerland

BBC's principal strengths are its technical reputation and its international network of production facilities, subsidiaries and licensees. But it has not yet become an established nuclear reactor vendor. It has lost its important stake in turbine-generated production in France and continues to be squeezed in the US and German markets. These threats to its position in the world industry make a clear strategy difficult to devise. Should it enter into new investments or joint adventures in major NICs? Should it increase the degree of specialisation between its existing facilities? Because of its stake in several European countries, BBC could well act as a catalyst in future efforts to reorganise the European industry.

Italy

The problems of Italy's industry stem mainly from ENEL's difficulties in securing new power station sites, although its plans have repeatedly gained parliamentary approval. Unless electricity shortages change public attitudes, it is unclear whether these plans will be implemented. The Italian industry, therefore, has to look for export orders. Lacking the size and resources of its major competitors, the Italian industry nevertheless has some political and technical advantages in exporting. However, given that export earnings are likely to remain limited in the next few years, much depends for the Italian industry (as for the US and German industries) on economic and political developments at home.

The UK

Poor prospects for electricity demand growth and surplus generating capacity means that the domestic market is likely to remain flat until at least the late 1980s. The few orders available since the early 1970s have been allocated mainly with a view to suppliers' needs. The future character of ordering is very uncertain, even though a large proportion of existing coal-fired plant will need to be replaced or refurbished in the 1990s.

The choice of nuclear reactor has still to be settled. Whatever the outcome of the Sizewell PWR Enquiry, the government and the CEGB could soon face renewed demands from major firms located in depressed areas for further orders for AGRs and coal-fired plants in preference to PWRs. The maximum ordering rate envisaged by the government and the CEGB for Westinghouse PWRs is in any case only one unit a year, compared with the two or three which are normally regarded as the minimum to justify investment in component manufacturing capacity. This could mean that major NSSS components would be imported for the whole programme rather than just for the first PWR.

Longer-term options for Europe

Opinions about future markets vary considerably. Some believe that demand will revive strongly in the 1990s, so that temporary measures such as advance ordering, accelerated scrapping and R & D subsidies may be adequate to keep the industry in a fit state. Others see over-capacity as a longer-term problem requiring structural initiatives and an effort to reduce the industry's size. The composition of demand is also highly uncertain and differences of view are especially pronounced regarding future investment in nuclear capacity. Yet another uncertainty concerns the willingness of utilities to support domestic suppliers. Whether private or state-owned, utilities might find patriotism too expensive under severe financial stringency or if plant reliability was below international standards. Decision-making is made even more difficult by the deterioration of the political and economic environment relating to power plant markets.

European power plant manufacturers are nevertheless confronted with a common problem of how to maintain international competitiveness. This problem defines the main concerns of industrial policy: production efficiency, management of technical change, and international trading arrangements. The two extreme policy positions that occasionally surface appear to us untenable. The first is that this is a strategic industry to be supported by governments whatever the costs. The opposite position is that governments should withdraw support and promote free trade. While the small size of the industry could hardly justify priority support, its long planning horizons and high development costs require the security afforded by a degree of nationalistic procurement. Moreover, trade liberalisation might so reduce the number of suppliers as to risk higher prices as the result of collusion.

At present the industry is burdened with overcapacity, but in the longer term, efficiency becomes more a problem of market size than of capacity utilisation. The illustrative figures in Table 6.5 suggest that average output per manufacturer over the next decades will be four to five times higher in the US than in Europe, and about double in Japan. The small base markets available to European suppliers will restrict their ability to obtain scale economies, not least in development and design engineering.

There is little further scope for national concentration in Europe. The situation is approaching where further concentration could only be pursued through transnational arrangements. Several moves have been made in this direction with limited results (for example Euratom and the SERENA agreement on the FBR). Intra-European approaches may hold more interest than in the past, partly because of the US industry's waning technological leadership. But the obstacles to far-reaching integration in an industry dominated by nationalistic procurement seem insurmountable, especially in recession. However, there is a more modest approach which appears to have a better chance of implementation. This approach would encourage an intra-European division of labour in the manufacture of large items which involved high fixed costs. The opportunities may be greatest in large steel pressure vessels and steam generators on the NSSS side where a variety of big components could be bought in and some machining operations could be subcontracted internationally.

This would require at least partial liberalisation of power plant trade. Cost pressures, US calls for reciprocal trade agreements and the aversion of some utilities (notably in Germany) to monopoly supply structures might help create the impetus. But such change is likely to be piecemeal and to take effect through private and public reactions to individual crises, rather than attempts to devise and implement a common policy through the EEC.

The industry now faces an array of possible new technical trajectories which give rise to difficult choices in managing technical change. As well as keeping abreast of technical change in traditional areas, the industry is now directing its efforts towards improving operating reliability (and safety in the case of nuclear power), raising efficiency (for instance, through electronic control systems), and establishing new energy-supply and conservation technologies. This technological agenda will increasingly require collaborative R & D, access to foreign technology, and government support. Increasingly, firms will also have to specialise in areas of comparative advantage.

Europe generally lags behind the US and Japan in electronic components in capital goods and in public spending on energy R & D. There is clearly some risk of Europe falling behind in power-plant technology while at the same time continuing to devote disproportionate effort to fast breeder technology. Technical collaboration and alliances may therefore be essential to competitiveness; but they have to be eclectic and flexible and it is dangerous if they are too restrictive (for instance, hindering the inflow of technology from the US or Japan or its outflow to developing countries).

The European industry is heavily dependent upon exports. In that sense it has a basic interest in widening the international market and in curbing non-commercial practices. However, European countries have been as guilty as any of such practices, including the increased use of bilateral trade packages to provide power plant exports. The trend towards import substitution in the Third World is probably irreversible, while some of the more proficient Third World producers are themselves likely to compete internationally. Relatively fast economic development, combined with Europe's acceptance of some specialisation between higher- and lower-cost suppliers, would be in the interests of both European and Third World producers.

There are a number of ways of promoting a collective European approach to export markets, including attempts to harmonise European export credit terms, to organise consortia to compete with the Japanese, and to restore confidence in the non-proliferation regime. In the long run, however, the capacity of specific sectoral policies to maintain the competitiveness of the European industry will be very limited unless these are accompanied by more general policies to promote international economic growth and assist developing countries with investment finance.

A summary view of the future

To summarise our own views of the industry's likely medium-term future: we believe that recession will hold back growth in electricity demand so that there will be continuing strain within the industry. While a few firms may succumb to market pressures, the core of the industry is likely to survive reasonably intact, although leading firms may gradually shift resources from power systems into expanding more profitable activities. Changes will largely occur in relative market power and in the pattern of alliances between firms. Such changes are unpredictable, although it is possible that European suppliers will turn more towards Japan than to the US for new technological alliances, loosening the transatlantic ties that have dominated this industry's international market structure since early this century.

Note

1. For greater details of assumptions about electricity demand growth, replacement demand, and plant lead-times, see pp. 48-9 of Surrey and Walker (1981).

Reference

Surrey, J., and Walker, W. (1981), *The European Power Plant Industry: Structural Responses to International Market Pressures*, Sussex European Papers No. 12, Brighton: Sussex European Research Centre.

7 PROCESS PLANT CONTRACTING: A COMPETITIVE NEW EUROPEAN INDUSTRY*

Tibor Barna

7.1 Introduction

At a time when many European industries are either unable to catch up with American leadership (for example, computers), or declining in the face of competition from Japan (for example, automobiles, cameras, watches) or newly industrialising countries (for example, textiles and clothing), it is useful to investigate industries in which Europeans *are* successful. One such industry is that which supplies process plant. Europeans have caught up with the US and up to now have been able to withstand challenge from Japan, while competition from NICs is still slight. It is an industry with long-term growth prospects, although demand for its services tends to be subject to wide fluctuations.

A key role in the industry is played by contractors, especially those able to carry out large contracts. They play a strategic role in the transfer of technology and the accompanying mobilisation of resources, which is especially important as regards relations between developed and developing countries. The significance of contractors far exceeds their size, which is small in terms of employment directly provided.

Process plant contracting as a separate activity is relatively new. The industry has become important in Europe only in the last twenty years or so. European firms are heavily oriented towards exports, especially outside the OECD. To be successful they have to respond to shifts in the geographical pattern of demand, shifts to a different type of client, changes in technology, and the emergence of new producers. This chapter explores how the industry adjusted to the changes which were particularly violent in the 1970s. (There are also signs that equally significant changes may take place in the 1980s.)

The emergence of a new activity, or the regrouping of already existing activities into a new industry, is always fascinating but its study is beset with difficulties because of lack of statistics and

---

* This chapter draws substantially on Barna, Aylen, Dosi and Jones (1981). In its preparation the author was greatly helped by comments and suggestions from Jenny Barna.

indeed lack of agreed definitions. In this particular instance the problem is enhanced by difficulties which are inherent in any business of contracting; the organisation of firms and of the industry is complex, flexible and constantly changing.

By *process plant* I mean the complete plant used by industries which employ mainly *chemical* processes to convert materials into semi-finished or finished products: such industries include petroleum refining, chemicals, steel, non-ferrous metals, cement and certain sectors of food processing. I use this definition for practical reasons even though some of the plant (especially in the steel industry) is used for mechanical and not strictly chemical processes. Conversely, characteristic process plant components, such as pressure vessels, are also used by other industries, for instance, electrical power plant, which is outside the scope of our enquiry. (On the power plant industry, see Chapter 6.)

A process plant contractor is defined here as a firm which has the capacity to manage the design, procurement and installation of one or more types of plant for the industries mentioned above. It has to combine technical, managerial and financial skills. Frequently, a large plant contains components which have to be ordered from several hundred manufacturers. The manufacturers of individual plant components, although they may have their own design and contracting facilities, are not regarded in this chapter as process plant contractors. Petroleum, chemical or steel companies, and on occasion financial groups, may, moreover, sign major contracts but I do not regard them as process plant contractors unless they have their own capacity for managing contracts.

This chapter concentrates on the two dominant sectors of plant-users: the chemical and allied industries (including oil and gas processing, synthetic fibres and pharmaceuticals) and the steel industry. The second section of the chapter examines the development and structure of the industry, and the role technology has played in this. Section 7.3 discusses the problems of adjustment; and Section 7.4 comments on government intervention in the industry.

7.2 The development and structure of the industry

Origins and growth

During the twentieth century there has been a rapid world-wide growth in the industries using process plant, especially since the Second World War. In all these industries technological change, larger markets and the exploitation of economies of scale have led to increasing size, complexity and automation of plant. Production processes are now made as continuous as is practicable to avoid, for example, handling of intermediate products and large temperature changes, thus minimising costs.

In earlier years it was customary for firms in, for example, the chemical industry to design their own plant (perhaps with the help of consulting engineers), to procure its manufacture, and to erect it with the aid of contractors in the construction industry. In the course of time, however, specialist process plant contracting firms emerged to undertake these functions.[1] They emerged for a combination of reasons but particularly because of the advance of technology and the growth of markets. It is common in any industry for specialist activities to arise as markets develop and specialisation becomes economical. This was certainly the case with the enormous growth in demand for all kinds of process plant. Process plant contracting is now dominated by specialist firms capable of achieving economies which are not possible in the contracting division of a plant user: for example, by offering a wider range of processes.

Specialist process plant contractors first developed around the US petroleum industry at the beginning of the twentieth century. The petroleum industry had a substantial demand for plant, the number of producers was large and many of them were relatively small so that there were obvious economies to be achieved by specialist suppliers of plant. In the first half of the century the importance of specialist contractors in the design and procurement of plant for the petroleum and chemical industries of the US grew considerably, mainly as a result of the rapid growth of the petrochemicals industry. In Europe, by contrast, the role of specialist contractors remained relatively small until the 1950s, even though some of the best-known European contractors were already well established by then. The European chemical industry was largely based on coal rather than oil and the monopolistic nature of the industry must also have hindered the development of independent contractors.

A great stimulus was given after the Second World War to the development of process plant contractors in the US as well as in Europe by the rapid growth of oil-refining and of chemical production based on oil. In the 1950s and 1960s the domestic European markets for plant were extremely important. American contractors came to Europe, especially to the UK, the Low Countries and Scandinavia, in the wake of US oil companies (although the first major American contractor had already come to Europe in the 1920s). They speeded up the transfer of technology from the US to Europe and, in a growing market, induced the emergence and growth of specialist European contractors. However, European firms only became fully competitive with the leading American firms in the 1970s.

The emergence of specialist contractors for the steel industry took place later and more slowly. The technology of steel-making is in general older than that of the chemical industries. Steel companies in the industrial countries are mostly well established and hardly any of them has gone multinational in the way that oil companies have. There used to be a strong tradition in the steel industry of relying on makers of plant within national boundaries. Change came, however, with the rise of steel industries in the NICs.

The leading process plant contractors of the world have various origins. Some started in plant manufacture and some in consulting engineering or civil engineering. Some firms have developed from the in-house contracting activities of chemical or steel companies. Financial independence is the exception rather than the rule. Many of the contractor firms are part of larger industrial groups in the mechanical engineering, civil engineering, petroleum, chemical or steel industries—reflecting the origin of the contractor—or belong to conglomerates. The reasons for this will be discussed later.

While technologically advanced firms may use a contractor for only some of the functions for which the contractor is qualified, this is not the case with new firms, particularly in countries which are short of technical or managerial skills. The scope for specialist process plant contractors has significantly increased because of demand for plant from Soviet-bloc and developing countries, notably those which are rich in oil or other natural resources. In the developing countries it has largely been lack of expertise, and in the Soviet-bloc countries strain on resources caused by rapid industrialisation, which have led those countries to commmission complete contract 'packages' from feasibility studies to installation, and often training of personnel. In some instances where infrastructure is lacking, the contractor may even take responsibility for the building of transport, communications and power facilities. Furthermore, the contract package tends to include provisions for finance and marketing services.

Since the Second World War there has not only been a large increase in exports of capital goods from industrialised countries, but an increasing share of such exports has consisted of items which are part of large projects (typically in electrical power plant, transport, telecommunications and civil engineering works, as well as process plant).[2]

Structure and economies of scale

Given the difficulty of valuing work done on projects lasting for several years, the relatively modest use of fixed capital by this industry, and the unreliability of data on orders outstanding, it would appear that, on balance, the most suitable measure of the industry's size is total employment in contractors' offices in the industry as I have defined it (excluding the contracting departments of major plant-using industries). Our data refer to 1980–1, since when there has been a substantial downturn in activity and employment as the result of a world-wide fall in demand for capital goods.

I have estimated that in 1980–1 there were 60,000 to 65,000 persons employed in process plant contractors' offices (including those in the field) in Western Europe. There were about 18,000 in both the UK and West Germany, 12,000 in Italy and perhaps 10,000 in France. These figures included more than 10,000 employees of US contractors. About eight or ten American contractors had a substantial presence in Europe, mainly in the UK where they accounted for 40 to 50 per cent of employment. Their share in other major countries was only 10 per cent or less. While two or three US contractors employed 2,000 to 3,000 in Europe, world-wide process plant contracting employment by the largest American firms was 15,000 to 20,000. (The largest was Fluor Corporation.)

Davy Corporation was the leading firm in the UK, employing 12,000 persons in contracting world-wide, of whom 6,000 were employed in Europe. It is the only European contractor whose total employment is in the range of the larger American firms. Some three other UK-owned firms employed in excess of 1,000. Chemical plant dominates total UK employment, mainly because of the presence of American contractors. Davy has a strong footing in both chemical and steel plant.

Lurgi, the leading firm in Germany, employed 5,500 persons (5,000 in Europe), while six other German-owned firms employed over 1,000. Employment was about equally divided between chemical and steel plant contracting. Lurgi, while excellent in both sectors, offers a more specialised range of technologies than Davy. Three of the large German contractors are entirely in steel plant and collectively the German position in steel plant is very strong, even though only one of them (the GHH group) can match Davy's range.

SNAM Progetti, the leading Italian firm, employed 5,000 persons (4,500 in Europe). There were only one or two other firms employing in excess of 1,000. SNAM Progetti is mainly concerned with petroleum-based chemical plant, while Italimpianti is a world leader in steel plant contracting.

The leading firm in France was Technip, with 4,500 employees (4,000 in Europe). Technip's main strength is in petroleum-based chemical plant. Three or four other firms employed in excess of

1,000 persons. Creusot-Loire is also a world leader in steel plant contracting.

On any estimate, the number of European-owned contractors employing more than 1,000 persons was unlikely to exceed two dozen. There are probably a further two dozen smaller process plant contractors (depending on definitions), but their share in total employment is small. They are mostly specialised parts of larger industrial groups and in some instances small firms marketing their own technology.

The wide range of numbers employed by process plant contractors—the smallest employing under 100—suggests that size does not have a dominant influence on efficiency and profitability. The major influence on size seems to be the nature and range of technologies provided. Thus the smallest firms deal in a single area while the largest firms can contract for a multitude of process plant types. Moreover, the design of some plant such as that for fertilisers requires a large number of relatively unskilled man-hours whereas plant involving more advanced technology may need a smaller amount of work, but it is highly skilled. Size also depends on the range of activities in which a contractor engages. A firm may concentrate on the front end of design—that is, creative and analytical engineering—or may engage in a full range of activities including construction.

A contractor needs almost no fixed capital assets. In centres of contracting the labour force is fairly mobile and employees transfer from one firm to another as workloads shift. Skills outweigh many of the factors normally associated with economies of scale. On the other hand, the risk factor is important since demand for most types of plant can fluctuate substantially. There are therefore economies in firms which supply a range of technologies since many of the resources can be shifted within the firm from one process to another.

The main reason why firms set up subsidiaries abroad is that their presence in the local market may be necessary to gain contracts and to carry them out, and often also to tap local finance.[3] Once offices are set up in more than one country, workload can be transferred from one to another according to need.

The actual structure of the industry cannot be explained, however, without reference to the size of available contracts. Contracts vary enormously in value, from under one million dollars for a plant making fine chemicals to over one billion dollars for a synthetic fuel plant. Large contracts tend to call for large firms.[4] Growth of large firms is reinforced by the fact that a customer will place a large contract only with a contractor who has been successful with similar contracts.

Process plant contractors can be integrated 'backwards' with chemical or steel firms, or 'forwards' with plant-makers. The general opinion of process plant contractors in the US and Europe is that there is little, if any, advantage from either type of integration from the point of view of the contractor, since the managerial skills required for success in contracting are entirely different from those required in manufacturing. Managerial independence enables them to acquire processes on the best terms and to procure plant in the cheapest market. The French example is telling: its success in chemical plant contracting is evidently related to the setting up of independent contracting firms. By contrast, it has had less success in steel plant contracting where the steel-makers have not relinquished their traditional control.

The opinion against vertical integration is, however, by no means universal. It does not appear to be shared by many Japanese firms. Indeed, in certain instances—for example, where a contractor wishes to exercise close control over the quality of a plant component—the weight of argument is in favour of integration.

Most contractors, as already mentioned, belong to large groups. The main argument put forward in favour of such an arrangement is financial and involves the nature of the risks in the contractor's business. The fluctuation in volume of business does not make process plant contracting different from many other activities. However, since contractors possess little capital assets of their own, a contractor may not be able to bear exceptional losses. This characteristic of the business concomitantly makes prospective customers wary of placing contracts.

There are, however, large independent contractors who argue that as long as the firm is efficiently managed, membership of a group gives no advantage to offset loss of independence. In the last decade contractors have tried to avoid risk by undertaking contracts on a reimbursable (cost-plus-profit), rather than a lump-sum, basis.

The distinction between full vertical integration and simply belonging to a group of companies for financial reasons is not easy to make where there are trading links within the group. In instances where the contractor claims managerial independence it is possible that in certain circumstances there are pressures within the group for the contractor to act in the interest of the group and not only itself. In certain contracts SNAM Progetti, for example, is subservient to the needs of the ENI group to which it belongs (although part of its high in-house procurement can be explained by the excellence of ENI's mechanical engineering subsidiaries).

Technology transfer and competition

A customer ordering chemical or steel plant must consider its performance characteristics, price and terms of sale (including credit). Different contractors may offer plant embodying different processes or at least variations in process design. In fact, each plant design is unique in some respect as it has to be adjusted to the customer's requirements for a particular volume of production and a particular location. Also, plant already in existence is never exactly copied. Contractors learn from experience and can incorporate improvements when new plant is ordered.

Usually, an improved design means cost reductions all round.[5] In order to offer a competitive process, a contractor must have property rights in the process: that is, patents of its own or licences to use other firms' patents and corresponding know-how. It must also have the necessary combination of skills to successfully complete a contract, fulfilling both technical and cost criteria.

The competitive position of the contractor depends on how far the innovation embodied in the plant design which he is offering is a radical one (offering new products or fundamentally different processes to make known products) or only a minor one.

Almost all product innovation and fundamental process innovation originated in oil, chemical or steel companies and in research institutes, not in contracting companies. Most major process innovation has a similar origin but here the role of contractors is not negligible and their role in minor process innovation is certainly important. Innovation by plant-makers tends to be confined to specific instances. Innovation by manufacturers is important in the case of components which are used in a range of plant (and not only process plant), for example, valves, pumps, or compressors, and is particularly important in steel plant.

For major process innovations, it is necessary to follow laboratory research by the building of one or more pilot plants and eventually, if the project promises success, by a 'demonstration plant', the first plant on a commercial scale. Pilot plants in the chemical and steel industries are expensive and tend to be built by firms in these industries rather than by contractors. Demonstration plants are even more expensive and are built to order and not speculatively.

The generalisation that contractors spend relatively little on process development is more valid for the US and the UK than for Germany. In the UK contractors have drawn heavily on research done by firms such as ICI (the largest UK chemical company), the British Gas Corporation and the British Steel Corporation (both nationalised). ICI has followed a fairly liberal policy, granting licences to a select group of contractors rather than to a single one. West German contractors tend to carry out more research and development themselves and this is explained, at least in part, by the restrictive licensing policy of the German chemical industry (apart from Hoechst which licenses through its subsidiary contracting firm, Uhde). The leading German contractor, Lurgi, is research-intensive compared with most other large contractors and does not have to rely on chemical or steel companies. In Italy, however, SNAM Progetti can make use of research within the ENI group and, in France, Technip has access to research by the Institut Français du Pétrole which was instrumental in creating it.

While in theory a contractor may offer almost any type of plant, effective competition in a given type of plant tends to be between relatively few contractors even where the market is open to international competition. This is so partly because of restrictions on processes and partly because the first in the field has an advantage over newcomers in attracting further orders.

Among 'major' plant sectors conditions are most competitive in refining. Here either patents are non-existent or licenses are freely available. Technological progress in refining is nowadays incremental and this is reflected in competition. Even so it is doubtful if there are more than about a dozen contractors capable of competing for large refinery contracts.

Steel plant is another major sector in which the main technology, using the blast furnace-basic oxygen process, is no longer new (see Chapter 3, Section 2). Technological advance is marked, however, in certain important plant components and in direct-reduction processes of steel-making (used mainly outside Western Europe). The number of competitors is limited both for specialised plant items where innovation may depend on the plant-maker, and for large integrated steel mills because of the sheer size of the contract and the range of components to be included in it.

In the third largest sector, fertiliser plant, there are several well-known processes and technological progress is relatively slow. Licences are available and prices for plant tend to be competitive.

In the case of other chemical products liberality in licensing is distinctly related to the rate of technological progress. But individual contractors invariably add their own contributions to process technology obtained from outside, and this is particularly noticeable with the scaling up of plant which usually implies more than just a change in dimensions.

In spite of the arguments favouring independent contractors, success in this industry crucially depends on close cooperation between firms in which innovation tends to originate (that is, oil, chemical or steel companies) and contractors and plant-makers. The three parties possess different skills and they need to interact, though not necessarily to lose their independence. Successful contractors have developed close relations with oil, chemical and steel companies, almost always in their own country for reasons of geographical and cultural proximity. They have developed similar relations, although perhaps these are slightly less important, with plant-makers which are usually in the same country.

Such cooperation helps explain the leadership of US contractors. By cultivating close relations with their domestic clients, they were able to dominate the world markets with plant proved at home. The success of the Italian contractors was partly facilitated by institutionalised collaboration within the state-owned groups (ENI in chemicals and IRI in steel), as well as in some major private groups.

Process plant contractors are the agents for the transfer, particularly to developing countries, of chemical or metallurgical technology wherever it originates. The activities of contractors enlarge the market for the application of innovation and speed up the spread of new technology. For this reason they enhance the value of innovation and increase the rewards of the innovator.

7.3 Recent and current problems of adjustment

The boom in European demand that had created the European contracting industry came to a sudden end in the early 1970s; orders for large steel works practically ceased (see Chapter 3), while oil refineries were particularly badly hit by the steep rise in the price of crude oil. While the fall in demand was universal in developed industrial countries, the supplying industry managed to switch its resources towards meeting increased demand from Soviet-bloc countries and from countries rich in oil or other materials. (For example, during the 1970s, one Italian contractor increased the proportion of exports in its order intake from 20 to 60 per cent, with the Soviet Union becoming the largest single market.) Even in the case of steel plant, demand from new steel-producing countries more than offset the decline in orders from developed countries.

Such shifts in demand gave additional benefit to specialised contractors, since both Soviet-bloc countries and developing countries make more intensive use of contractors than do developed countries. European contractors particularly benefited from these changes because of traditional relations between their home countries and the countries where new demands arose, because of geographical proximity, and because of the virtual absence of exports of process plant from the US to the Soviet Union.

European contractors, however, also improved their position because they mastered new technologies, gained experience in large contracts, and thus could offer a stronger challenge in export markets to US contractors. For the first fifteen years after the Second World War, US firms were dominant in steel plant and for twenty-five years in chemical plant. They were helped in securing and maintaining this position by a large home market and innovation in the domestic steel and chemical industries (particularly in petroleum-based products). Technological leadership in steel plant, however, passed to European firms in the 1960s, largely as a result of the vast investment pro-gramme of European steel industries which enabled contractors and plant-makers to gain experience with new technologies. By the end of the 1960s European contractors had also gained positions among the leaders in some types of chemical plant; for example, SNAM Progetti in oil refineries and Davy in methanol plant (of which it became the foremost supplier during the 1970s).

The leading European contractors undoubtedly improved their position both in absolute terms and in international competition during the 1970s. The shift to export markets and the shift to large and comprehensive contracts gave business to the large contractor but the smaller ones may not have had the marketing and financial strength to exploit the new situation. Some survived due to excellence in technology; some were merged into large contractors; and some diversified into related fields (such as nuclear power plant or, particularly in the UK, offshore oil-mining).

Japanese process plant contractors were also becoming increasingly successful in the 1970s, although the threat to Europeans posed by the Japanese is by no means as great as in a number of other indust-ries. In the first place Japanese competition is hardly evident in the domestic markets of Western Europe and the US, and this is probably due predominantly to technological and market factors and not to protectionism. Japanese competition, however, has increased, and is increasing, in export markets. It is based on cheap supplies of plant, and is strongest in plant requiring low levels of technology (such as refineries, fertiliser plant). It is greatest in steel plant because of the expansion of the Japanese steel industry and less in chemical plant where overall the Japanese chemical industry is not as advanced as that of the US or Europe.

Following the increases in oil prices in the 1970s, Japan's need for large international contracts is at least as great as that of any other country. There is evidence that in some instances the Japanese have obtained contracts on terms unlikely to have been remunerative and in countries which were not favoured by their competitors. Moreover, it is questionable whether the Japanese have yet acquired skills peculiar to contracting. The Japanese contractor, usually part of a large integrated company, appears to derive both advantages and disadvantages from being part of a group.

The Japanese are much stronger in exports of process plant than in international contracting.[6] This is made possible because American and European contractors tend to procure plant in the cheapest market and indeed, in some instances, the customer obliges them to do so. Japan is very competitive, for instance, in heavy pressure vessels which require large quantities of steel. In medium pressure vessels, however, which require a somewhat lower level of technology, there are a number of NICs which are now competitive in price, although not always in quality or delivery time.

It has become clear that further changes are taking place in demand in the 1980s. The growth of the world economy has slowed down considerably and strains in international financial relations have become evident. It is doubtful whether orders from Soviet-bloc countries can return to rates experienced in the 1970s. Some of these countries have run up excessive debts to Western countries and in some cases find it difficult to meet obligations. Secondly, political relations have deteriorated since 1981. Thirdly, in a number of instances, over-ambitious investment plans in the 1970s resulted in delays in construction. As regards the oil-producing countries, the collapse of the price of oil in 1981–2 may interfere with some of their investment programmes. Thus there are uncertainties in two categories of markets which in the 1970s came to the rescue of process plant contractors.

The pattern of change in the composition of demand has tended to reflect the international relocation of the steel and chemical industries, especially in relation to supplies of materials and sources of energy. This has resulted in substantial excess capacity in Europe in steel, petrochemicals and synthetic fibres. The European process plant industry has gained from these changes as it supplied a substantial proportion of plant for the new industries.

Further new demands arose as a consequence of the two oil crises of the 1970s. First, there is demand for plant to produce fuels, especially transport fuels, from substitutes for petroleum. Secondly, there is demand for processes which take account of the new energy economies, in particular the refurbishing of refineries to make them more energy-efficient and to produce a mix of outputs which better corresponds to the new pattern of demand. Both types of demand depend on the expected price of oil, and the violent fluctuations of the latter during the early 1980s must be a cause of uncertainty. This is especially true for synthetic-fuel programmes which are long-term, ambitious and risky.

One particular problem facing European contractors is that the largest market for plant, in the US, has in the past been virtually impenetrable by foreign contractors. Several European contractors have acquired subsidiaries in the US so as to have a presence in the market, as well as access to technology. The most important of these acquisitions was that of McKee by Davy in 1978. Such connections between Europeans and Americans should promote the flow of technology in both directions, and thus benefit both sides of the Atlantic, but it is not at all certain whether Europe will gain any substantial increase in exports of plant to the US.

On the supply side, changes are likely to continue to occur as a result of the fact that a major project can usually be broken down into parts. Not only can different items of plant be procured in different countries but the contractors' own activities need not be carried out in one place. There are a few countries, which may not have the capacity to undertake creative and analytical work for all kinds of plant, but which may have the capacity for lower levels of design work for most kinds of plant.

7.4 Government intervention

The rationale of intervention

The function of process plant contractors as agents for the transfer of technology benefits innovators inasmuch as the reward for innovation is enhanced. The same function can be of larger, national benefit. By encouraging the interaction of innovators and contractors within national boundaries, governments encourage technical progress to take concrete shape and to lead to export. Furthermore, technology in its concrete form can be used for political purposes as a bargaining counter to obtain scarce materials or diplomatic advantage, or in helping economic development abroad.

The other function of contractors is even more important. They must have close relations with makers of plant which embodies technology and this cooperation tends to take place within national boundaries (see pp. 170–6). It may induce what those connected with ENI refer to as 'engineering culture'. In many instances plant manufacturers would not have had the opportunity or ability to export except through contractors located in the same country. This tendency is reinforced by government policy (as will be explained).

These functions accord contractors a strategic position in the economy that is more important than that suggested by the size of the contractors themselves. We believe that figures for employment in contractors' offices have to be multiplied by at least six to estimate employment in plant manufacturing. On this basis about 500,000 jobs in Western Europe are dependent on specialised process plant contractors. Indeed, this total employment, together with a parallel effect on the balance of payments, is of paramount importance for most governments. Nor should the spin-off effects—or what has been referred to as the 'flagship' role—of successful projects abroad be forgotten.[7]

Government intervention takes the form of direct or indirect subsidisation of projects, initiative or help in the establishment of contracting firms of international stature, and the use of the apparatus of government to promote their interests.

The financing of exports

Subsidies to projects consist of: export credits on favourable terms, usually given to buyers rather than to suppliers; government underwriting of credit insurance; and grants-in-aid to customer countries tied to projects.

Export credits are particularly important for process plant projects where the repayment period is long. Such credits are important in sales to Soviet-bloc and developing countries, but not so much in sales to developed and some oil-rich countries, or when the buyer is a major oil company. Export credit is government-subsidised, although technically often given by private banks as well as government departments, and it is normally stipulated that a high proportion of the plant financed by the credit must be purchased in the creditor country. In certain instances—for example, when suitable items are not available—an exception is made.

It is not easy to assess credit arrangements and indeed to define the meaning of the term 'subsidy'. A financial package includes the rate of interest applicable to the credit, and the period and terms of repayment, but there are also other conditions and circumstances which are difficult to describe let alone measure.

Interest rates for export credit are lower, sometimes much lower, than domestic interest rates. Over the years efforts have been made to reduce excessive competition in export credit between industrialised countries since subsidisation by governments is regarded as undesirable within the framework of current international trading arrangements. Agreements to limit competition in export credit have been made by the OECD countries since 1978. Minimum rates of interest and maximum repayment periods are fixed and developing countries are treated somewhat more generously than industrialised countries.

The principal underlying difficulty in the credit markets is that while inflation is world-wide, its rate is different in different countries. In the long run countries with a higher rate of inflation are bound to depreciate their currencies against those countries with lower rates of inflation. Furthermore, rates of interest reflect rates of inflation and thus prospective changes in exchange rates. In other words, low interest rates (for example, in West Germany, Switzerland and Japan) are associated with currencies which are likely to appreciate. This being so, it is difficult to justify uniform rates for export credit which do not take into account the currency in which credit is given. (Indeed, from November 1981, credit in certain currencies was permitted at interest rates below those agreed for the rest of the OECD group.)

An apparent problem is that payments for some exports of plant (especially to Soviet-bloc countries) are made not in money but in kind, in most instances in commodities produced by the new plant, with the process plant contractor being responsible for disposal. In fact, this is not an additional problem, but part of the more general problem of the relocation of world steel and chemical production. These 'counter-trading', or 'buy-back', arrangements bring out dramatically, however, the conflict of interest between the process plant contracting industry and the domestic steel or chemical industries.

A further problem is that aid to developing countries is often tied to particular projects on condition that contracts are given to the donor country. In a number of instances attractive financial packages are offered (not necessarily to the most deserving countries) which include both credit at agreed OECD rates and aid. These 'mixed credits' are tantamount to a further lowering of average interest rates.

Even if there were an agreement on the general conditions of credit, it would be difficult to ascertain whether different governments subsidise exports to the same extent or not. In the case of large projects each transaction is unique; not only is each project different from each other in some respect, but the commercial and political risks attached to each customer are also different.

The least scope for subsidising exports from Europe through financial arrangements is found in West Germany where the difference between domestic and export rates of interest is the smallest. Among European countries France appears to be at the other extreme.

In particular, the French compensate exporters for domestic inflation during the construction period. The British have also introduced compensation for inflation, but this appears to be more restricted than that in France.

Direct support to process plant contractors

In view of the importance they attach to large process plant projects, and in the belief that only large contractors are capable of winning such contracts, governments have ensured that, where needed, suitable companies are created.

The most explicit example of government involvement in the process plant industry was the creation of Technip by the French authorities in a conspicuous attempt to establish a major international contractor. It was established in 1958 and has grown rapidly since 1975. The present form of Technip is the result of French industrial strategy which brought together public agencies as well as French oil, chemical and engineering companies. The close relations between the contractor, research organisations and the industrial companies are of great benefit (Technip is one of the leaders in gas processing technology), and the rigidities which occur in an integrated company are avoided.

Government involvement in Italy is indirect, through the state enterprises ENI and IRI which respectively control SNAM Progetti in chemical and Italimpianti in steel plant. SNAM Progetti is highly successful in the field of oil-related process plant. Italimpianti employs about 1,500 and is capable, with the backing of its parent company, of winning large international steel plant contracts. Both firms are backed by highly developed plant manufacturers belonging to the same state enterprises so that a very substantial proportion of plant procurement takes place in Italy. In both cases plant manufacturing developed in parallel with the respective needs of the oil, gas and steel industries of Italy.

Davy has grown rapidly through acquisition, especially in the 1970s, to become the largest European contractor. It has done so with the blessing and encouragement of the British government. Although Davy is unique among contractors in having a substantial presence in three countries—the UK, West Germany and the US—it is nevertheless recognised as a company representing British interests. In 1981 the Monopolies and Mergers Commission prevented a foreign take-over of the company. In doing so, it explicitly recognised the high degree of support developed countries often give to contractors in view of their potential innovatory role with respect to the chemical or steel industries and with respect to their suppliers.

As regards Davy, it also recognises the importance to the British economy of the business it generated for suppliers.[8]

Indeed, the national character of Davy's successful bids in 1981 for some major steel plant contracts, supported closely by UK financial institutions, is evident from coincident visits to the purchasing countries by royalty or senior ministers, and the granting of aid to outbid competitors.

While UK efforts to gain steel plant contracts have been influenced by regional unemployment problems, the efforts of other European countries have been motivated by the need to secure supplies of oil and some other materials, although the French effort has been greater in nuclear and military contracts than in process plant. In Italy ENI pursued an effective policy to secure oil supplies. In Germany direct government involvment is less evident and indeed there is less need for it in view of the technological excellence of German plant-makers and the fact that the leading contractors belong to large groups. This is especially true for Lurgi since its parent, Metallgesellschaft, can handle finance and counter-trade.

Government involvement is in fact hardly avoidable where trade takes place within the framework of bilateral treaties, which is the case for trade with Soviet-bloc countries. Further, governments are involved in substantial programmes to support the development of synthetic fuel technologies for which demonstration plants are very expensive. German and UK firms which have long experience with coal-based technologies are participating in the programme of the US Department of Energy. In Europe the largest programme is that funded by the German Federal Ministry of Technology.

The impact of intervention

It is not easy to say how far the success of European process plant contractors has been due to government intervention. With the shift away from the internal markets of the industrial countries towards exports to developing countries and the Soviet bloc, government policies obviously had an influence on contractors and, indeed, in certain instances trade could not have taken place without arrangements between governments. Subsidised export credit is the clearest but not the only manifestation of the role of governments. In the post-1973 world especially, governments were keenly interested to redirect industries into serving specific export markets. The large process plant contracts that could be obtained were a particularly attractive target.

But the role of government intervention can be exaggerated. First, a great deal of intervention is defensive—for instance, to match intervention by other governments or to offset some other perceived advantages of foreign industry (for example, close links between US oil companies and contractors). Secondly, intervention could not have been effective without a qualified and competent industry able to take advantage of it. Because of the development of European process-plant-using industries, the contractors supplying them had reached a stage at which they were ready to attack world markets.

In various parts of this chapter we have pointed out differences between the four major countries as regards the origin and structure of the industry and as regards government intervention. There were substantial differences between them as regards problems of employment, balance of payments and inflation. West Germany has the strongest position, based largely on its innovative mechanical engineering industry, and the least need for intervention. In the case of the other countries, exports of process plant depend to a significant extent on the success of their contractors. This is clearly perceived by governments. There are, of course, different traditions of intervention in different countries, common to a whole range of industries. One of the most interesting developments has been the gradual strengthening of British governmental intervention in specific instances, as against generalised aid. For example, the British government made it clear in 1980 that aid programmes are to be used for political, industrial and commercial purposes.

A role for developing countries.

The benefits derived from the technology-transfer activities of contractors have hitherto been confined to relatively few developing countries. A major reason for this is that the technologies on offer are not necessarily appropriate for the scale of operations possible in a number of developing countries or for materials available there. There is a need especially to develop energy-saving and oil-substitute plant for the poorer countries. At the same time, when the advanced countries are facing heavy unemployment, particularly in the capital goods industries, it should be possible to create a scheme whereby process plant contractors gear their activities towards both supplying the needs of developing countries and improving employment possibilities at home.

Notes

1. Freeman (1968) estimates that in the mid-1960s three-quarters of major new chemical plant were supplied by contractors whereas before the Second

World War the chemical industry did most of its own designing and procurement.

2. According to Vitry (1977), French exports of complete plant, for instance, in the seven years up to 1976 increased their share of exports of capital goods from 8 to 22 per cent.

3. One informant said that it pays to set up an office in France to get into certain markets in Africa and to make use of French government credit facilities, even for one contract.

4. Davy, for instance, has argued the limits to inter-firm cooperation. See Monopolies and Mergers Commission (1981), para. 5.2.

5. On this and other points in this subsection, see Freeman (1968).

6. Trade statistics, of course, only indicate flows of hardware, not of contract income. Given the problems of classification, our best estimates suggest that the share of the four major European countries in total OECD exports of process plant remained unchanged, at a little over 50 per cent, throughout the 1970s. (Germany accounted for one-half of this figure.) Japan apparently gained at the expense of the US.

7. See para. 3.23 of Monopolies and Mergers Commission (1981).

8. See paras. 9.5, 9.6, and 9.16 of the Monopolies and Mergers Commission (1981).

References

Barna, T., Aylen, J., Dosi, G., Jones, D. (1981), *The European Process Plant Industry*, unpublished report to the Commission of the European Communities, Brighton: Sussex European Research Centre.

Freeman, C. (1968), 'Chemical process plant: innovation and the world market', *National Institute Economic Review*, London.

Monopolies and Mergers Commission (1981), *Enserch Corporation and Davy Corporation Limited: A Report on the Proposed Merger*, London: HMSO.

Vitry, G. (1977), *Les Usines Clés en Main*, Études de Politique Industrielle, No. 18, Paris: La Documentation Française.

8 MACHINE TOOLS: TECHNICAL CHANGE AND A JAPANESE CHALLENGE

Daniel T. Jones

8.1 The nature of the industry

The products of the metal-working machine tool industry are not as well known to the general public as those of the other industries discussed in this book. Except perhaps in Germany and Switzerland they are rarely seen outside an engineering workshop or assembly line. The industry is small in national terms, at between 1 and 3 per cent of GDP and manufacturing employment. Despite its small size it is often thought as one of the central subsectors of the engineering, metal goods and transportation equipment industries. Historically the diffusion of new machine tools embodying the latest machining technology was an important transmission mechanism for spreading new technology and techniques throughout these industries. In turn the structure and competitiveness of the machine tool industry is very directly related to that of the engineering industry as a whole. Despite the growing degree of intra-industry trade and international specialisation, there is still a strong link between a healthy domestic machine tool industry and a competitive engineering industry. Those countries which are technological leaders in this industry have the important advantage of controlling to some extent the international division of labour in engineering products. Countries which are dependent on importing the most advanced machine tools experience a certain delay in the diffusion of the latest machining technology. This, of course, can be a disadvantage in relying on exporting high value added engineering goods. This disadvantage becomes acute vulnerability in times of war, as Britain found at the start of both world wars.[1]

The most notable features of the machine tool industry are the relatively small scale of production and the vast range of types of machine tools produced. Individual machine tools vary in price from $1,000 to $450,000 in 1980 prices (see Table 8.1). Often, however, machine tools are sold as part of a large package—for instance, a complete line to produce engine cylinder blocks. Firms in this industry are generally small (with the partial exception of Japan), those employing more than 2,000 persons being the exception.

Table 8.1 Machine tool production and unit values by type, 1980

	Production ($ millions)				Average unit values ($'000)			
	Germany	UK, France and Italy*	Japan	US	Germany	UK, France and Italy*	Japan	US
NC boring†	107	62	36	93	451	342	349	411
NC lathes	380	364	678	481	172	129	56	176
NC milling	68	152	84	163	393	122	58	62
Machining centres	260	202	298	413	::	::	::	::
Transfer machines	356	334	178	793	::	::	::	::
Boring	71	74	101	100	187	86	42	64
Drilling	103	121	51	154	5	4	1	4
Gear cutting	159	30	68	130	128	122	58	140
Grinding	571	384	319	523	10	20	29	54
Lathes	495	451	302	346	57	18	13	23
Milling	388	232	183	177	81	25	20	12
All cutting	3,314	2,880	3,033	3,718	24	22	17	15
Presses	649	392	628	441	55	37	31	21
All forming	1,395	1,009	824	1,097	15	19	29	15
NC cutting	1,289	712	1,507	1,260	::	::	::	::
Share of NC in all cutting (%)	38.9	24.7‡	49.7	33.9	::	::	::	::

* The distribution of production by type and average unit values were similar for France, Italy and the UK; therefore they were aggregated.
† NC = numerically controlled.
‡ Italy 18.6 per cent, UK 20.6 per cent and France 40.1 per cent.

Sources: CECIMO, *International Statistics of Machine Tools*, 1980; author's estimates.

Median plant size is over 1,000 employees in Japan, just over 400 in Germany and the US, and somewhat lower elsewhere. According to figures for the early 1970s, Germany had only twelve plants employing more than 1,000 employees, the US ten and the UK seven.[2] At an industry level the concentration of production in the largest companies is low; the largest five firms account for between 10 per cent of total output in Germany to 20 per cent in the UK, with the other European producers and the US in between. In particular product lines, however, the concentration is much higher, even at the international level. This is particularly so in specialised types of machine tools where competition is less in terms of price than in terms of performance, reliability, spares availability, operator-training schemes, and so on. In less sophisticated machine tools barriers to entry are low, concentration is low and price competition is important. The Japanese industry is slightly different in that both plant and firm size are larger.

With such a wide spectrum of product types production methods clearly differ widely, most machines being produced in small batches with many customer-specific features distinguishing each order. This certainly applies to all the more sophisticated types of machine tool, accounting for the bulk of machine tool sales by value (see Table 8.1). Flow-line production methods are only possible with more standardised machine tools, such as simple drilling and grinding machines, lathes and punching and shearing machines, produced in thousands and not hundreds per year. Table 8.2 shows that while these kinds of machine tools might account for about 60 per cent of output by volume they only account for between 20 and 45 per cent of output by value.

For a long time there has been a discussion in the industry about the relative merits of a strategy based on specialisation in advanced machine tools or one of mass production of standardised machine tools. The successful entry of newer countries, such as Korea and Taiwan, in these product lines makes the latter a risky strategy for a country with high labour costs. Machines embodying a great degree of human skill are obviously more suited to production in developed countries. However, the issue is not quite so clear cut and significant advances have been made in utilising mass-produced standardised components and design modules in more sophisticated machine tool production.

An important prerequisite for a competitive machine tool industry is the existence of a substantial skill base in the workforce, from skilled fitter to design engineer. The other main determinant seems to be the existence of a dynamic and technologically sophisticated

Table 8.2 Volume of machine tools produced, 1978 ('000)

	Germany	Italy	UK	France	Japan	US
Drilling	22	14	11	9	35	52
Grinding and polishing	53	6	9	20	8	110
Lathes	12	8	18	4	23	13
Milling	8	4	6	3	8	15
Other cutting	43	7	8	6	63	67
Punching and shearing	52	2	4	6	4	14
Presses	15	6	6	2	12	17
Other forming	25	3	7	13	2	38
Total	230	51	70	61	155	327
Total (tons '000)	*293*	*147*	..	*72*	*335*	..
NC cutting tools	2.4	0.7	1.0	0.8	7.3	5.9
NC lathes	1.9	0.6	0.3	0.5	5.0	1.5
Drilling, lathes, grinding, punching and shearing machines as per cent of total:						
By volume	60.4	58.8	60.0	63.9	45.2	57.8
By value	31.1	28.0	44.8	17.4	23.2	31.9

Source: CECIMO, *International Statistics of Machine Tools*, 1980.

market for machine tools. This is true also of small countries such as Sweden and Switzerland where close contacts have been established between customers and machine tool designers to meet specific customer needs and gain initial learning and operating experience before commencing exporting. In some countries, such as the US and the UK, the latest developments in machine tools were closely related to aerospace and military demand, while elsewhere they are oriented towards more sophisticated engineering products, as in Germany, or light, precision engineering, as in Japan and Italy. While downstream linkages are extremely important, the upstream linkages with the electronics industry are becoming more important as electronic controls comprise a growing proportion of the selling price of advanced machinery.

Historical development — technological leaders and followers

The development of the machine tool industry can be summarised as two phases of relative stability among the major participants and two phases where rapidly changing patterns of demand and new entrants caused a major shake-up of the industry world-wide.

The UK machine tool industry, which emerged between 1770 and 1850, maintained its dominant position until the latter decades of the nineteenth century when it was successfully challenged by

Germany and the US. The challenge came in two different directions. In America it came from the development of machinery, such as turret lathes, with interchangeable, standardised parts suitable for the mass production of consumer products such as cycles, motor cars, and so on, rather than from the heavier custom-designed machine tools for producing mining equipment, steam engines, railway equipment and ships that were the origins of the UK industry. The Germans developed a world lead in more sophisticated machine tools and advanced machinery of all kinds and retained a technological lead in this direction in part because of the early establishment of a system of technical education that was the envy of other countries in Europe and was later copied by the Japanese. The need to compete on world markets and successful rationalisation programmes in the inter-war period reinforced this lead. The UK industry was slow in adapting to these challenges and was to a large degree cushioned from having to respond during the inter-war period and immediate post-Second World War period by relying on her captive empire markets. There is a considerable literature on these changes during that period.[3]

Table 8.3 shows the relative stability in trade shares of the major producers from 1930 to 1970, with Germany and the US dominating world trade, although US export shares declined in the 1960s. This

Table 8.3 National shares of world trade in machine tools, 1913–80*
(per cent)

	1913	1937	1965	1970	1975	1980
Germany	48	48	31	34	36	32
Switzerland	†	5	9	10	9	10
Italy	†	†	7	10	9	9
UK	12	7	13	11	8	7
France	†	†	6	6	7	6
Japan	†	†	3	5	6	16
US	33	35	22	16	12	8
Other	7	5	9	8	13	12
Total	100	100	100	100	100	100

* Non-communist world.
† Included under 'Other'.

Sources: UNIDO, *The Machine Tool Industry*, Vienna, 1974; Committee on Industry and Trade, *Survey of Industries, Part IV: Engineering*, London: HMSO, 1928 (Balfour report); Hornsby, W., *History of the Second World War—Factories and Plant*, London: HMSO, 1958; UN, *Yearbook of International Trade Statistics*, New York, various years.

stability did not result in technological stagnation; many advances were made during the inter-war period, in high speed steel and tungsten carbide, for instance. These made higher machining speeds and less frequent tool changes possible. The post-war period saw the beginnings of the development of numerically controlled (that is, computer-controlled) machine tools, although the widespread diffusion of these only took place during the 1970s.

8.2 Adjustment pressures in the 1970s

Demand

The period of growth in output and employment came to an end in 1970. In almost all countries this proved to be a watershed after which employment continued to fall. This decline predates the events of 1973 but was certainly magnified by them and by the subsequently prolonged recession amongst the developed countries. The engineering and metal-using industries suffered from the slow-down in growth rates in the 1970s and falling investment levels. The impact on the steel and machine tool industries, both of which found themselves with surplus capacity as a result, was even more serious. The machine tool industry is in any case a highly cyclical industry as customer industries postpone or speed up their investment pro-grammes. A slower rate of growth of economic activity in the developed economies makes it more difficult for the machine tool industry to cope with these cyclical swings. In addition, the geo-graphical location of demand has shifted back and forth considerably during the 1970s. Up until about 1978 exports to the developing countries and the CMEA countries expanded rapidly, only to fall back again sharply by 1980. This left many producers oriented towards those markets in difficulties, particularly Germany, France and Italy. At about that time the US market picked up as the air-craft industry expanded production and the automobile industry retooled to downsize their product to meet Japanese competition and Federal energy-saving regulations. Among the main beneficiaries of this surge in demand were the Japanese producers. Both of these markets have since contracted again in the US in the face of falling demand.

In addition to these changes in demand the fact that the rapidly growing industries of the future, such as electronics and information processing, are not major consumers of machine tools may have a permanent impact on machine tool demand. Even some of the traditional customer industries, such as motor cars and aerospace, may also increasingly use composites, plastics and ceramics which involve less pressing and machining in the next decade. Offsetting this is the fact that successive generations of production technology, incorporating not only machine tools but also transfer lines, robots, and so on, are rapidly making existing tooling in the engineering and motor car industries out of date, thereby creating a demand for retooling ahead of the normal replacement cycle. Switching to new markets takes time and cannot be accomplished overnight.

Technological change

The most important development in this industry in the 1970s was the accelerating diffusion of machine tools controlled by computer, that is, numerically controlled (NC) machine tools. The take-off in the diffusion of these machine tools was the result of the gradual refinement of these types of machine tool, in particular with the advent of cheaper microprocessor controls, and was not directly related to the interruption of the period of stable market shares and the turnaround in the conjunctural situation. The US airforce first commissioned research into electronically controlled machine tools at MIT in 1952 and much of the early development was geared to the needs of the aerospace industry in the US and the UK.[4] The diffusion to other industries was initially hampered by the high capital costs and reliability problems of early models. As the cost of the control units came down with the advent of the micro-computers in the early 1970s and microprocessors in the late 1970s, more and more machine tools were fitted with NC units and the diffusion began to accelerate. These became known as computer numerically controlled (CNC) machine tools. They also had the advantage of greater flexibility and versatility, with the possibility of reprogramming to perform a wider variety of tasks. The cost of control units tumbled as they were mass produced, particularly by the leading Japanese producer Fujitsu Fanuc which currently produces something like 10,000 control units a year. Leading European producers such as Siemens and Philips have so far only achieved about 1,500 a year.

The next step was to link a series of CNC machine tools through a central computer, thereby achieving a greater utilisation of the machines by automatic routing of production pieces and adjusting machine speeds to feed rates. These developments are beginning to revolutionise machine tool design which is increasingly incorporating adaptive controls, local testing and fault diagnosis. The later 1980s should see the introduction of distributed intelligence networks and the integration of the whole production process with the widespread use of industrial robots. Prototype unmanned factories are in existence and under development in a number of countries, notably Japan, and flexible manufacturing systems (FMS) are being introduced in many plants world-wide. In one example a factory would manufacture 2,000 different machine items in lot sizes up to 25 pieces and assemble them into 50 different products. Automatic operations, including forging, welding, machining, painting, tool replacement, machine self-diagnosis and repair, are all achieved by a hierarchy of microprocessors and a large central computer.[5] In addition many plants are now able to run an extra unmanned shift at night, called the 'ghost shift', thereby increasing the utilisation time of the machinery. While it may take time for these developments to gain widespread acceptance, the continuing reduction in the cost of electronification will continue to increase the range of applications. By 1980 NC machine tools accounted for close to 50 per cent of Japanese production by value, for 20 per cent in Italy and the UK, for 33 per cent in the US and nearer 40 per cent in Germany and France (see Table 8.1).

For the user industries this means that, in addition to the benefits of greater automation, the whole trend of this direction of technological change is to achieve mass production levels of efficiency even at small batch production scale and to blur the traditional choice between dedicated automation and flexibility. It is, for instance, having a major impact on production methods and economies of scale in the motor car industry (see Chapter 5, Section 4). Although NC machining technology developed in response to the highly specialised needs of the aerospace industry, countries which either did not have a substantial aerospace industry or were latecomers to this technology, such as Japan and Italy, focused the application of numerical control on much simpler general purpose machine tools that could be used throughout the engineering industry, in particular by smaller engineering firms.

Not only was the machine tool industry faced with much more rapid technological change and the need to commit larger resources to research and development, but NC technology had a number of important impacts on the operations of machine tool firms and on the structure of the industry. Machine tool firms had to acquire and integrate electronics skills alongside the well entrenched mechanical engineering skills. This in some cases proved difficult to do. Machine tool firms had to initiate links with electronics producers, which in some cases also joined the industry. Apart from the domestic availability of electronics skills, access to the latest electronics hardware and software became increasingly important. In this respect countries with a well-developed electronics industry, such as Japan, have a substantial advantage. A typical response to these pressures was to subcontract many previously in-house production steps to highly specialised subcontractors, reversing the traditionally highly vertically integrated structure of the industry. Machine tool firms therefore concentrated much more on design, assembly and marketing rather than manufacturing the whole product in-house.[6]

Another important change is in the marketing of machine tools, which, with the integration of machine tools into production systems, is in some cases becoming a specialised function. Firms like Comau, the machine tool subsidiary of Fiat, are custom-designing complete production systems (including automatic welding, machining, transfer systems and warehousing) to optimise the degree of electronic sophistication and machine tool choice to match the requirements of the customer in terms of the desired degree of flexibility and the sophistication of the back-up skills available locally. In many ways this begins to resemble the process plant industry (described in Chapter 7). There are no clear advantages in being either an electronics or machine tool firm to perform this specific function, although one needs a capability in both. The opportunity for new entrants, particularly from large system users, who could exert a very powerful position in this industry, is wide open.

Changes in comparative advantage

The third major change in the 1970s, related to the two already discussed, is the changing comparative advantage of different countries. So far most of the European countries have maintained their share of world trade since the 1950s (see Table 8.3). The exception is the UK. In constant prices the value of current UK output has not grown since the mid-1950s, and for the first time the UK is experiencing a net deficit in machine tool trade. Germany, still the dominant exporter, and Switzerland managed to maintain their trade shares by moving up-market into more advanced machine tools, despite the revaluation of the DM and Swiss franc throughout the 1970s. The other country consistently to lose market share is the US (Table 8.3), although it was never so reliant on exports as other major producers (see Table 1.2, p. 7).

The challenge from Japan, particularly in NC machine tools and their derivatives, poses the greatest question marks over continued German dominance in this industry (see Table 8.3 and 8.4). Japanese firms carefully focused their export strategy around the two most important NC machine tools, NC lathes and machining centres, for which the market was large enough to gain substantial production

Table 8.4 World production and consumption of machine tools, 1960-80

Production	($ millions at current prices and exchange rates)			(per cent)		
	1960	*1970*	*1980*	*1960*	*1970*	*1980*
North America	786	1,478	4,995	25.0	18.9	18.8
Germany	501	1,479	4,693	15.9	19.0	17.7
Other Western Europe	741	1,713	5,853	23.6	22.0	22.1
Japan	164	1,109	3,818	5.2	14.2	14.4
Sino-Soviet bloc	938	1,795	5,875	29.8	23.0	22.1
Others*	14	230	1,301	0.4	2.9	4.9
Total	3,144	7,804	26,535	100.0	100.0	100.0
Consumption						
North America	629	1,428	5,846	20.0	18.3	22.0
Germany	334	891	2,610	10.6	11.4	9.8
Other Western Europe	759	1,581	4,705	24.1	20.3	17.7
Japan	214	1,179	2,586	6.8	15.1	9.7
Sino-Soviet bloc	938	1,746	6,317	29.8	22.4	23.8
Others	270	979	4,471	8.6	12.5	16.8
Total	3,144	7,804	26,535	100.0	100.0	100.0
Trade balances						
North America	157	50	− 851			
Germany	167	588	2,083			
Other Western Europe	− 18	132	1,148			
Japan	− 50	− 70	1,232			
Sino-Soviet bloc	0	49	− 442			
Others	− 256	− 749	− 3,170			

* Production in Argentina, Brazil, Mexico and India may have been underestimated in 1960.

Sources: *American Machinist*, January 1972 and February 1981; UNIDO, *The Machine Tool Industry*, Vienna, 1974; author's estimates.

economies (see Tables 8.1 and 8.2). They have come to dominate trade in these products to the extent that in 1980 they accounted for over half the imports into EEC countries of NC parallel lathes and 25 per cent of total NC machine tool imports. The reasons for this phenomenal success are discussed more fully below (Section 3). In the now familiar way this challenge began in third markets, particularly in South-East Asia (see Tables 8.5 and 8.6), and only later moved to the US and finally to Europe.

Another challenge to the competitive position of the European machine tool industry is emerging from the more recently

Table 8.5 Direction of machine tool exports, 1970 and 1980*

Exports to	Exports from ($ millions at current prices and exchange rates)						
	Germany	Italy	UK	France	Japan	US	OECD
1980							
Western Europe	1,475	462	332	268	354	358	4,486
Eastern Europe	584	159	51	185	89	40	1,351
North America	327	79	196	45	586	255	1,862
Latin America	305	89	45	31	51	315	970
Africa	130	62	96	75	56	26	525
Asia and Oceania	467	122	147	57	432	256	1,728
Total	3,288	973	867	660	1,568	1,250	10,922
1970							
Western Europe	380	86	82	58	10	89	922
Eastern Europe	104	48	35	28	30	8	309
North America	54	12	33	5	14	78	235
Latin America	33	20	8	5	3	36	120
Africa	7	4	3	8	1	1	27
Asia and Oceania	111	21	41	13	33	94	364
Total	690	191	202	116	90	305	1,977

* Exports from OECD countries only.

Source: OECD, *Statistics of Foreign Trade: Series C*, Paris, various years.

industrialising countries such as Spain, India, Poland, East Germany, Taiwan and Korea, which are producing less sophisticated types of machine tools, such as simple lathes, which are very price sensitive. The challenge initially takes the form of the substitution of European exports by local production in domestic markets but is now turning into a reverse flow to the developed economies. Countries such as the UK and to a certain extent France and Italy, which have relied heavily on exporting these kinds of machine tools in the past, are increasingly finding themselves squeezed between these developing countries in simple machine tools and the leading nations in technologically advanced machine tools. Although this challenge from the developing countries is still of small proportions, this trend is clear and will become significant during the 1980s.[7]

Table 8.6 Shares of machine tool export markets, 1970 and 1980*
(per cent)

Importing country	Country of origin					
	Germany	Other Western Europe	Japan	US	Other	Total OECD
1980						
Western Europe	32.9	50.9	7.9	8.0	0.3	100.0
Eastern Europe	43.2	47.2	6.6	2.9	0.1	100.0
North America	17.5	30.3	31.5	13.7	7.0	100.0
Latin America	31.5	29.9	5.2	32.5	0.9	100.0
Africa	24.8	59.4	10.6	4.9	0.3	100.0
Asia and Oceania	27.0	32.4	25.0	14.8	0.8	100.0
Total	30.1	42.6	13.4	11.4	2.5	100.0
1970						
Western Europe	41.2	47.9	1.1	9.7	0.1	100.0
Eastern Europe	33.7	54.3	9.6	2.4	–	100.0
North America	23.1	32.7	5.9	33.0	5.3	100.0
Latin America	27.3	40.0	2.3	29.8	0.6	100.0
Africa	26.4	66.6	3.3	3.7	–	100.0
Asia and Oceania	30.5	34.1	9.1	25.8	0.5	100.0
Total	34.9	44.3	4.5	15.4	0.9	100.0

* Exports from OECD countries only.

Source: OECD, *Statistics of Foreign Trade: Series C*, Paris, various years.

8.3 Private and public responses to adjustment

Germany

The German machine tool industry has demonstrated a remarkably strong performance throughout its history. Even after the two world wars and the inter-war depression the industry recovered its leading position rapidly. Although less affected by these events, the UK, French and American industries did not manage to improve their positions in times of temporary German weakness. The fundamental strength of the whole German engineering industry, including machine tools, is the sustained investment in human skills and technical training, the basis of which was laid in the second half of the nineteenth century.[8] Upon this foundation an enormously strong engineering industry grew up which prided itself on high-quality products embodying the most sophisticated engineering knowledge available. One key ingredient in maintaining this lead in sophisticated engineering is the close contacts that have been built up over the years between the leading customers and the machine tool producer in the early design and prototype stage. Designing machine tools for the specialist requirement of the leading textile or printing machinery companies in the world, for example, laid the basis for subsequent success in export markets. Inter-war government programmes to develop industry-wide standards and rationalise the number of machine tool types helped to improve efficiency and competitiveness.

Such a long history of industry dominance led to a number of problems when a serious challenge was mounted. An early disbelief on the part of German machine tool firms in the seriousness of the challenge posed by the Japanese perhaps had its origins in a reluctance to attach sufficient importance to electronic engineering in an industry long dominated by mechanical engineers. Moreover, the Japanese did not tackle the Germans head on in the most sophisticated kinds of machine tools. Instead they achieved a completely new combination of advanced electronic controls, previously only thought worthwhile on the most sophisticated and specialised machine tools, that they applied to smaller general-purpose machine tools suitable for widespread use throughout the engineering sector. This new situation particularly caught off balance those German firms that were heavily committed to lathe manufacture. The largest two of these, Gildermeister and Pittler, have not paid dividends since 1973 and 1975 respectively. By 1980 the Japanese had captured over 30 per cent of the German market for NC lathes and accounted for over 50 per cent of all NC lathe imports.

Although earlier the most reluctant to support attempts by the Federation of European Machine Tool Associations (CECIMO) to initiate studies of the Japanese threat, the German industry association (VDMA) late in the day commissioned its own report from a leading consultancy firm. This reported in 1981. In part as a direct result of the impact of this report many German companies have switched their strategy to adopt new product strategies and production methods akin to the Japanese. It is too early to assess the success of these changes. It is, however, very characteristic of the German engineering industry that a consensus should develop through the industry association. This plays a very important role in coordinating opinions, representing the views of industry to government and disseminating new technical and strategic information. The German government, while it has many schemes for supporting new technology initiatives and small- and medium-sized firms, has never had a specific strategy for the machine tool industry. The task of rescuing a number of individual companies has been undertaken by the banks, not always successfully. The most dramatic case was the rescue of Pittler.

Italy

The Italian industry grew very rapidly in the post-war period and it is now the second largest producer of machine tools in Europe (see Table 8.7). The industry is highly concentrated in the Turin and Milan area and supplies an extraordinarily diverse network of small companies that comprise the Italian engineering industry. The size of

Table 8.7 Indicators of level of activity in the machine tool industry, 1962–80

	Germany	Italy	UK	France	Japan	US
Employment (000)						
1962	113.0	..	72.9	..	34.6	82.2
1966	112.5	17.2	71.3	21.9	33.7	108.2
1973	112.0	37.0	52.1	27.0	45.2	86.9
1979	97.0	..	50.9	20.2	31.0	102.6
Production (\$ millions)						
1980	4,693	1,635	1,190	970	3,818	4,820
Production per employee (\$ 000)						
1980	48.4	44.2	23.4	48.0	123.2	47.0

Sources: National Machine Tool Builders Association, *Statistical Yearbook,* 1981; *American Machinist,* February 1981; author's estimates.

median Italian machine tool plant, in most cases the same as the firm, at 150 employees is less than half that elsewhere.[9] The Italian dualism is also evident in the machine tool industry, with many highly versatile small firms at one end and a few large companies, like Comau (the Fiat subsidiary), with 16 per cent of the industry workforce, and Olivetti, at the other. There are important subcontracting relationships between the two groups. The main obstacle to the rapid growth of machine tool demand in Italy in the early post-war period was the small scale of the potential customer firm in the Italian engineering industry. What was required was a mechanism for bringing together a technical advisory service for purchases of machine tools with a credit package with attractive terms and a generous grace period. The framework for such a package was laid down by the Sabatini Law which allowed the Italian machine tool industry association UCIMU to provide just such a service. It runs two financing companies that run on a break-even basis and, using various tax advantages, provide credit at favourable terms and at a subsidised rate of interest. This has been so successful that about 80 per cent of machine tool sales in Italy have been made under the Sabatini Law provisions.[10] It has also acted as a subtle form of protection as only Italian-built machine tools qualify. Italian machine tools also benefit from an export credit subsidy.

UCIMU is quite unique among industry associations throughout Europe in that it provides many commercial functions centrally to its member companies, in addition to the usual export promotion and market intelligence functions. An example is the training company that provides complete training packages for engineers in Third World countries. Training on Italian machine tools is a good base for further export sales. UCIMU was also one of the first to study the Japanese challenge, even though Italian producers are somewhat protected by preferential credit. The success of UCIMU has meant that the pressure for larger units has not been so strong in Italy and the uniquely Italian design flair and technical ingenuity have flourished in a decentralised industrial structure. Apart from providing the legal basis for the Sabatini financing the state has not had to become involved in company restructuring and so on. One might call the activities of UCIMU a 'private industrial policy' for the machine tool industry.

France

The French machine tool industry has always been much weaker and more fragmented than in other European countries. This reflects the narrower base of the French engineering industry, concentrated around the motor car, nuclear, aerospace and defence industries, in contrast to Germany's more broadly based engineering industry. Although the machine tool industry was frequently described as a priority sector by the government, the reality has been that the French engineering industry has equipped itself principally with German machine tools. (Until recent years France was the leading export market for German machine tools.) This situation is a reflection of the political bargain struck in the creation of the EEC, namely German support for French agriculture in return for the opening of the French market to German industrial goods. Like the UK the French machine tool industry has been on the defensive throughout the 1970s.

Again as in the UK the main thrust of government policy was to promote mergers to achieve economies of scale in production and sufficient size to invest in developing new NC machine tools. As a result the industry is now dominated by four major companies which are intended to provide the 'poles' of its development. The largest machine tool producer in France, the motor car group Renault, has consistently refused to take over ailing machine tool firms despite its nationalised status. The second largest producer, Ratier Forest, one-third publicly owned (by the Institut pour le Développement Industriel), received a cash injection in 1979 to absorb a series of take-overs of smaller companies. More recently attention has focused on rescuing the Line Group and in this case the French government even approached the Japanese industry, through MITI, for help. Other government policies have from time to time included funds to launch new projects, funds for R & D, preferential loans for overseas sales, and subsidies tied to 'growth contracts' (where firms agree to achieve certain financial targets). Despite the enormous attention the machine tool industry has received from successive governments, its performance has not been very successful. Further difficulties were created with the collapse in 1982 of the Eastern European market, to which 47 per cent of French non-Western European exports went in 1980 (see Table 8.5). Most of these sales were tied to political trade deals and did not reflect increased competitiveness. Both the French and the UK industries have been active in demanding curbs on Japanese imports into Europe.

The UK

The UK machine tool industry's problems are symptomatic of the relatively poor performance of the country's engineering industries in the post-war period. The machine tool industry faced a slower rate of growth of domestic demand for its products than its main competitors and, apart from the government subsidised aerospace and defence industries, a market that placed less emphasis on technological sophistication. Like the rest of the engineering industry, the machine tool industry historically relied on captive, relatively unsophisticated Commonwealth markets until these were also lost during the 1960s. The industry was, however, responsive to the advent of NC machine tools, particularly in relation to the aircraft industry, and the UK was amongst the initial leaders in the diffusion of NC machine tools.[11] However, having tooled up for these machines, the machine tool industry faced great reluctance from other engineering sectors to purchase NC tools. From the mid-1960s the UK motor industry, traditionally one of the largest customers for machine tools, entered a decade of decline (see Chapter 5, Section 3). In the absence of sufficient domestic demand, the industry found it increasingly difficult to adjust to more open competition in the 1970s and to meet the NC revolution and Japanese competition in the early 1980s. World market share continued to fall, imports took an increasing share of the domestic market as in France, production continued to be geared to low unit value and tools like simple lathes (which in 1978 still accounted for 45 per cent of production by value compared to 20 to 30 per cent elsewhere), and productivity remained low (see Tables 1.2, 8.2, 8.3 and 8.7). By 1982 employment was only half that in the peak year of 1970.

The response of successive British governments was on the one hand to try to rationalise the structure of the industry to achieve larger units and on the other to promote R & D and product development. However, the fundamental reason for the poor competitiveness of the UK engineering industries, namely the weak skill base, goes back almost a century and has remained unresolved.[12] Although the many schemes to assist the development and diffusion of new products were fully taken up, they were unable to reverse the market situation facing the industry. Expensive and prolonged attempts to try to create in Alfred Herbert the largest machine tool firm in Europe were in the end a failure and the firm went into receivership in 1981.[13]

The US

The US machine tool industry had the unique advantage in the first half of this century of a much earlier diffusion of mass-produced consumer goods than Western Europe. This large domestic market, reinforced by wartime production during both world wars, continued to grow in the post-war period with the expansion of the aerospace and defence industries. Until 1970 imports were under 10 per cent of domestic demand (see Table 1.2). Although the US continued to export about 20 per cent of its production, its share of world trade has continued to fall (see Table 8.3), and in 1980 it ranked behind Germany, Japan, Italy, Switzerland and, very nearly, East Germany in the league of exporters. The industry has failed to rise to the Japanese challenge and recent surges of demand associated with the retooling of the automobile industry for downsized cars have sucked in imports, which now account for nearly 30 per cent of the market. A number of US firms have pulled out of production in continental Europe and there is growing pressure for tighter controls on Japanese imports. Apart from government support of the aerospace and defence industries, there has not been any assistance to the machine tool industry.

Japan

The Japanese machine tool industry has pursued a strikingly successful strategy in the last decade, rising to second place after West
Germany in exporting and third place after West Germany and the
US in production. In the production of NC machine tools the
Japanese are already world leaders (see Table 8.1). The industry grew
up in tandem with the rapidly growing motor car, consumer durable
and light engineering industries. This is reflected in its dominant
product strategy, which was never deflected away from smaller
general-purpose machines towards the large sophisticated machines
produced by others. This route, rather than the trickle down from
advanced machines, turned out to be the key to achieving the
widespread diffusion of NC machine tools. The Japanese industry
identified NC machine tools and NC machining centres as the basic
machine tools for general metal-working automation and set out to
produce them in volume. Currently 50 per cent of its production is
in NC machine tools and forecast to rise to over 70 per cent by
1985–6. The lower unit prices of Japanese NC lathes in Table 8.1
reflects both the smaller size of these machines and the efficiency
advantage from large-scale production.

The industry in Japan, unlike most other countries, is dominated
by relatively large companies. Median plant size is over 1,000
employees. Many of these companies began machine tool production
for their own use. There are many independent Japanese machine
tool producers, but many are also part of the larger Japanese industrial groups. This was important in bringing them together with
electronics firms within the group to integrate and develop advanced
NC control systems. Fijitsu Fanuc quickly came to dominate the
market for NC control units, and is currently holding over 50 per
cent of the world market. The Japanese machine tool producers
are also amongst the leading firms in developing new levels of factory
automation from flexible manufacturing systems to full so-called
unmanned factories. The proportion of resources devoted to R & D
is higher than elsewhere and the rapidly growing patenting performance in the US (see Table 8.8) reveals a continuing effort to become
world leaders in automated manufacturing technology.

The Japanese machine tool industry has rapidly gained a substantial share of world trade in the last decade (see Table 8.3). This
is particularly impressive when it is realised that 60 per cent of their
exports in 1980 were NC lathes and NC machining centres. The value
of Japanese exports of these two products alone exceeds the total
exports of machine tools from the US, Italy and the UK. This shows

Table 8.8 Machine tool patents granted in the US, 1966–81*

	Patents granted				Shares (%)			
	1966	*1971*	*1976*	*1981*	*1966*	*1971*	*1976*	*1981*
US								
Companies	1,170	1,406	744	281				
Individuals	410	494	339	1,143				
Foreign								
Germany	129	262	152	193	29.6	28.2	23.3	27.8
Japan	28	124	131	160	6.4	13.3	20.1	23.0
UK	98	135	78	67	22.5	14.5	12.0	9.6
France	45	85	52	32	10.3	9.1	8.0	4.6
Switzerland	26	55	36	27	6.0	5.9	5.5	3.9
Sweden	32	54	42	25	7.3	5.8	6.4	3.6
Italy	12	32	22	25	2.8	3.4	3.4	3.6
Other	66	182	139	166	15.1	19.6	21.3	23.9
Total foreign	436	929	652	695	100.0	100.0	100.0	100.0

* US SIC 354, numbers of patents granted in each year.

Source: Compiled from data supplied by the US Office of Technology Assessment and Forecast, Washington DC, to the Science Policy Research Unit, University of Sussex.

the degree to which the Japanese have focused their export strategy on these key products, for which a number of years there were few direct equivalents available in Europe or the US.

As with most other successful Japanese industries the government played an extremely important role in the early years, by protecting the home market with high tariffs and capital controls, by monitoring the licensing of foreign technology, and through various schemes to subsidise R & D. This continues to the present day with a seven year MITI-sponsored programme for machine tools incorporating lasers.[14] Probably more important, many of the customer industries, including the motor car, motor car components, machinery and electronics industries, have, at different times, been the beneficiaries of schemes to promote the acquisition of new machinery. Apart from very specialised machinery, there is little chance of selling into Japan where extremely close working relations exist between machine tool manufacturers and customers, and imports continue to be negligible (see Table 1.2). However, the major government action in relation to exports was in administering a price cartel for the US and Canadian markets since 1978 and for the European market after 1981. In the face of this situation, not only have Japanese machine tool firms prospered but almost all of them are now forming links with producers in the US and Europe for local production, either on a joint-venture or licence basis. A similar pattern is developing in robots.

8.4 Adjustment paths, policy choices and strategies for the future

We have seen that national machine tool industries have followed quite different paths of development, with varying degrees of success at different times. In the 1920s the US machine tool industry expanded at the time when the US developed a world lead in the mass production of consumer goods and in the scientific management of large complex organisations. Both of these developments had to wait until after the Second World War to take off in Europe. During that time the orientation of the US industry shifted towards the more specialised needs of the growing aerospace industry, incorporating successive generations of numerical controls to cope with even more complicated machining operations. By the 1980s it became clear that the Japanese had developed a completely new state of the art of production management which turned many of the conventional wisdoms upside down.[15] This formed the basis of the Japanese challenge in many consumer goods in world markets (see the case of cars, Chapter 5). The Japanese also challenged the assumption that the widespread diffusion of NC machine tools could trickle down from specialised machine tools. The focus of the Japanese industry was instead to incorporate NC into the most important general-purpose machine tools used throughout the general engineering industry, namely lathes and machining centres. By doing so, it gained a world lead in these kinds of machine tools and caught the industries of other countries unprepared. But it also initiated the widespread diffusion of NC tools across sectors world-wide.

The German, Swedish and Swiss industries have maintained their world lead in the most advanced, high-quality machine tools because of the existence of a domestic engineering industry that also places great emphasis on these factors. The Italian industry, however, developed in the quite different circumstances of a uniquely dispersed network of small engineering firms relying on design flair, flexibility and low costs. These firms fed into a few large companies, such as Comau, specialising in custom-designing production systems which have been very successful in world markets. The Italian industry led the way towards a new vertically disintegrated division of labour in the machine tool industry now being followed by others. It was only able to do so on the basis of legislation enabling an exceptional industry association to channel credit to small-firm customers and that protected the domestic market. The UK and French industries never found the right strategy and were in different ways hampered by the characteristics of their domestic markets. Public policy initiatives directed towards defensive restructuring of the industry were in these circumstances bound to fail.

Apart from one or two areas, it has proven extremely difficult in this sector to find the right policy instruments to make a significant impact on the direction and competitiveness of this industry. The modest impact of government intervention reflects two principal factors. First, the machine tools industry is only part of a closely linked chain: in particular, intervention in the industry will fail if domestic demand is insufficient. Second, intervention in an industry consisting of many firms is in itself difficult. Direct restructuring efforts have not been successful and neither have subsidies for R & D and product development. What has been more significant was the creation of the right legal and fiscal framework where the industry could collectively organise its own 'private industrial policy'. The German industry association has a position defined by law in German society and the Italian association used the opportunities opened up by the Sabatini Law. In times of change both of these associations played an extremely important role in developing a consensus on the nature of the challenge being faced and in the Italian case devised a very successful set of instruments to bring change about. The domination of the French industry by four major companies with close direct contact with the government left no place for a strong industry association and in the UK the historical tradition of representing both manufacturers and importers left that industry association weak and ineffective.

Having successfully identified the product strategy that leads to a rapid diffusion of NC machine tools, the Japanese are now going on to integrate these and other basic elements of the automated manufacturing systems of the future. Thus it is no longer appropriate to think of the machine tool industry in isolation, since it provides only one of the elements, albeit a vital one, of such a system. This phase of the technology places even greater emphasis on the need for major customers to become involved as the designers and builders of these systems. While many large customer firms in France, Germany, Italy and Japan are doing so, it is quite against the tradition of 'arm's-length buying' from specialist suppliers in the US and the UK. The presence of such firms interacting with a less vertically integrated set of suppliers is more important than having large machine tool firms as such. For the machine tool industry in each country to go up-market to evade the Japanese challenge is not a realistic option in these circumstances. There is no doubt that there is a considerable learning process going on in Europe at the moment, with some European machine tool firms independently bringing out comparable equipment to the Japanese and others entering into joint ventures or licensing agreements with Japanese firms.

All the major European countries have come to the conclusion that a domestic presence in these manufacturing systems of the future is essential and that the domestic industry cannot be allowed to disappear in the short term. It is for this reason that, in the early 1980s pressure has come to be applied on the Japanese for some restraint on their exports. So far this has taken the form of price cartels administered by MITI. All such curbs have their limitations. This one gives the Japanese added profitability and slows down the diffusion of these machine tools in Europe. However, its major significance was to signal that the Japanese had to switch from direct exporting to local investment in Europe. This has begun and the presence of Japanese ventures in Europe should provide adequate competitive pressure on those European firms able to revise their product and production strategies in the next few years. Strong industry associations able to cover all the elements of automated production systems and not just machine tools would enhance this process and act as a focus for any government assistance.

Notes

1. See Hornby (1958).
2. See Daly and Jones (1980).
3. See Habbakkuk (1962), Saul (1960 and 1977), Rosenberg (1976), Clapham (1938), Rolt (1965), Floud (1976), and Kindleberger (1975).
4. For a history of NC technology, see Rendeiro (1983) and Real (1979).
5. See Dixon and Marsh (1978).
6. See Rendeiro (1983).
7. See Jacobsson (1982).
8. see Daly and Jones (1980), Prais *et al.* (1981), and Kindleberger (1975).
9. See Daly and Jones (1980) and Taranto *et al.* (1979).
10. See Rendeiro (1983).
11. See Nabseth and Ray (1974).
12. See Jones (1981) and Daly and Jones (1980).
13. See Daly (1981).
14. See Rendeiro (1983).
15. See Jones (1983) and Schonberger (1982).

References

Clapham, J. H. (1938), *An Economic History of Modern Britain, Machines and National Rivalries 1887–1914*, Cambridge University Press.

Daly, A., and Jones, D. T. (1980), 'The Machine Tool Industry in Britain, Germany and the United States', *National Institute Economic Review*, May.

Daly, A. (1981), 'Government Support for Innovation in the British Machine Tool Industry: A Case Study', in C. Carter, ed., *Industrial Policy and Innovation*, London: Heinemann.

Dixon, K., and Marsh, J. (1978). *The Microelectronic Revolution: A Brief Assessment of the Industrial Impact with a Selected Bibliography*, Birmingham: Technology Policy Unit, University of Aston.

Floud, R. (1976), *The British Machine Tool Industry 1850–1914*, Cambridge University Press.

Habbakkuk, H. J. (1962), *British and American technologies in the 19th Century*, Cambridge University Press.

Hornby, W. (1958), *History of the Second World War, Factories and Plant*, London: HMSO.

Jacobsson, S. (1982), 'Electronics and the Technology Gap: the case of Numerically Controlled Machine Tools', *IDS Bulletin*, Vol. 13, No. 2, Brighton: Institute of Development Studies.

Jones, D. T. (1981), 'Industrial Development and Economic Divergence', in M. Hodges and W. Wallace, eds, *Economic Divergence in the European Community*, London: George Allen & Unwin.

Jones, D. T. (1983), 'Technology and the UK Automobile Industry', *Lloyds Bank Review*, April.

Kindleberger, C. P. (1975), 'Germany's overtaking of England, 1806–1914', *Weltwirtschaftliches Archiv*, Vol. III, Nos. 2 and 3.

Nabseth, L., and Ray, G. (1974), *The Diffusion of New Industrial Processes: an International Study*, Cambridge University Press.

Prais, S. J., Daly, A., Jones, D. T., and Wagner, K. (1981), *Productivity and Industrial Structure*, Cambridge University Press.

Real, B. (1979), *Report of an Enquiry into the Machine Tool Industry*, Paris: OECD.

Rendeiro, J. O. (1983), *Policies for Change in the Machine Tool Industry in Portugal: a Study of Market Processes and Public Policies*, Brighton: Sussex European Research Centre, mimeo.

Rolt, L. T. C. (1965), *Tools for the Job*, London: Batsford.

Rosenberg, N. (1976), *Perspectives in Technology*, Cambridge University Press.

Saul, S. B. (1960), 'The American Impact on British Industry 1895–1914', *Business History*, Vol. III, No. 1.

Saul, S. B. (1977), 'The Mechanical Engineering Industries of Britain 1860–1914', in B. Supple, ed., *Essays in British Business History*, Oxford University Press.

Schonberger, R. J. (1982), *Japanese Manufacturing Techniques*, New York: Free Press.

Taranto, R., Franchini, M., and Maglia, V. (1979), *La Industria Italiana della Macchina Utensile*, Milan: Il Mulino.

9 SEMICONDUCTORS: EUROPE'S PRECARIOUS SURVIVAL IN HIGH TECHNOLOGY*

Giovanni Dosi

9.1 Semiconductors and the microelectronics revolution

From time to time scientific discovery produces a new technology with a potential for wide diffusion throughout the economy. Semiconductors—essentially a miniaturised way of controlling electrical circuits with great speed and accuracy and at falling cost—are such a technology, developed in the last thirty-five years. Many observers are likening the impact of semiconductors to that of such all-pervading innovations of the past as the steam engine, the internal combustion engine or the early stages of the production of electricity itself.

What is a semiconductor?

Semiconductors are materials (generally silicon, but germanium and gallium arsenide can also be used) with the property, in the right conditions, of acting alternatively as conductors, allowing electrical current to flow, or as insulators, cutting off the flow (see Marsh, 1981). The material can be used to control an input of electric power, thus transmitting coded signals to the piece of machinery, which may be a giant computer or a digital watch, in which it is embodied. In this function semiconductors replace the far larger, less reliable, much less rapid and much more expensive thermionic valve or tube.

The first stage in the application of semiconductor materials was the development around 1948 of the *transistor*, a tiny globule of treated semiconductor material whose main function is to amplify, or rectify, the electric current. The transistor is the basic building block.

The second landmark (around 1960) was the development of the *integrated circuit* (IC) which packs together on a single unit, the silicon chip, a number of connected transistors (or other components), to be used either to pass on the electric signals within the computer or other machine or to serve as memories, storing information.

---

* This chapter is a condensed, and partially updated, version of Dosi (1981a). See also a longer study, dealing at greater length with the theoretical issues of technological change, with a semiconductor case study, in Dosi (forthcoming).

The third stage (early 1970s) was the *microprocessor*, a still further miniaturisation linking together on a single chip the size of a button the logical (that is, arithmetical) functions of hundreds, or even thousands, of transistors as well as memory chips and other components. The advance made by the microprocessor is that its components include integrated circuits containing the programme instructions for performing the sequence of functions required.

The uses of semiconductors

These tiny semiconductor devices are incorporated in a great variety of electronic machines. The first (and still the most important) end-use of the semiconductor was in the refinement of the electronic computer (developed in the Second World War and then operated by great numbers of thermionic valves). Computers probably still account for somewhat near one-third of the total world use of semiconductor devices. The technological history of semiconductors is closely bound up with that of the computer. Semiconductor devices have by now allowed a computer the size of a small domestic refrigerator to do the work of the 30-ton computer which came into operation in the mid-1940s.

The second major end-use for the semiconductor device, accounting for maybe a sixth of the world market, is in a variety of consumer goods, radio and TV being probably the most important but extending also to pocket calculators, microwave ovens, refrigerators and washing machines, electronic games, electronic watches and many others. Roughly similar shares of the market are held by end-uses in industrial equipment—process control, product testing and now industrial robots—and by telecommunications equipment. Then comes office equipment of various kinds. One of the largest outlets in future—although so far quite small—is likely to be the incorporation of semiconductor devices at a number of control points in motor vehicles as well as in the increasing automation of vehicle production (see Chapter 5). The range of uses steadily widens as the product is improved and its cost reduced. It is not therefore surprising that the development of semiconductors is intimately bound up with the production and sales of the end-use appliances. The closeness of this inter-relationship has been a vital factor in the development of the whole electronics industry. While the chip is only a tiny piece of the machine or appliance in which it is embodied, accounting for only a fraction of the cost (some estimate an average for the electrical industry as a whole of about 5 per cent), it is its essential driving force—its 'brain'.

The world's semiconductor industry

Commercial production of semiconductors has taken root in three areas of the world (apart from the centrally planned economies which are not discussed here for lack of information): the US, Japan, and Western Europe (principally the UK, France, Germany, Italy and the Netherlands). Smaller-scale production is also carried on in other industrialised countries, largely by the firms from the major centres, while a number of other areas (notably South-East Asia) assemble under subcontract. Production is thus highly concentrated geographically: over half in the US, about a quarter in Japan and about a sixth in Western Europe. (Production of integrated circuits is even more concentrated in the US.) The most significant change in these proportions in the last decade has been Japan's increase in share.

World consumption of semiconductors is differently distributed: over 40 per cent in the US, and a quarter each in Western Europe and Japan (see Table 9.1). The US has an export surplus, Western Europe a considerable deficit, while Japan is enjoying a growing surplus.

Further, the bulk of production is heavily concentrated in a few major firms. About nine US firms, five Western European, and six Japanese make up the 'big league', accounting for over 70 per cent of production (1978 figures; see Table 9.2).

Distinctive characteristics of the industry

It is difficult to define semiconductors as an 'industry' in the old-fashioned sense. Quite a few of the major enterprises are giant concerns making a large range of electrical and electronic products (see Table 9.2). However, in several major firms and in most of the American ones, semiconductor production in 1978 exceeded one-fifth of total turnover (Table 9.2). For major producers in Western Europe, this figure is less than 5 per cent. Precise data on activity in the 'industry' are therefore not easily available; the statistics given here are largely compiled from a variety of company and consulting organisations' estimates, often differing in coverage and definition; they must be interpreted with caution.

The economic significance of the 'industry' does not lie in its size. Estimates for 1978 put total Western-world semiconductor output at little over $10,000 million[1] and employment at around 260,000—130,000 in the US (0.6 per cent of manufacturing employment), 30,000 in Japan (0.3 per cent), and 60,000 in Western Europe (less than 0.3 per cent).[2] The semiconductor industry is thus close to the smallest of the industries reviewed in this book.

Table 9.1 Estimates of major world markets for semiconductors, 1980–5

	All semiconductors				Integrated circuits			
	1980	1981†	1982‡	1985‡	1980	1981†	1982‡	1985‡
*In $ millions**								
North America	6,148	6,028	6,973	13,091	4,817	4,634	5,468	11,165
Western Europe	3,774	3,411	3,726	6,094	2,408	2,071	2,337	4,310
Japan	3,488	4,617	5,694	8,606	2,308	2,965	3,795	6,427
Rest of world	1,015	966	1,114	1,962	502	402	474	956
Total	14,425	15,022	17,507	29,753	10,035	10,072	12,074	22,858
In per cent								
North America	43	40	40	44	48	46	45	49
Western Europe	26	23	21	20	24	21	19	19
Japan	24	31	33	29	23	29	31	28
Rest of world	7	6	6	7	5	4	4	4
Total	100	100	100	100	100	100	100	100

* At current prices.
† Estimated.
‡ Forecast.

Source: Estimates in $ millions by Nomura Research Institute, quoted in *Electronics*, 13 January 1982, p. 151.

Table 9.2 Major world semiconductor producers, 1978*

	Country of ownership	Semiconductor (SC) turnover			Main areas of firm specialisation									
		Total[c] ($ million)	Share in total firm sales (%)	In-house consumption as (% of total SC)	S	D	O	T	C	P	I	H	E	M
Texas Instruments	US	1,292	51	87	S	D			C					
IBM	US	750	4	100		D	O		C					
Motorola	US	782	33[f]	5[i]	S			T	C					M
Nippon Electric (NEC)	Japan	581	20[f]	25[i]	S	D		T	C		I			
Philips[a]	Netherlands	500	3[f]	...[i]		D		T	C	P		H		
Hitachi[b]	Japan	450	6[f]	20[i]		D		T	C		I			
Fairchild[b]	US	389	73	2[i]	S				C					
Toshiba	Japan	386	7	15[i]	S	D		T	C		I			
National Semiconductor	US	364	51	93										
Siemens	Germany	300	2	..[i]	S	D	O		C		I			
Intel	US	298	75[f]	10[i]		D		T	C			H	E	M
Matsushita Electronics	Japan	232	3[f]	49[i]										
Western Electric	US	200	..[g]	100[i]					C					
Mitsubishi Electric	Japan	197	4[f]	9[i]		D		T	C		I			
ITT	US	170	1[h]	:		D		T	C			H		
Thomson-CSF	France	160	3	:		D		T	C			H	E	
AEG-Telefunken	Germany	150	3	:		D			C			H		
RCA	US	130	2	:		D			C			H		
SGS-Ates	Italy	120	100[f]	..[i]	S	D		T[j]	C					M[.]
Fujitsu	Japan	106	5[f]	47[i]	S	D		T	C		I			M[j]
Others (estimated)		(2,843)[d]												
Total		10,400[e]												

* See p. 214 for notes and source.

The industry's importance rests, rather, on its character as supplier and diffuser of a technologically vital input in a growing number of electronics and electronics-related industries and in industries which can use electronics as a minor but invaluable input. Hence—as in other high-technology industries—the growth of the industry depends on links between producers and end-users. The presence or absence of this 'synergy'—involving continuous close contact and feedback of innovations—do much to explain the differing patterns of development of the semiconductor industry in different parts of the world.

The industry's growth rate, from the beginning of commercial production around the 1950s, has been extremely rapid. From 1958 to 1976, US semiconductor production grew, in current terms, at about 18.5 per cent a year. Because prices fell vertiginously, increases in real terms exceeded 40 per cent a year (Table 9.3). Similar, if somewhat less rapid, growth rates were achieved in Western Europe. Growth was particularly fast in production of integrated circuits.

At the same time, continuous technical progress has meant a very rapid increase in labour productivity, but only modest increases in employment. In terms of *direct* employment, the industry cannot be expected to offer much significant contribution to the solution of the unemployment problem in the industrial West. The powerful employment effect is likely to be *indirect*, the consequence of the adoption of new products and new cost-reducing technologies in which semiconductors play a part.

A marked characteristic of the industry, helping to explain the dynamics of its structure, is the importance of technological

---

Notes to Table 9.2

Key to main areas of firm specialisation; S: Semiconductors; D: Data-processing, small and large computers; O: Office equipment; T: Telecommunications; C: Consumer electronics; P: Professional goods; I: Industrial electronics; H: Household electrical goods: E: Heavy electrical engineering; M: Military markets.

a Including Signetics (producing in the US).

b Taken over by Schlumberger (France) in 1979.

c Including in-house consumption.

d Major Western European firms included in this residual figure are (with nationality, semiconductor turnover and specialities): GEC (UK, $30 million, CIHEM); Plessey (UK, $20 million, TM); Semikron (Germany, $40 million, S); Ferranti (UK, $25 million, DTM). Major Japanese firms included in these figures are: Sharp ($37 million, C); Tokyo Sanyo ($23 million, C); Sony ($11 million, C).

e Total (excluding centrally planned economies) is taken from Table 2 of Dosi (1981a).

f As per cent of parent company.

g As per cent of total for American Telephone and Telegraph (ATT).

h As per cent of total for the group.

i Figure for 1980, calculated from Table 10.7.

j Specialisation of holding company (STET-IRI).

Source: (Except as otherwise specified above): Dosi (1981a), Tables 10, 14 and 24.

Table 9.3 US: production, price and productivity indices for semiconductors 1958-76 (1963 = 100)

Year	Shipments (constant prices)	Prices	Output per worker-hour*
1958	11	380	22
1965	246	54	217
1970	980	22	575
1972	2,174	18	1,235
1974	4,128	15	1,519
1976	5,424	12	2,912

* Value added at constant prices.

Source: Calculated from Dosi (1981a), Table 7.

capabilities, R & D and economies of scale in production. Labour productivity appears to be a direct logarithmic function of the cumulative volume of production: the well-known 'learning curve' effect. There is accordingly a very high degree of concentration: the four largest companies accounted in 1978 for one-third of world production and the ten largest for 55 per cent.[3] Thus barriers to entry are high except for radical innovators and large diversified companies already well established in related industries and with an existing capacity for advanced research. Company estimates (1979 figures) place the minimum viable level of production for a fairly complete range of semiconductor devices at around £70 to £80 million a year, the minimum investment required at £25 to £100 millions. Hence—and this is not peculiar to the semiconductor industry—international competition basically takes the form of a race between great firms. A place remains, however, for smaller enterprises specialising in a limited range of products, typically 'custom' devices suitable for a narrow range of applications, by contrast with the mass-market producers of standard devices.

Finally, although its structure has become more stable in recent years, the industry and its users face a continuous problem of adjustment to a fast-moving technology. There is every reason to suppose that the technological boundaries in electronics will continue to dominate investment (in both equipment and research) and the strategic decisions of producers and users.

9.2 The growth of Western Europe's technology lag

The birth of the industry is usually placed in 1948, when Shockley, Bardeen and Brittain at Bell Laboratories in the US developed the first transistor. It is reported that Philips developed its first transistor just a few weeks after Bell's announcement; but, in spite of the significant involvement of Philips and Siemens in the early stages of the new technology, it was in the US that the bridges between scientific research and commercial exploitation were first crossed. The commercial leadership then established in the US has been maintained *vis-à-vis* Europe.

The American lead

The capacity to bridge the divide between pure science, applied science and technology has always been strong in the US. In the 1950s, Bell laboratories accounted for about half of the major product and process innovations in semiconductors, and the very big established electrical firms, General Electric, Westinghouse and RCA, for more than a quarter. On the other hand, commercial exploitation and diffusion have often occurred through new firms (in many cases spin-offs from established companies) which have become the industry leaders, while the big electrical firms have performed poorly. The entry of new firms was possible because in the early years development depended on people rather than expensive equipment. When increases in capital requirements began to create barriers to entry, the number of spin-off companies progressively declined.

The second reason for the US lead was that the Federal government, particularly through military and aerospace programmes, was heavily involved from the beginning in research-financing and semiconductor-purchasing. In the mid-1950s, military-related demand accounted for around half of the total production of semiconductors (Dosi, 1981a, Table 8). The proportion has since fallen to not much more than a tenth as civilian users have grown.

Military and space programmes made a crucial contribution in helping to define the specific path—or trajectory—of technical change that the semiconductor industry was to follow in the US, hence in the world.[4] On the supply side, these programmes set precisely defined directions for R & D; stimulated the exploration of alternative paths of technical change and its pursuit at the fastest rate possible; subsidised expansion of production capacity to reach target levels necessary for defence needs; and encouraged the standardisation of production. On the demand side, these programmes served to guarantee a future market for the appropriate products, assumed much of the burden of risk, and contributed to rising productivity.

Very often, the history of military-sponsored research shows an impressive number of failures. The success of the military-related 'synergy' in semiconductors can be attributed to the coincidence, early on at least, between military and civilian technological trajectories and their many common requirements, especially in the development of computers. The military aerospace role was decisive in establishing the early American lead, albeit a high cost. Innovation and diffusion were thereafter to become increasingly the product of market forces. The expansion and technical progress of the industry brought about, and were promoted by, the dramatic and sustained fall in semiconductor prices in the highly competitive US market: prices were reduced, it is estimated, by over 75 per cent in 1963–70 and by almost a half in 1970–6 (see Table 9.3).

The European lag

Several factors help to explain why Western European semiconductor production in 1978 was little more than a quarter of the value of that in the US. In the first place, military and public-sector procurement was far less significant than in the US. Nevertheless, military purchases had some importance in the UK and France and nationalistic public procurement policies—notably for telecommunications, aerospace and computers—have been favoured in all major countries.

Despite pioneering research in a few companies, the development of the semiconductor industry in Western Europe was slower and more haphazard than in the US. The large European companies entered the field at different times and, with a few exceptions, devoted comparatively few resources to semiconductors in the 1950s and 1960s. Since most of them were involved in consumer electronics (Philips in the Netherlands, Thomson in France) or heavy electrical engineering (Siemens in Germany, AEI in the UK), they tended to neglect, relatively, the military and computer-related applications where the greatest technical advances were being made. This is illustrated by the large difference in the pattern of end-uses of semiconductors between the US market, where computers are relatively important, and the Western European market where consumer products are most important (see Table 9.4). This contrast also reflects the differing promptness of end-users to embody the new technologies in their production.

In general, the European firms tended from the beginning to follow a pattern of technological imitation, with significant time lags, of up to three or four years, against the US in first commercial production. These lags have not changed much over time and help to explain the relative absence of new spin-off firms from established firms. The innovation process tends to be cumulative, in the sense that the probability of advance is likely to be proportional to the

218   *Giovanni Dosi*

Table 9.4 End-uses of semiconductors in US and Western European
markets, 1978 (per cent)

	US	Western Europe
Computers	56	20
Consumer products	9	30
Automotive	2	
Industrial	11	18
Communications	9	14
Government	13	5
Distributor	*	13
Total	100	100

* Attributed to estimated end-user.

Source: Dosi (1981a), Table 4.

already occupied *vis-à-vis* the technological frontier. This has
reinforced the relative stability of European lags. In fact, European semiconductor producers have found themselves running
hard to stay in the same position relative to the fast-moving
Americans.

Five major producers now dominate the Western-European-owned
industry (see Table 9.2 for major characteristics of these firms and
Table 9.5 for the evolution of their shares in Western European
markets). Siemens and Philips have clearly emerged as Europe's
strongest semiconductor producers. They are in the same league as
the major American and Japanese producers.

Philips, by far the largest European-owned firm, is based in the
Netherlands but tends to operate as a national firm in each of the
countries in which it, or its subsidiaries, are established: the Netherlands, Germany, France, the UK, the US and elsewhere. In 1978 it
held almost 20 per cent of the total Western European market, but
its market shares have fallen since the 1960s in the face of US competition. It is on the technological frontier in many fields, especially
as a result of huge efforts to improve its technological capability in
integrated circuits, but Philips remains relatively weak in some
crucial new areas such as microprocessors and metal-oxide silicon
(MOS) devices. Although Philips firms in the UK, Germany and
France (but not in the Netherlands) have received considerable
official help, the proportion of government support in Philips'
R & D expenditure has probably been smaller than for other European firms. It has basically progressed independently of governments.

Table 9.5 Share of major Western-European-owned firms in Western European semiconductor markets (per cent)

	All Western Europe	Germany		France		Italy	UK	
	1978	1968	1978	1968	1978	1978	1962	1977
Philips*	19	25	15	22	14	10	49†	18
Siemens	11	22	21	—	—	5	—	—
AEG-Telefunken	6	9	9	—	—	3	—	—
SGS-Ates	5	6	3	7	6	19	—	3
Thomson-CSF	4	2	9	20	16	5	—	—
Ferranti							10‡	1
GEC	55			18	4	58	7‡	6
Other non-US-owned firms								8
US-owned firms		36	43	33	60		34	64
Total	100	100	100	100	100	100	100	100

* Valvo in Germany, RTC in France and, from 1968, Mullard in the UK.
† Production in ASM, a joint venture of Mullard (Philips) and GEC, entirely taken over by Mullard in 1968.
‡ Production in AEI, purchased by GEC in 1967.

Source: Dosi (1981a), Table 15.

Because of its size and experience in the field since the beginning of the industry, Siemens would probably have been able to undertake the cost of expanding and improving its semiconductor activities alone. In fact it has had considerable support from the German government; yet even now it still lags behind in integrated circuits and microprocessors.

Thomson-CSF, AEG-Telefunken (Germany) and SGS-Ates (part of STET, the Italian telecommunications holding company within IRI) make up the remaining three major European producers, with far smaller output levels. After these five, with even smaller output levels, come a number of more specialised firms: for instance, GEC, Plessey and Ferranti in the UK, and Semikron in Germany.

The most immediate problem for many of the existing European firms remains that of survival in the markets where they are already operating. This depends on ability to finance both heavy research and increasing investment when most companies can expect to make losses in semiconductors for a considerable time. (Philips is said to be one of the few European firms to have made profits on semiconductors.) This survival problem can be illustrated with the emergence and diffusion of integrated circuits from the mid-1960s. Europe's lag was very long and its efforts to catch up particularly expensive, while US competition was bringing prices down. European firms had a choice between withdrawing from production or trying to seize a share in the new market despite the costs and risks. Shorter-run profitability criteria would have suggested withdrawal. Thus GEC is hardly to be blamed by sheer profitability criteria for leaving the standard-device market in 1970-1. Thomson partly withdrew and would have withdrawn further had not the French government intervened.

On the other hand, Siemens and Philips, reluctant to retreat from a rapidly expanding market and with the advantages of size, vertical integration and technological inter-relatedness among their various activities, *were* prepared to move into the new field despite the unlikelihood of early profit. It is likely that decisions to stay in or leave semiconductor production were also influenced by the national environment in which firms operated: the far-sightedness of financial markets, the role of banks and relationships with the labour force and government.

The changing national and international structure of the industry

Rapid technical change has had a major influence on the structure of the industry. Vertically integrated companies, whose oligopolistic market power is based on the success of older technologies, have had their position eroded by the emergence of new vertical integrations based on new technologies. The large electrical and electronic groups (including Philips and Siemens) have struggled to maintain their position against US producers of final products (computer and electrical manufacturers such as IBM, Honeywell, Sperry-Univac and Xerox) which tried to move upstream into semiconductors in the late 1970s. As part of this process there has been a wave of acquisitions of small American semiconductor producers in which European and Japanese companies have also played a role.[5] The most prominent European purchases were Philips' acquisition of Signetics (US) in 1975 and Schlumberger's (France) acquisition of Fairchild Camera and Instrument (US) in 1979. The reverse aspect of this trend is the expansion of semiconductor firms downstream into user industries (such as the entry of Texas instruments into computers and watches).

Given the fast-widening range of applications, this trend towards vertical integration is likely to continue. The next drive will probably involve the motor car industry which, with its enormous potential demand, may well rival computers as the major end-user for semiconductors.

American leadership in the new technology has naturally led to significant trade surpluses in semiconductors throughout the history of the industry. At the same time the US lead and the unification of the world market were also promoted by very substantial American direct investments abroad, particularly in Western Europe. In 1976, for instance, US-owned firms accounted for something around one-third of Western European production.[6] Through investment, the more advanced foreign firm pre-empts the market for the advanced products which national companies cannot yet produce. Although this increases the difficulties for national firms seeking to imitate, this process could also benefit end-users. It does not appear that the transfer of semiconductor technology to Europe by US investment has so far been overwhelming. Most of the R & D has remained in the US (though ITT is a noted exception). So, normally, has production of the most advanced devices, with some exceptions (such as National Semiconductor's production in Scotland).

In general, the evidence suggests that the net consequences of direct US investment in Europe have been negative for European national industries. This conclusion cannot, of course, be generalised. In some other industries, competition from foreign-owned firms has stimulated national producers to become more aggressive and innovative. In semiconductors some recent trends in European firms' strategies suggest that competitive reactions have been aroused.

In addition to direct investment by US firms in Europe, a certain number of joint ventures has been established, notably between US and French firms, which have largely been exchanges of European cash for US technology. Licensing of US technology to European firms has also developed in recent years: for instance, Thomson with Motorola and Intel's deals with a few European producers. Like joint ventures, licensing is in part a reflection of financial constraints on growth in the US.

In general, however, the various forms of internationalisation involving the European and US industry all seem to reflect a defensive strategy on the part of the Europeans. Such strategies may improve the competitiveness of some European companies, but they are unlikely to bridge completely the technological gap.

A new challenge from Japan

The recent emergence of Japan as a major semiconductor producer puts a new pressure on the Western European industry. Since the mid-1960s, when the Japanese industry was if anything behind Europe's, a huge effort has been made to close the technological gap with the US. By the end of the 1970s, Japan had generally caught up in many areas, having gained a pronounced lead in some of these. (Japan has notably come to dominate the world market for 64K Random Access Memories, the first generation of very large-scale integrated circuits which have only been in commercial production since 1981.) Japan still imports quite heavily, but has had a growing trade surplus in semiconductors since 1977. While the US and Western Europe have been through a comparative slump in electronics since 1979, Japan managed to double its output of semiconductors in the space of just three years (in 1978–81).[7]

By 1982 the share of the Western European market that Japanese exports had come to enjoy was approaching 10 per cent (compared to 2 per cent in 1978). Japan's rapid advance has, in a short space of time, created a new set of flows of foreign investment and, to a lesser extent, technology licensing. First, important foreign investment initiatives have been taken by the major Japanese producers in both the US and Western European markets. This has been partly to pre-empt some of the protective measures that have recently been taken in other industries (in cars for instance; see Chapter 5, Section 2); and partly to overcome the EEC's Common External Tariff on semiconductors (see Section 3 below). Japanese production—for the most part assembly rather than fabrication—is under way or envisaged by: NEC in Scotland and Eire (and the US), Hitachi and Toshiba in Germany, and Fujitsu in Eire. Secondly, Japanese firms are sometimes prepared to license production; Toshiba for instance, licensed production of certain advanced devices (CMOS circuits) to SGS in 1981. Finally, major US producers (plus Siemens, so far the only Western European firm) are envisaging joining Texas Instruments—till recently the only foreign semiconductor producer in Japan—by setting up production in Japan.[8]

9.3 Public policies towards semiconductors

The arguments for a national semiconductor industry

The key argument in favour of public support to create a national competitive semiconductor industry concerns the relationship between technical progress in semiconductors and progress in many end-uses for these devices. This 'synergy' is undoubtedly of great importance where technology is fast moving, but could it not be achieved if users bought the most advanced devices on the international market? Is it possible for a country to specialise in downstream applications by relying solely on the market mechanism?

On the one hand, it is true that the market mechanism is central to the transmission of technical change. On the other hand, the increasing embodiment in the integrated circuit of functions specific to a particular end-use inhibits the efficacy of the international market system. Trading at arm's length, especially across national frontiers (more so across the Atlantic), limits the possibilities of establishing a close producer–user relationship. Certain non-market factors, such as the opportunity for the flow of technical knowledge, technicians and scientists between producers and users, are very important. One obvious example is the effectiveness of the geographical concentration of competing firms in California's Silicon Valley. The efforts of diversified electronics firms to move up-stream into semiconductors can be seen as an effort to internalise within the firm the potential technological advantages which the invisible hand of the market cannot transform into tradable commodities.

There are examples, particularly in small countries, of successful electronics-based industries with no significant local production of semiconductor components, for example, Norwegian robotics. The argument, however, applies with force to big countries with a large variety of inter-related electronics-based producers and great opportunities for downstream diffusion.

Other arguments of a more or less political nature may also apply, such as the strategic importance of the industry for military objectives, for national prestige or for securing technological autonomy.

Finally, there are conflicting views on the benefits of local production by foreign firms as an alternative to an expensively created indigenous industry. In some respects, US direct investment has made positive contributions to the diffusion of the most advanced technologies. Yet foreign investment may be a second-best choice, involving slower feedbacks of innovative stimuli. Whether the first-best alternative is practicable is, of course, a different matter.

The growth of Western European intervention

Western European policy-making has had to face two particular problems. The first is that of deciding on the allocation of support between semiconductor production and the production of final products, notably computers, given the inter-relationship between them. The second problem is to distinguish between the paths that are already being followed by the existing producers and the long-term interests of the national economy. In general, the Western European solution to both problems has been support policies designed to reinforce the existing strategies of the firms. This has meant, for the most part, a certain concentration of public support on computers rather than components. Only in the mid-1970s—notably in Britain, Germany and France—was substantial active support given to semiconductors.

Policies have tended to be based on two connected assumptions: that it is impossible for governments to tell firms what they should do; and that the objectives of the firms can be taken as coinciding with the national interest. It may be that no other course was possible, but the support of existing strategies of firms has so far done little more than hold steady Western Europe's technological gap, as well as the gaps between the European producers themselves.

Western European policies have passed through three stages. Up to the mid-1960s non-intervention on the whole prevailed, apart from defence-related R & D and some preference for national producers in government procurement. From the mid-1960s to the mid-1970s, official interest in the development of computers, particularly in the UK and France, led, rather as a by-product, to some interest in support for research in semiconductors. In neither stage does it appear that public policies had a significant effect on the semiconductor firms' innovative capacities. From the mid-1970s, however, as the pervasive effect of progress in semiconductors became more obvious, official support started to focus on technological inter-relatedness within the whole area of electronics. In all four main producing countries, specific support for semiconductors began to gain ground.

Instruments of government support

European governments have used a variety of instruments to support the semiconductor industry. By far the most important and the most commonly employed is the support of *research and development* activities by subsidies, research contracts, low interest loans, and research work in public institutes and agencies. In the UK and France, military research establishments (in France, also the tele-communications and nuclear research establishments) have played a part in the development of semiconductors. In Germany, and to a lesser extent Italy, publicly sponsored research and advisory organisations have been active. The effectiveness of public support to R & D has been much discussed. If the aim was to narrow the technological gap with the US, European policies seem fairly weak: first, because firms have tended to pursue research strategies based on their existing strengths and markets; secondly, because subsidies can be substitutes for private financing, adding little to what the firms would have achieved without them.

Investment grants and subsidies have played a certain part, especially in the UK. But mostly such financial supports are linked either with general investment incentives or with regional policies, not specifically to semiconductors or electronics. Regional subsidies have played an important role in the substantial US and Japanese foreign investments in electronics that have been made in Scotland's 'Silicon Glen', although some of these projects might well have been undertaken in a different UK locality without such subsidies.

Controls on *inward foreign investment*, mainly from the US and Japan, have played a role for France. But Germany, Italy and the UK have in practice adopted a non-discriminatory policy, although some earlier schemes excluded foreign firms from the benefits of public support.

Government purchases, both for military and telecommunications uses, have been effectively directed towards local suppliers in the UK and France, although less in Germany and Italy. But their influence has been small compared with the US experience. Moreover, the share of public procurement, accounting for about 20 per cent of the market in the major countries, has been falling.

Tariff and non-tariff barriers do not in themselves appear to have much affected imports into Europe, at least for the more advanced products. However, the EEC Common External Tariff, at 17½ per cent, is the highest among industrial market economies (compare the US at 6 per cent). The Community, unlike Japan and the US, did not agree any reductions in the Tokyo Round negotiations. National technical standards, especially for telecommunications and military components, may also act as a form of protection. It is claimed, too, that in France and Italy import licensing represents a particular barrier.

The *promotion of structural change* in semiconductors has been particularly important in France where official policies have long favoured mergers in a variety of industries. The government played an active role in the concentration of all French-owned semiconductor production in the Thomson Group by 1978, and again in financing two joint ventures with US companies (St Gobain-Pont-à-Mousson with National Semiconductors and Matra with Harris), in both cases requiring a 51 per cent share for the French partners. Public plans for specialisation in French semiconductors became even more explicit after the socialist electoral victory of 1981. Thomson and Matra were both taken into public control and designated as the two poles of the industry. Matra has concluded a new joint venture with Intel (US), while Thomson was negotiating at the end of 1982 to take over St Gobain's joint venture with National Semiconductors. French electronics ambitions took on a European colour in 1982 when Thomson, with full government backing, bid to take over Grundig, the German electronic consumer-good producer. However, this bid, which immediately concerned the organisation of Europe's television industry but had longer-term implications for European electronics as a whole, was disqualified by Germany's Cartel Office in early 1983. Acquisition of AEG-Telefunken's radio and television interest was a consolation prize for Thomson and the government.[9]

The British government followed no explicit structural policy until the controversial establishment of INMOS in 1978. INMOS was set up and financed by the government's National Enterprise Board in a large and ambitious attempt to return the UK to the fold of producers of standard devices. This was to be achieved by leapfrogging into production of very large-scale integrated circuits. The outcome cannot be known at the very least until INMOS sales begin in volume (expected in 1983). The risks are high but, given the remarkable staff recruited on both sides of the Atlantic, appear worthwhile. Previously, attention has been mainly devoted to computers, where the government played a role in the series of mergers that led to the constitution of ICL (International Computers Limited), the main UK producer of computers.

In Italy, the most important action has been the purchase by STET of SGS (originally a joint venture of Olivetti, Telettra and Fairchild) and a number of other electronics companies. STET's acquisition must be seen primarily as part of the strategy of a company acting to a great extent independently of official industrial policies. It is, however, doubtful whether any private company would have been willing or able to take over SGS and cover its persistent losses.

No significant structural policy has been formulated in Germany, and no clear need for one appears to have arisen.

A comparison by countries

While national policies have tended to follow similar defensive and imitative objectives, there have been impressive differences in their comprehensiveness, their timing, the initial structural conditions which policy-makers faced, and the size of intervention.

A summary of the limited and not always comparable information available on financial support programmes affecting semiconductors is given in Table 9.6.

Germany emerges as the best placed. Public support programmes for electronics in general—in money terms at least as large as in the UK, France or Italy—have also been more comprehensive, covering data processing, components, applications and software. The importance of the interaction between producers and users seems to have been recognised earlier than elsewhere. German programmes for data processing have, since 1969, given significant support to semiconductors which benefited after 1974 from a specific plan. Moreover, the industrial environment was favourable: the specialisations of the major manufacturers were already well established and Siemens was able, thanks to its vertical integration, to internalise improvements in semiconductor technologies. The companies were also willing to take their own risks: one estimate is that the German firms financed 60 to 80 per cent of their R & D compared with only about 20 to 30 per cent in France. Germany's strategy has been a rapid imitation of new technologies and a quick diffusion in applications, rather than ambitious leapfrogging. Significant results have been achieved and the imitation lag is probably somewhat shorter in Germany than elsewhere in Europe.

The *UK* policy has until recently concentrated, not unsuccessfully, on computers. It may be that public support could have done little for semiconductors in view of the great number of rather small producers mainly interested in their own special applications. For instance, the £10 million available under the 1973 Microelectronics Support Scheme, restricted to UK firms and to projects which were regarded as unlikely to be undertaken without support, was not fully used up for six years. Later programmes were developed on a larger

Table 9.6 Government support for the semiconductor industry
in the UK, France, Germany and Italy, 1964–82[a]

	Period	Amount (US $ m)
UK		
1. Microelectronic support scheme	1973–9	21
2. Component Industry Scheme[b]	1977–	10
3. Microelectronic Support Scheme[cd]	1978–	111
4. INMOS	1978–82	101
5. Microprocessor Application Project[cd]	1978–82	111
6. Support for microelectronics under Product and Process Development Scheme[d]	1979	54
7. Other (annual average)[e]	1964–77	2–4 p.a.
8. Military (annual average) (estimated)	1970–9	4–6 p.a.
9. Non-business institutions and universities (annual average) (estimated)	1966–78	4–6 p.a.
Germany[f]		
1. BMFT support	1969–72	23
2. BMFT Electronic Component Programme	1973–8	118
	1979–82	74
3. 2nd Data Processing Programme	1969–76	32
4. 3rd Data Processing Programme	1977–8	n.a.
5. Synchroton Radiation Project	1981–2	26
6. Military and space	1964–8	n.a.
	1969–76	33
	1977–82	n.a.
7. German Research Association	1964–76	22
France		
1. 1st Plan Calcul[g]	1967–70	36
2. 2nd Plan Calcul[g]	1971–5	33
3. Plan Circuits Intégrés	1977–80	132
4. Non-business institutions and government laboratories (annual average) (estimated)	1964–75	10 p.a.
	1976–82	n.a.
5. Military	1964–82	n.a.
Italy		
1. Technological Evolution Fund		
(a) grants	1968–78	1
(b) loans	1968–78	4
2. Electronics Plan (Law 675)[h]		
(a) grants	1980–2	96
(b) loans	1980–2	60
3. Military	1964–82	n.a.
4. National Research Council project on solid state physics	1964–82	n.a.

[a] Figures cover grants, subsidies and transfers on capital account unless otherwise stated. Regional incentives are excluded, also low-interest loans except in Italy.

[b] Total scheme involves $40 million, of which amount shown in the table went to semiconductors.

[c] Amounts are estimates of what the Conservative government might retain from schemes introduced by their predecessors.

(Notes and source continued opposite.)

scale, but the potential breakthrough in semiconductors came only in 1978 with the establishment of INMOS.

Public intervention in *France* played a decisive role in the survival of the semiconductor industry, particularly through a well-articulated structural policy. But it failed in the more ambitious task of increasing its relative technological and market strength. French experience illustrates the difficulty of identifying and enforcing the national interest as against the preferred strategies of the firms. The actual policies and their outcome can be represented as the result of a stalemate between the government's view of the national interest, which it seldom has the power to enforce, and the conflicting interests of the companies. Often a government has been forced into agreements on support strategies which are compromises between the divergent private interests.

There are, however, signs of a clear bid to catch up with the world technology leaders. Thomson has become increasingly committed to semiconductor development. The massive government programme for modernising and expanding its telecommunications services and the plan for 'Informatisation de la Société' have given a push towards technological progress in the whole area, with a potentially profitable market secured by government procurement policy.

An explicit policy for *Italian* electronics has appeared only more recently, in the Industrial Restructuring, Rationalisation and Development Law of 1977. This law provides support (for 1978–82) for a dozen industrial sectors regarded either as technologically strategic or as facing strong adjustment pressures. In semiconductors (within the electronics sector) the central objective seems to be to strengthen the capacity of SGS-Ates. Although the amounts of money involved are substantial, effective decisions on the allocation and management of funds appear to have been delayed by conflicts within the administration, as well as by a lack of civil service expertise in the execution of industrial policies. By early 1981, no money is believed to have reached the industry. Consequently, the results cannot yet be judged, but the support could somewhat reinforce technological and manufacturing capability (already fairly good by European standards) in SGS-Ates.

d There may be some overlapping in these items.

e Includes funds from the Advanced Computer Technology Project of 1964.

f Figures include R & D performed by industry and by other institutions.

g Includes expenditure on other electronic components, but the bulk of the sums shown are believed to be attributed to semiconductors.

h Grants, subsidies and other transfers to the business sector only. It should be noted that these figures refer to proposed and approved amounts, which differ from the actual cash available at the time of writing.

Source: Dosi (1981b), Table 8.1.

The development of the Japanese semiconductor industry

It is instructive, if not too encouraging, for European producers, to compare the experience of Japan's semiconductor industry with Western Europe's. The similarity lies in the common objective of reducing the technological lag with the US; the differences lie in Japan's success in virtually eliminating this lag and the planning philosophy that helped achieve this. (For a more detailed account of the development of the Japanese industry—which, however, gives greater emphasis to the role of private enterprise than the following —see Chapter 10, Section 4.)

Briefly, it appears that the successful development of the Japanese industry is due to two factors: first, to the aggressive and far-sighted technological and marketing strategies shared by the major competing companies; secondly, to the fact that these strategies could be harmonised with the national objectives of policy-makers. There was a strikingly effective relationship between the firms and the government (notably MITI). In this environment, 'planning' appears less as the exercise of government authority than as the result of a natural harmony between social groups and individual decisions. To a lesser extent these Japanese characteristics are shared by West Germany, but much less so by the other major Western economies.

The instruments devised by the Japanese government have essentially taken the form of removing constraints hindering the national long-term objective adopted by the firms of catching up with the US industry. The main instruments included: (a) very restrictive controls on foreign investment (formally until 1974, informally thereafter); (b) official monitoring of the terms of licence agreements, which were required to be made available not only to a single firm but to the whole industry; (c) import controls (formally ended in 1974); and (d) the setting of technological targets and establishment of research facilities to achieve them (including research centres with joint public and private participation).

To summarise, Japanese policy was characterised by: a determination to improve the country's position in the international division of labour, rather than to accept an inferior position as inevitably given by market forces; a willingness to render privately profitable what was considered to be good for the country; and the acceptance of competition as a positive stimulus as long as it operated among national companies in the domestic market or with foreign companies in foreign markets.

9.4 The future for semiconductors in Western Europe

The important constraints that Western European firms and governments are likely to face in the future include the following:

—The rapid pace of technical progress which has so far given a cumulative advantage to producers already on the technological frontier (US firms, but also now the Japanese), and the continuing trend towards vertical integration between producers and users. These maintained formidable barriers to the entry of any but very large firms, except as specialists in a small part of the field. Reducing the lags behind the leaders will be no easier than it was in the past.

—The progressive unification of the world market, leading not only to a more or less unified price structure but also to rapid international integration of the industry. Although technological innovation will continue, the structure of the world industry—the newly emerging electronic-based oligopoly—may now begin to stabilise. None the less, increasing Japanese investment in Europe (to the extent governments permit this) and Japanese efforts to conquer a larger share of the world market are beginning to impose a heavy strain on the European firms.

—The great difficulties that national European governments have so far had in formulating and carrying out active policies comparable with the Japanese-styled strategy, a strategy distinguished by a wide but consistent battery of policy instruments, a rigorous definition of targets and a powerful commitment of government and firms to common objectives.

Three possible scenarios for the future of the Western European semiconductor industry may be suggested. These represent a continuum of possibilities rather than the only alternatives. Each assumes a continuing trend towards vertically integrated pan-electronic enterprises, in which semiconductor capabilities would represent a technologically crucial part.

Scenario A: a combined European offensive

The essence of this scenario is a substantial measure of cooperation among the Western European semiconductor firms and among their governments to establish a combined European strategy. It would also necessarily involve the wide range of producers of electronics-based products.

The components of such a strategy could include the following measures on the part of the firms: cross-frontier collaboration in research, technological transfer, and manufacturing (on the mode of the Airbus agreements, for instance); a consensus with governments on objectives; and a strong commitment by the major companies, especially Philips and Siemens, to expansion in semiconductors. For their part governments would have to concert their efforts at a European level, most appropriately through the EEC, with the aim of: making national policies more consistent by reducing duplication of research activites and monitoring the allocation of local and foreign investments; sharing some national R & D results within Europe as well as funding some collective research (like Euratom); making efforts to create a European telecommunications network to promote procurement in favour of European firms; and building up technological capabilities in other electronics sectors (for instance, consumer electronics, computers).

Such a strategy might allow not only the survival of the European-controlled industry, but some growth in its market share. It would, however, require: first, a greater capacity for national governments to act independently of the immediate interests of their firms; secondly, a political will to harmonise government action; and thirdly, a willingness to allow 'national champions' to fade away with the trend towards more international firms.

Scenario B: a continuation of present trends, optimistically viewed

It is possible to construct a moderately optimistic view of the future based on the strengthening of present national policies, focused mainly on R & D support and primarily responding to firm strategies (although in France a greater consistency between company strategies and national goals is being achieved). Of the major companies, Philips would remain among the world's largest producers, while Siemens would pursue its efforts to join the 'big league'. SGS-Ates would remain an important European company in spite of its weak finances and uncertainties about government support. Thomson and INMOS could become important producers. More joint ventures could be expected with American and Japanese companies.

Thus, a European semiconductor industry would survive, with beneficial effects on end-user sectors, and somewhat improve its relative performance on world markets. But the industry taken as a whole would still lag well behind the US and Japan and the differences between the national European industries would remain.

Scenario C: a continuation of present trends, pessimistically viewed

An opposite outcome of the kind of assumptions made under Scenario B might be that national policies would be powerless to prevent anything more than two firms, Philips and Siemens, surviving in the mass market for semiconductors, while other European companies either retreated into small, specialised market niches or disappeared. Some joint ventures or subsidiaries of American or Japanese firms would remain. The consequences would probably be to weaken Europe's whole electronics-based industry. While Philips and Siemens might then be represented as 'European champions', they would not necessarily have a European commitment in their allocative decisions or strategies; they would simply be the major European participants in an international electronics oligopoly.

An assessment of the prospects

The coordinated European solution of Scenario A offers the best opportunities for improving the competitiveness of European semiconductor production (and the electronics industry generally). But the obstacles are formidable. Both Philips and Siemens appear to believe that they can do best on their own, and both the Dutch and German governments have always been sceptical about any kind of European industrial policy. French official views have been more changeable: at one time the French favoured a European microelectronics plan, but their withdrawal in 1965 from UNIDATA (in which France's CII was to cooperate on computer development with Philips and Siemens) in favour of links with American companies brought that experience in European cooperation to an end and the French established their own microelectronics plans. Thomson's attempt in 1982–3 to take over Grundig suggests that France under the Mitterrand government is once more experimenting with European solutions, although only, it seems, under clear French leadership. The British interest, in view of ICL's relatively strong position, appears to have been in a European computer plan rather than in any comprehensive electronics programme. The Italians favour an initiative on the European level, but still have little bargaining power.

A possible chink of light is provided by a new cooperative venture, ESPRIT, announced in 1982. The Commission of the European Community and twelve leading European electronics companies are to look at the feasibility of undertaking joint basic (that is, commercial) research on various aspects of information technologies, including very large-scale integrated circuits.[10]

This can hardly yet be described as having created an integrated European approach. Indeed, the recent evidence just as strongly emphasises a continuing national approach, which often favours cooperation with non-European countries. First, the foundering of Thomson's 'European' strategy in its attempts to take over Grundig surely reflects a certain nationalism on the part both of French and German public authorities. Secondly, leading national firms (Siemens, Thomson and Matra) have opted for important extra-European link-ups through licensing or joint ventures in the recent period. Finally, Germany, the UK and Eire already play host, or will soon do so, to foreign investments from four of Japan's top seven semi-conductor producers.

A more probable outcome may lie somewhere between Scenarios B and C: a continuation of nationally oriented policies and a continuing technological lag. If so, then the important aims should be to make the policies as comprehensive as possible, with integrated support to both end products and semiconductors, and to promote wherever possible increasing cooperation between European companies both in research and manufacturing. Government support in Europe may not so far have done much more than help hold together a somewhat precarious industrial structure. The opportunities are now open for more positive and consistent programmes, even if such programmes continue to concentrate mainly on national objectives.

Notes

1. Dosi (1981a), Table 2.
2. Employment magnitudes from Dosi (1981a), Table 3.
3. Calculated from Table 9.2. See also Dosi (1981a), Table 6.
4. For a more detailed and theoretical treatment of factors influencing the nature and direction of technical change, see Dosi (forthcoming).
5. See Dosi (1981a), Table 11.
6. Calculated from Table 2 of Dosi (1981a).
7. In current yen. See the Japan Economic Journal (1982), pp. 85–6.
8. On foreign investments in Japan, see the Japan Economic Journal (1982), p. 55; on the SGS-Toshiba link, see *Financial Times*, 18 May 1982; on Japanese investment in Western Europe, see *Financial Times*, 31 March and 10 December 1982.
9. See *Financial Times*, 10 March 1983.
10. See Commission of the European Communities (1983).

References

Commission of the European Communities (1983), *ESPRIT: A New Venture in Cooperation,* ISEC/B1/83, London.

Dosi, G. (1981a), *Technical Change and Survival: Europe's Semiconductor Industry*, Sussex European Papers No. 9, Brighton: Sussex European Research Centre.

Dosi, G (1981b), 'Microelectronics in Europe', in Carter, C. F., ed., *Industrial Policy and Innovation*, London: Heinemann.

Dosi, G. (forthcoming), *Technical Change and Industrial Transformation: The Theory and an Application to the Semiconductor Industry*, London and Basingstoke: Macmillan.

Electronics, 13 January 1982, New York.

Financial Times, 31 March, 18 May, 10 December 1982; 10 March 1983, London.

Japan Economic Journal (1982), *Industrial Review of Japan 1982*, Tokyo.

Marsh, P. (1981), *The Silicon Chip Book*, London: Sphere Books.

(Dosi (1981a) and Dosi (forthcoming) provide an extensive bibliography on the history and structure of policies for the semiconductor industry.)

10 SHIPBUILDING, MOTOR CARS AND SEMICONDUCTORS: THE DIMINISHING ROLE OF INDUSTRIAL POLICY IN JAPAN

Mototada Kikkawa

10.1 The background to industrial policy

Policy does not operate in a vacuum. Its effectiveness and its character can be understood only by appreciation of the economic, political and social conditions of the nation, the soil in which policy is cultivated. Observers of Japan have often stressed the importance of such specific features of Japanese society as the 'intellectual consensus' for industrial development, which is deep-rooted in the national culture. In this light, Japan's industrial success, and European apparent weaknesses, cannot be attributed simply to differences in industrial policy; a policy on the Japanese model could not, for example, produce the same results in a stagnant or complacent society (such as the UK often appears to be).

Japan, with her world-scale industries, is sometimes regarded as a demonstration of successful industrial policy, based on a strong relationship between government and industry ('Japan Incorporated'). It is true that industrial policy, executed mainly by the Ministry of International Trade and Industry (MITI), contributed to the early post-war development of Japanese industry. But we cannot attribute the more recent success to the effects of official policy. Moreover, the character and importance of the policies have differed widely among industries and over the course of time.

In the period of rehabilitation after 1945, Japanese efforts were directed to restoring production capacity destroyed during the war. This required strong regulation of industry, such as the Priority Production System introduced in 1946 for the most urgently needed commodities (coal, iron and steel, for example). After the peace treaty (1952), the main national goal became economic independence: a sound international balance of payments without the aid of US military procurement. Policies for developing such industries as iron and steel, synthetic fibres, fertilisers and motor vehicles with good export prospects were carried out in the 1950s. In view of the chronic shortage of money, industry was attracted by low-interest loans from the Japan Development Bank (JDB), a government institution set up in 1951 to supply funds for investment. At the same time, imports of goods, technology and capital were strictly regulated—although it was assumed that liberalisation of imports would follow.

The 1960s were a period of unprecedented economic growth in Japan. The 'National Income Doubling Plan', presented by the Ikeda cabinet in 1961, was followed by the revised 'Medium Term Economic Plan'.[1] The plans stressed the development of chemicals and heavy industry and especially their orientation to exports. In the 1960s, petro-chemicals and engineering products—first motor cars, then machinery and computers—became the main objectives for policy support because of their strategic importance. It was recognised that international competitiveness must be the national goal, since liberalisation of imports was to come from the mid-1960s. Eventually (except for a few minor industries such as sugar-refining) Japanese manufacturing could cope with liberalised imports with the help of careful policy assistance.

Rather ironically, MITI's policy influence has tended to diminish since the instrument of import control lapsed and its efforts to maintain control through other legislative measures have failed. The environment of industrial policy changed immensely in the 1970s, when Japanese industries basically caught up with the US and Europe and no longer needed policy support. Moreover, new national needs emerged, such as pollution control and consumer protection; popular pressures backed important political measures for these purposes.[2] Thus the role of policies for industrial development was reduced, while it proved difficult for policies to meet new national needs.

After the 1973 oil crisis new problems arose, requiring some assistance under new legislation: the rescue of 'structurally depressed' industries, and the need for conservation and new sources of energy.[3] Recently, in the difficult world economic situation, Japanese opinion has become increasingly sensitive to overseas complaints about the excessive Japanese presence in the world market; but problems of conflict in international trade—which go beyond the problem of Japanese competitiveness alone—cannot easily be solved by industrial policy.

These developments in industrial policies will be illustrated in this chapter by an account of three industries: shipbuilding (depressed); motor vehicles (growing but mature); and semiconductors (fast growing). (For parallel developments in these three industries in Europe and North America, the reader may refer to Chapters 4, 5 and 9 respectively.)

10.2 The shipbuilding industry

Compared with other industries, the Japanese shipbuilding industry before the Second World War was remarkably large and comprehensive. The main reason was not only Japan's geographical situation but also the backing of the Japanese navy. The conditions sustaining the rapid growth of the industry from the end of the war until the early 1970s are different, but the close association with government operations still remains, and the importance of policy influence cannot be underestimated. The recovery in the early post-war years was helped by a variety of policy measures. Later the industry enjoyed the indirect benefits of interest subsidies to shipowners. When the industry was declining in the later 1970s—in strong contrast to motor cars and semiconductors—its painful curtailment was guided by the Ministry of Transport.

'Programmed' shipbuilding

In 1945, Japan's usable merchant fleet was reduced to 1 million tons. Reconstruction of the fleet was an urgent need and government supports were essential since the shipping companies were in far too fragile a condition to order new vessels. In 1947 a Shipping Public Corporation was established by the government to provide 70 per cent of the total cost of new ships in loans to shipowners repayable over ten years. Although this corporation was abolished a few years later, the essential feature of the scheme, which came to be known as 'programmed' shipbuilding, has been retained: a proportion of the cost of new ships is supplied by official institutions to shipping companies fulfilling certain terms and conditions. The amounts supplied have varied from time to time. In 1947–53, when programmed shipbuilding covered 90 per cent of their operations, the scheme was vital to the industry. It was still insufficient to cover more than 400,000 tons a year out of a capacity of 1.8 million in those years, but it allowed the gradual modernisation and reconstruction, indeed the survival, of the shipyards.

In addition, shipbuilders were able to add to their output by taking orders from those shipbuilders who had their own finance and from such potential shipowners as oil, cement and iron and steel companies—which helped the shipbuilders to establish independence from the shipping interests. But the most promising market proved to be exports and several policy supports triggered the ability of Japanese shipbuilders to overcome their weak international competitiveness.

One measure was the plural exchange rate system providing

preferential rates for ship exports, until 1949 when the exchange rate was fixed. Another measure came later, the 'Raw Sugar Link Scheme', under which the enormous profits of sugar importers, due to the foreign exchange allocation system, were taxed and the proceeds issued to shipbuilders for exported ships which would otherwise have been unprofitable. This scheme operated only in 1954 when it applied to 400,000 tons of ships. Fortunately for Japanese shipbuilders, the world-wide boom in shipping then began.

Since 1953 the main support for shipbuilding has been the shipbuilding interest subsidy: shipping companies receive loans for the purchase of new ships, in accordance with a shipbuilding target settled annually by the government, at officially subsidised interest rates. The main channel is the Japan Development Bank which was able to offer loans at 3½ per cent compared with a normal 7½ per cent (the subsidy was in fact 1½ per cent but another 2½ per cent could be postponed). Interest on loans from commercial banks was also subsidised. The terms and volume of loans have varied from time to time as economic conditions and the freight market changed; for example, preferential treatment was given to the shipping companies which were consolidated, under official guidance, into six groups in 1964.

It can safely be said that the provision of official finance was essential to the building-up of the national fleet. By 1974, about 30 million tons (1,000 vessels) had been built under these schemes (with a peak of 3 million tons a year in 1971 and 1972), the cumulative total of official funds reaching about $5.3 billion.

Export promotion measures

Throughout the 1960s and early 1970s, the growth of the Japanese shipbuilding industry has depended heavily on exports, to which various forms of assistance have been granted. Shipbuilders have long enjoyed a special export price on their purchases of iron and steel. Although government guidance may have played a part originally, the price discount resulted basically from commercial deals between shipbuilders and iron and steel producers. In addition, shipbuilders benefited from schemes applied to promote all kinds of exports (for example, the favourable tax treatment applied to reserves set aside for overseas market development). But the most important help must be export finance on favourable terms from the government's Export–Import Bank of Japan to meet shipbuilders' (and other exporters') cash-flow problems when exporting on deferred payments terms. Such loans to shipbuilders accounted for about three-quarters of all loans extended by the Bank in the 1960s. Similar financial assistance has been given to ship-exporters by other

Western countries (since 1978, the OECD regulations on the terms of such finance have been strengthened—see Chapter 7, Section 4).

Exports accounted for over 70 per cent of orders received by the Japanese shipbuilders in every year in the 1960s and early 1970s, reaching a peak of 82 per cent in 1973 as a result of the world-wide tanker boom. In that year, new orders totalled 34 million tons, a historic record.

Policies for decline and adjustment

Since the first oil crisis of 1973–4, the situation has entirely changed. The collapse of the world shipping market led to a decline in new orders received by Japan. These fell to 9.4 million tons in 1974 and there has been a further decline since then. (Figure 10.1 shows new orders and completions.) At the same time, many earlier orders were cancelled (cancellations in 1976 reaching 7.6 million tons against 8.4 million tons of new orders received). The decline in

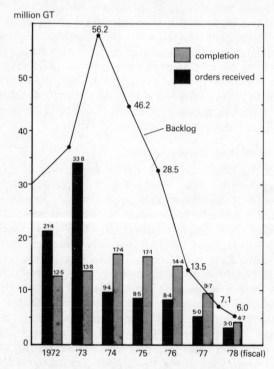

Figure 10.1 Japan: business trends for shipbuilders, 1972-8. *Source*: Japanese Ministry of Transport; Shipbuilders' Association of Japan.

Japan, although part of the world-wide collapse, was accelerated by the competition from new shipbuilding countries, such as Poland, South Korea and Brazil, and also by the floating up of the yen. Up until 1975 Japan had built about 50 per cent of the world total of ships launched (see Table 4.3, p. 90), but by 1978 her share had fallen to 35 per cent while the lower-wage countries had increased their shares. By 1980–1, however, Japan had regained her former share.

Japanese completions remained at a fairly high level up to 1975, as ships ordered earlier reached completion, but since then the orders have been declining sharply, and the gap between capacity and production has been rising. After 1974, as a result of the desperate shortage of work, thirty-seven medium and small size local shipbuilders fell into bankruptcy (twenty-two of them in 1977). Then in 1978, Sasebo Heavy Industry, Japan's eighth largest shipbuilder, was almost ruined. Several big shipbuilders announced 'voluntary' retirement schemes for their employees (for example, in 1979, thousands were retired in the second largest firm, IHI). Shipbuilding became generally regarded as a 'structurally depressed' industry.

To alleviate the situation, the Ministry of Transport issued in 1976 and 1977 recommendations to large shipbuilders to reduce working hours in fiscal 1977, 1978 and 1979 to 75 per cent, 70 per cent and 63 per cent respectively of hours worked in the peak year 1974. In early 1979, even lower percentages were recommended for fiscal 1979 and 1980: a reduction to 39 per cent of the level of the 'standard years' 1973–5 (in gross tonnage a reduction to 3.8 million tons against 9.6 million). The recommendations were differentiated, allowing smaller reductions for the smaller firms (see Table 10.1). At the same time, with the approval of the Fair Trade Commission, the thirty-nine main shipbuilders formed an anti-depression cartel to operate from August 1979 to March 1981 in conjunction with the reduced rates of activity.

Surplus capacity scheme

Policy is also directed towards long-run adjustment of the industry by reducing surplus capacity. Under the 1978 Law on Temporary Measures for the Stabilisation of Specific Depressed Industries, the Council for the Rationalisation of the Shipping and Shipbuilding Industries submitted a programme for the shipbuilding industry to the Ministry of Transport, recommending the scrapping, freezing or sale of about 35 per cent of existing capacity. Given favourable assumptions about world demand and a Japanese share of 35 per cent, the demand for new Japanese ships in 1985 was expected to be only

Table 10.1 Japanese shipbuilding: targets for reduction of capacity and output by 1980

Number of companies*	Size category (annual completions) (000 grt)	Capacity			Output	
		Before scrapping (000 cgrt)	Ratio to be scrapped (by March 1980)	After scrapping (000 cgrt)	Recommended percentage of base year (annual average 1973–5)	To be made by fiscal 1979/80 (000 crgt)
Big 7[†]	above 1,000	5,731 (58.5%)	40%	3,447	34%	1,860
Medium 17(2)	100–1,000	2,900[‡] (29.5%)	30%	2,030	45%	1,350
Medium 16(6)	Below 100	790[‡] (8.1%)	27%	580	49%	560
Other 21(5)		400[‡] (4.1%)	15%	340		
Total 61(13)		9,821 (100%)	35%	6,397	39%	3,770

grt: gross registered tons.
cgrt: compensated gross registered tons (for definition see Chapter 4, note 1).

* Figures in parentheses indicates number of companies bankrupted afterwards.
† Mitsubishi, Ishikawajima, Kawasaki, and Sumitomo Heavy Industries, Hitachi and Mitsui Shipbuildings, Nippon Kokan.
‡ Approximate figure.

Source: Japanese Ministry of Transport.

6.4 million tons against an existing capacity of 9.8 million tons in sixty-one companies. The recommendation was that the 3.4 million tons of surplus capacity (35 per cent) should be disposed of by March 1980. Again, larger companies were invited to reduce capacity by larger proportions than the smaller companies (as shown in Table 10.1); compromises were made among the complicated interests, and account was taken of the fragile base of the smaller shipbuilders.

Policy assistance was given to facilitate these operations. An Association for the Stabilisation of the Shipbuilding Industry was established to buy production facilities (at book value) and shipyard land (at current market value) from medium and small size firms who were short of funds. The necessary finance was provided from several sources including of course the government budget (a quarter of the total). It was expected that about 1 million tons of the 3.4 million tons of surplus capacity would be disposed of by this method.

At the same time, shipbuilders reduced their labour force; by the end of 1978, employment in the industry had fallen to 100,000 from the 1974 peak at 163,000. The unemployed were covered by the Depressed Industry Law, which offered various grants. Shipbuilders demanded special legislation for their unemployed workers, comparable with the special arrangements for unemployed coalminers when that industry declined in the 1950s, but without success.

Stimulating demand

Recently, attempts have been made to generate (rather artificially) the demand for new ships. The government put through a 'three-year urgent programme for building ocean-going vessels', based on a revival of the subsidised interest loans to shipping companies and related to the amounts of tonnage scrapped—a 'scrap and build' scheme. The subsidies (3 per cent off interest rates) are higher than in the past, resulting in interest rates of 4.1 per cent on loans from the Japan Development Bank and 5.1 per cent on commercial bank loans (in the case of tramp steamers, the principal items affected), and the share of loans from the JDB is greater. It was expected that 1 million tons of new demand would emerge under this scheme in fiscal 1979, and more later, against the scrapping of 0.8 million tons a year. Also, scrapping is to be promoted by a subsidy to owners of obsolete ships through an Association established for this purpose; the scrapping of 1 million tons a year is the objective. The real purpose of these schemes, offering very favourable incentives to shipowners is to assist shipbuilders by stimulating demand. The government had further given direct help to shipbuilders by allocating budgetary funds for buying new vessels; although the amounts are limited, many small shipbuilders have benefited from orders for small ships (such as coastal observers).

The evidence seems to suggest considerable success in the capacity cutting programme, and in 1981 output limits were relaxed from 39 per cent to 51 per cent of peak output (1973–5). Certainly, Japan was one of the few shipbuilding countries to increase output in the years after 1979. Following the end of the cartel in April 1982, the number of building berths had been reduced from 138 to 88.

To sum up: careful policy supports and government interventions have played an important part in helping the Japanese shipbuilding industry through its vicissitudes and changing fortunes, a major reason being the longstanding close relationship between the industry and the government. The variety of official approvals and monitoring to which the industry is subject has helped to render the policy effective; in these ways, shipbuilding is rather exceptional among Japanese industries. In addition, the dependence of some local economies on the industry is a feature of shipbuilding. The Sasebo case (when in 1978 the government finally decided to rescue Sasebo Heavy Industry which related business interests thought was going bankrupt) illustrates how the difficulties of an individual shipbuilder could become a political issue.

Since 1979, the inflow of new orders into the Japanese shipbuilding industry has been recovering, apparently quite rapidly. However, whether Japan's shipbuilders—so highly dependent on exports, with their dominant share of world trade in ships, and thus so subject to fluctuations in world demand—can sustain their position as in the past, is open to doubt. Shipbuilding is fundamentally an assembly industry, not requiring a highly sophisticated technology and with a large proportion of labour costs. It is quite probable that Japan will gradually lose her competitiveness, at least in standard non-sophisticated vessels, and be overtaken by new shipbuilding countries such as Korea. Also she will be affected by exchange rate fluctuations. Policies have hitherto tended to be time-buying *ad hoc* measures to meet urgent needs. Policies for the future should aim at finding an appropriate and stable place for the Japanese shipbuilding industry in the changing world market.

10.3 The motor industry

The 1950s: fast growth begins

In the early 1950s, the motor industry (at least for passenger cars) was virtually non-existent in Japan. Of the 130,000 cars in the country, 100,000 were imported. Car production was held to be at least twenty years behind the US and Europe. Prevailing opinions may be illustrated by a dispute in 1953-4 between the Ministry of Transport and the MITI in which the Ministry of Transport asserted that users, unable to wait for home-made cars, must have imports, and the MITI insisted on development of the domestic industry. In the event, the car industry gradually found its place in the policy of economic independence. A report by a MITI committee recommended that 'in order to construct the passenger car industry most fitted to Japan, a mass production system must be set up through the introduction of foreign technology'. Cost reductions and quality improvement could then be expected. The aim was to build a passenger car industry based on rationalising the existing truck production.

Principles for policy and guidelines established by MITI in 1952 restricted 'unnecessary' introductions of foreign capital and technology into Japanese companies, while encouraging desirable ones, especially for mass production. Some car companies rushed to bring in technology, mainly from European companies. Thus Nissan (already producing the Datsun car) made a seven-year agreement with Austin (UK), approved by MITI, in 1952. Nissan was to assemble CKD kits for 2,000 cars a year, under royalty, and domestic production of the components was to be achieved within three years. Isuzu came to an agreement with Rootes (UK) and Hino Diesel with Renault (France)—both arrangements being approved in 1953. But seven other similar proposals failed to be realised, mainly because MITI rejected them.[4] Although MITI was anxious for car production to catch up quickly, it did not want the limited Japanese market to become overcrowded with a multitude of small firms. This combination of aims was largely achieved.

In 1955, MITI proposed a National Car Development Programme, based on a model with a speed of 60 mph, a price of 150,000 yen ($420), and a production of 2,000 a month. MITI would select the best from test products to be submitted by the companies and would arrange financial support from the Treasury and loans from the banks. The scheme never materialised in this form. The manufacturers successfully resisted discrimination in favour of one company. Moreover, the specifications proposed were not feasible at that time.[5] However, the MITI programme demonstrated the possibility of a popular car—no longer a status symbol—and encouraged a national consensus to foster the car industry. This may indeed have been MITI's main aim.

Modernisation of the productive equipment of the car industry then began, with a variety of official supports. The industry benefited from a general reduction in corporate taxes. A Special Taxation Law allowed accelerated depreciation for specified items of machinery, including 20 per cent of the car industry's investments. The industry benefited from exemption from import duties on certain 'new and highly efficient machines which are difficult to produce domestically and which help Japan's economic independence'. Direct financial assistance came in a low-rate loan from the JDB which, although equal to only 4 per cent of the car industry's investment, had a catalytic effect on financing from private sources. At the same time, in view of the weak balance of payments, a tariff quota was applied to car imports in the mid-1950s. The government also tried with some success, by arrangement with the US government, to limit 'disguised imports' in the form of cars brought to Japan by the American military for private use but subsequently sold on the Japanese market. A 'Buy Japanese cars' campaign was instituted, together with pressure on official bodies to buy Japanese cars.

The 1960s—fast growth and liberalisation

By 1960, total output of 4-wheel motor vehicles had reached 500,000, but two-thirds were trucks and buses and only 165,000 cars. The size of the car industry, despite its fast growth (Table 10.2), was still minimal in relation to that of the major producing

Table 10.2: Japan: production of passenger cars, 1952–80

	Units (000s)	% of previous year shown
1952	4	
1955	20	500
1960	165	825
1965	696	422
1970	3,179	457
1975	4,568	144
1980	7,038	154

Source: Japan Automobile Manufacturers' Association, *Motor Vehicle Statistics of Japan 1981*, Tokyo, 1981.

countries. But popularisation of the small-size car—the 'My Car' period—spread rapidly with the fast economic growth of the 1960s. At the same time the government decided to accelerate liberalisation of imports, to be followed by liberalisation of capital movements. So the motor industry in the 1960s was characterised both by massive investments and by strong competition, with a number of new entrants. This led to the institution of policies for reinforcing the structure of the industry.

In 1961, MITI's Industrial Structure Council presented MITI's first attempt at a strategy in preparation for liberalisation, known as the 'Three Groups Plan'. The car industry was to be treated as consisting of three groups: the mass production car, the high class or special use car and the mini car. For the first two of these groups desirable production scales were set at 7,000 a month and 3,000 a month. Within each group, the excessive number of companies was to be consolidated into two or three.

However, this plan lacked effective measures for its execution and seems to have been no more than an 'ad-balloon' of MITI. A new law was then drafted by MITI, based on a report recommending restraints on new entries, control of new models, priorities in the allocation of a Treasury loan and a reorganisation of the industry. These proposals became part of a comprehensive Law for the Development of Specified Industries drafted by MITI in 1963 as a countermeasure against the forthcoming liberalisation. The draft, however, gave rise to opposition, mainly from the Zaibatsu groups which disliked both the reinforcement of MITI's authority and the interference with enterprise economy; the Japanese industries could do very well without any such law. Despite a cabinet decision in its favour, the law was never enacted and the regulations proposed by MITI did not materialise.

However, MITI did not renounce its aim of consolidating the car industry into an oligopoly. In 1965, when there were eleven car producers in Japan's still small market (600,000 cars a year), a merger of Nissan and Prince was announced—a merger largely due to an initiative of MITI. It can be said that this merger was supported by a national consensus in favour of large-scale firms (at that time the largest Japanese car producer, Toyota, had only a twentieth of the sales of General Motors, see Table 10.3).

The immediate reasons for the merger were the deteriorating profits and weak financial position of Prince, despite its high technical level, and, on Nissan's side, anxiety to catch up on its lag behind Toyota, which called for drastic measures. The merger helped to form the 'Big Two' structure which had been MITI's aim for more than ten years. Other links followed, although MITI did not play an important role. Hino, the largest truck producer, came to an agreement with Toyota in 1966 to come under Toyota's umbrella for development and sales of new cars; Daihatsu did the same in 1967. But some other links (for example, Isuzu-Fuji, Isuzu-Mitsubishi,

Table 10.3 The world's major manufacturers of cars and commercial
vehicles, 1965 and 1980

	1965		1980	
	Units produced ('000)	Rank	Units produced ('000)	Rank
General Motors (North America)	6,125	1	5,517	1
Toyota	478	11	3,293	2
Nissan	345	12	3,118	3
Volkswagen-Audi	1,448	4	2,529	4
Ford (North America)	3,340	2	2,323	5
Renault	503	10	2,133	6
Peugeot–Citröen–Talbot	736*	8	2,051	7
Fiat	1,026	5	1,554	8
Ford (Europe)	926	6	1,395	9
Toyo Kogyo	274	13	1,121	10
Mitsubishi	165	15	1,104	11
GM (Europe)	631†	9	985	12
Honda	52	17	957	13
Chrysler (North America)	1,611‡	3	883	14
Daimler-Benz	233	14	717	15
Isuzu	98	16	472	16
Suzuki	42	18	469	17
British Leyland	798	7	396	18

* Peugot 291; Citröen 445.
† Production in Germany only.
‡ Production in US only.

Source: *L'Argus de l'Automobile*, annual statistical supplements, June 1966 and June 1981.

Nissan-Isuzu, all in 1966–8) were later dissolved, largely as a result of the liberalisation of capital movements allowing the entry of foreign producers (which is described below). MITI's objective of a wholly Japanese-owned car industry was thus to be modified.

Faced with the prospects of liberalisation of imports, policy aimed at reducing to the minimum the expected impact on the Japanese economy. A phased programme of liberalisation was devised for products such as motor vehicles where imports might have a damaging effect on strategic industries. Imports of trucks and buses, in which Japan was sufficiently competitive, had already been liberalised in 1961: that is, foreign exchange was allocated automatically. But the import of passenger cars was liberalised only progressively and after a number of steps were taken, such as gradually increased allocations of foreign exchange, to moderate its impact. Final liberalisation came only in 1965. Moreover, the high tariff on engines (the most important part of the car) was maintained, although the ceiling on imports was later raised. Because of this careful step-by-step approach, the car industry was not seriously affected by the liberalisation.

Other government measures also provided favourable conditions for the car industry's expansion. For example, the tax structure on cars was revised in 1966 so as to favour the small cars mostly produced in Japan: the tax on big cars (3,000 or more cc), mostly imported, was put at 40 per cent; on medium cars (2,000 to 3,000 cc) at 30 per cent; and on the smallest cars (under 2,000 cc) at only 15 per cent. High taxes on 'luxury' items are not uncommon in the Japanese tax structure, but it can be argued that this discrimination contributed substantially to the sales of the small car. Moreover, the fast tempo of motorway construction stimulated car ownership. Road construction generally was financed by specific taxes on motor fuel so that increasing revenue, improved and extended roads and expanding car ownership reinforced each other.

Rationalisation and modernisation of the manufacture of motor *components* was also supported by policy. The industry was one of seventeen specified for rapid modernisation by the Law for the Development of the Machinery Industry of 1956. The Law provided for establishing a detailed programme of rationalisation, for funds to be made available and for joint actions such as limitation on production items. Prices were to be reduced and quality improved to reach US levels in a number of items. By 1960, the rationalisation of about two-thirds of the items specified (twenty-two out of thirty-two) was effected. To accelerate the process, in view of the coming liberalisation of car imports, the Law was extended in 1961 and 1965. Investment was stimulated, about 20 per cent of the funds used in 1961–6 being supplied by the Japan Development Bank and the official Smaller Business Finance Company. Later, in 1971, the Law was replaced by the Law for the Development of the Electronics and Machinery Industry, in which motor components were again specified as a priority objective.

The policy-supported reduction of component prices—estimated at about 30 per cent in 1955–65 for the principal items—was particularly important in establishing the Japanese industry's international competitiveness along with that of the car industry. MITI's role in fostering this once very fragile industry was essential at that time. But MITI's other objective, the formation of a few large components manufacturers strong enough to confront the carmakers, has not yet been realised, although there has been some concentration of production of several components. But in general the components industry remains subordinate to the car industry.[6]

By the late 1960s the Japanese motor industry had become established among the world's major producers. In 1967, Japan was the second largest producer of four-wheel motor vehicles, although trucks and buses still exceeded passenger cars both in current output and in the total stock (Table 10.4). The rapid development of the industry no longer called for strong measures of support from the government.

Table 10.4 Japan: production and number of vehicles in use, 1967 and 1980

	Production				In use			
	1967		1980		1967		1980	
	000	%	000	%	000	%	000	%
Passenger cars	1,376	43.7	7,038	63.7	3,836	39.1	23,660	63.8
Trucks	1,743	55.4	3,913	35.4	5,856	59.6	13,177	35.5
Buses	27	0.9	92	0.8	129	1.3	230	0.6
Total	3,147	100.0	11,043	100.0	9,821	100.0	37,067	100.0

Source: *L'Argus de l'Automobile*, annual statistical supplements, June 1966 and June 1981.

The 1970s: international links, pollution and energy-saving

With new developments in the 1970s MITI's role was modified. In the first place, the entry of foreign capital into Japan was finally liberalised in 1971, sooner than originally anticipated, and the opportunity was taken by some weaker car firms to link up with the big three US car companies (which MITI probably did not expect). In 1971, General Motors took a 34 per cent share in the capital of Isuzu, which preferred GM, with its world-wide sales network, to the alternative of deepening its existing cooperation with Nissan. Although MITI may have preferred the link with Nissan, the Ministry at least retained authority to limit the share of foreign capital; thus GM's 34 per cent was within the limit of 35 per cent set by the Minister. MITI's guideline was also effective in limiting an increase in the 15 per cent share in Mitsubishi Automobiles held by Chrysler since 1970 to 35 per cent. Later, in 1979, Ford acquired 25 per cent of the capital of Toyo Kogyo and appears content with this modest share together with the benefits gained from the good components capacity of Toyo. The tie-up, on which the Sumitomo Bank, rather than MITI, exercised much influence, was thus by no means a 'bargain sale' by a firm in financial distress. These three links have since developed in different ways, reflecting the vicissitudes of the American parents (see Chapter 5). Isuzu has become increasingly involved in GM's network and is now GM's major subcontractor in the Far East. The future of the Chrysler-Mitsubishi link is uncertain in view of Chrysler's financial crisis. And the sharp decline in Ford's profitability has cast a shadow over the future of the Ford-Toyo link.

The second development concerns safety standards. Accidents attributed to defective cars aroused much public attention in the late 1960s, leading to an order from the Transport Ministry directing inspection of certain models found to be in some respects defective. Following discussions between a Diet committee and the car firms, the Japanese Automobile Manufacturers' Association initiated a system for reporting and recovering defective cars (similar to the system established earlier in the US). Safety standards were regularly strengthened throughout the 1970s by the Ministry of Transport (for example, seat belts were made compulsory in 1972), following the Federal Safety Standards of the US. The Japanese industry was significantly affected by these regulations.

Thirdly, a number of new regulations were introduced for control of noise and pollution emissions. Noise control was introduced by the Environment Agency in 1974 and has been continuously stiffened. More important, probably, is the control of the polluting emissions HC, CO and NOx (high nitrogen oxides). After temporary regulations in the late 1960s, more effective ones were introduced in the mid-1970s (based on the 'Muskie Law' in the US). Quite severe objectives were announced in 1975, arousing resistance from some car producers and, reportedly, from MITI in view of the heavy burden thought to be imposed on the industry. However, after developing a new engine, Honda accepted the regulations, as did some other producers, and the 1975 regulations came into effect. But still stiffer regulations proposed in 1976, including in particular a 75 per cent reduction in the emission of NOx, the main cause of photochemical smog, led to disputes between the Environment Agency and car producers who insisted on the technical impracticability of so severe a control of NOx. As a result, enforcement of the 1976 proposal was postponed and a milder regulation of NOx made effective temporarily. It was only in 1978 that the 1976 proposal was made effective as originally intended.

These regulations—the most severe in the world, but necessary in Japan's narrow territory—have been a success. By directing technological development in the appropriate direction they have helped to reconcile Japanese society with the motor car industry.

The fourth development, resulting from the energy problems in the later 1970s, has been the general need for energy conservation. Passenger cars have already achieved (thanks to their small size) the ambitious targets announced for 1985 by President Carter in the US (27.5 mpg). In late 1979, new standards for 1985 were set by the Ministry of Transport and MITI. These new standards imply an improvement of over 12 per cent in average mpg (to 36 mpg, far surpassing the US target for 1985 of 27.5).[7] They are not regarded as unrealistic and will give Japanese producers additional possibilities for penetration of the US market.

Finally, the success of Japanese motor vehicle exports, rising from 1.1 million units in 1970 to 6.0 million in 1980 and accounting recently for more than half of production, has made Japan the largest car exporter in the world (see Table 5.5, p. 118). North America takes half of Japan's car exports and Europe a quarter (Table 10.5). Thus the avoidance or alleviation of trade conflict

Table 10.5 Japan: vehicle exports, 1980 (000 units)

	Cars	Trucks	Buses	Total	%
North America	1,977	616	–	2,593	43.5
Asia and Middle East	475	628	21	1,123	18.8
Oceania	190	124	3	317	5.3
Europe	1,008	218	1	1,227	20.6
Africa	85	202	36	322	5.4
South and Central America	212	165	5	382	6.4
Total	3,947	1,954	66	5,967	100.0

Source: Japan Automobile Manufacturers' Association, *Motor Vehicle Statistics of Japan 1981*, Tokyo, 1981.

between the major car-exporting countries must be an important objective for Japanese policy. The definition of this aim remains unclear, however, and MITI does not possess effective instruments for it. The difficulty is that policy intervention will directly injure the present interests of car producers.

However, MITI has tried to exercise its influence to ease trade conflicts with the US and Europe in some special cases. In 1978, in view of Japan's immense export surplus, eight main export items were brought under MITI's control. Car exports were monitored with a view to limiting their volume to that of the previous year.

This control was abolished in mid-1979 when Japan's balance of payments worsened.

By 1981 protectionist pressures had built up to the point where Japan was compelled to introduce 'voluntary' restraints on car exports to the US, Canada, Germany, Belgium and the Netherlands. Since exports to the UK, France, Italy and Spain had already been limited, voluntarily or unilaterally (see Chapter 5, pp. 119–20), Japan thus found the major part of its world export markets under restraint.

Protectionist pressures have had a clear effect on the foreign-investment activity of the Japanese car industry. In the early 1980s, Japanese car exports increased fast enough to take about 20 per cent of the US new car market—owing to the attraction of low fuel consumption as well as of price competitiveness and high reliability. Pressures arose from the US government and Congress, joined by trade unions, not only for 'orderly marketing' but also for Japanese car producers to invest in production in the US. Honda has now begun car production there. The bigger Japanese producers, Toyota and Nissan, were at first reluctant although MITI made vigorous efforts to persuade them, suggesting that they could make use of public funds from the Japanese Export–Import Bank. MITI's persuasion was not effective, basically because MITI was in no position to take any responsibility if the investment proved a failure. However, the Japanese government anxious to avoid a worsening of political relations with the US, made some concessions—for example, by removing the import tariff on car components. More recently, however, Nissan has decided to produce a pick-up truck in the US, while Toyota, which has proven more reluctant to invest abroad, is now considering a joint venture with General Motors to produce a small car in the US. In addition, Honda and Nissan have acquired a few modest interests, through cooperative arrangements or share acquisitions, in Western Europe (see Chapter 5, pp. 129 and 131). Also, Nissan has been examining the feasibility of setting up a new factory in the UK to produce passenger cars on an economic scale.

To sum up: the development of the Japanese motor industry has been an autonomous process, not attributable to the influence of government policy. The secret of the emergence of world-scale firms such as Toyota and Nissan lies in their superior product technology and know-how,[8] effective use of labour based upon strong work ethics,[9] and market-oriented sales operations. However, it is also true that the development follows the basic objective pursued by MITI for the last three decades: the dominance in Japan of a Japanese-owned motor industry; and the early policies of the

1950s must not be forgotten. By contrast, the major concerns of official policy in the 1980s are likely to focus on moderating trade conflicts, especially between Japan and the US and Western Europe, Japan's most important export markets for cars. This implies quite different tasks for policy than the fostering of industry, tasks of which other countries have relatively little experience.

10.4 The semiconductor industry

A general sketch of the world's semiconductor industry is given in Chapter 9. The reader may be reminded of some special features of the industry which form the background to its development in Japan: the rapid technical progress represented by the scaling-up of integration—the increasing number of elements that can be crammed into an integrated circuit (IC, or chip) followed by remarkable reductions in costs and prices;[10] the great benefits of large-scale production arising from the 'learning curve', creating competitive advantages for the big producers (see Figures 10.2 and 10.3); and the importance of cost reduction or a high yield rate (or low wastage rate)—the proportion of good quality chips to the total produced— still difficult to stabilise and even more to improve. Successful IC production, despite new and highly efficient machines, still requires human skill (and is sometimes regarded as closer to agriculture than to industry). The great variety of industries and end-products in which the chip has found, or will find, its place must also be stressed.

Japan's semiconductor industry (meaning here mainly production of integrated circuits rather than the discrete semiconductors forming transistors, diodes, and so on) now accounts for about a quarter of world output, supported by the large domestic market (see Table 10.6) and by continuous expansion of exports (exceeding imports after 1977). The technological lag behind the US—very marked in the 1960s—now appears to be rapidly disappearing. Japan's international competitiveness is well established (as is indeed demonstrated by trade conflicts with the US).

The building up of the Japanese industry

There are no firms in Japan (except for some minor ones) specialising wholly in the production and external sales of semiconductors. The four largest suppliers (see Table 10.7) developed their semiconductor operations out of other activities. The largest is NEC (Nippon Electric Co.), which was originally the supplier of telecommunications equipment to the NTT (Nippon Telegraph and Telephone Public Corporation). NEC entered semiconductors in 1962 using the US

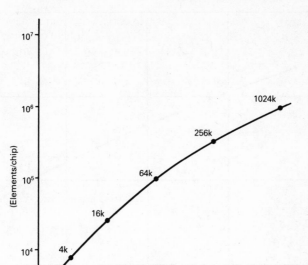

Source: Gnostic Concepts Inc.

Fig. 10.2 Change in the degree of integration for memory integrated circuits, 1970–85.

Table 10.6 Forecast of world consumption of integrated circuits US $ million

	1977	1980	1982	1977–82 Increase p.a.
North America	2,659	3,934	4,867	12.9%
Europe	1,639	2,412	3,174	14.1%
Japan	1,616	2,473	3,337	15.6%
Others	396	771	1,250	25.8%
Total	6,310	9,590	12,628	14.9%

Source: Data Quest Inc., *Data Quest* (monthly), various issues.

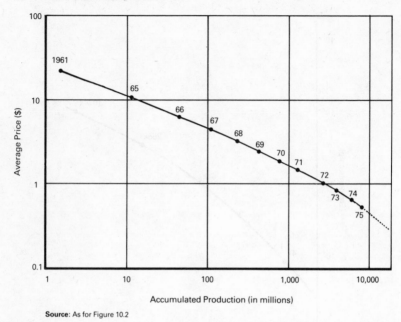

Accumulated Production (in millions)

Source: As for Figure 10.2

Fig. 10.3 Learning curve for integrated circuits

firm Fairchild's planar technology; until the late 1960s, NECs semiconductors were used wholly in-house, for telecommunications and
computers. Now, about 80 per cent are sold to outside customers,
and these make up more than 20 per cent of the company's total
turnover. NEC has become (in 1980) the third largest producer in
the world of semiconductors and the second largest (after Texas
Instruments) of ICs. The other three large semiconductor producers,
Hitachi, Toshiba and Mitsubishi Electric Corporation, with much
larger total sales than NEC, are all comprehensive electrical engineering companies producing a wide range of electrical machinery using
ICs, but selling most of their ICs outside; semiconductors represent
less than 10 per cent of their turnover. Four other firms are smaller
producers of semiconductors: Matsushita Electronics, Tokyo-Sanyo,
Sony and Sharp; these are basically makers of domestic electrical
appliances but all started production of ICs as a necessary input for
their end-products as did Fujitsu, originally a producer of telecommunications and now specialising on a large-scale computer.

The sources of the rise of Japan's IC industry are thus to be found
within the industry itself. The first is the emergence of a strong and
highly competitive market in electrical appliances in which the semi-

Table 10.7 Main Japanese semiconductor producers, 1980

	Sales (yen billion)*		(B)/(A) (%)	Share of Japanese market (%)	In-house use (yen billion)	Export (yen billion)
	Total (A)	Semiconductors (B)				
Nippon Electric (NEC)	720	161	22	16	40	35
Hitachi	1,698	124	7	12	25	37
Toshiba	1,428	97	7	10	15	24
Matsushita Electronics	180	81	45	8	40	12
Mitsubishi Electric	1,075	44	4	4	4	4
Tokyo Sanyo	258	43	17	4	9	11
Fujitsu	501	43	9	4	20	3

* US $ 1.00 = 227 yen; £1 = 527 yen.

Source: Estimates by Industrial Bank of Japan.

conductor naturally played its part as a key input. Because of the rapid spread of domestic appliances in Japan, the discrete semiconductor dominated until the late 1970s. Subsequently, ICs became the more important with the development of pocket calculators, computers (especially microcomputers), electronic watches and musical instruments—all made possible by the dramatic cost reduction as the learning curve took effect.[11] The virtuous circle of falling prices, rising sales volume and so further cost reductions came into play. Furthermore, the fact that the principal makers of ICs originally developed the IC mainly for use in their own end-products, providing an assured demand, is also significant. (The importance of this 'synergy' between producers and end-users of semiconductor appliances is stressed in the review of the international semiconductor industry in Chapter 9.)

A second internal source of Japanese success is the establishment of high standards of quality in production, giving the industry high 'credibility'. For example, the NTT, probably the major end-user of ICs in Japan, is known to demand the highest possible standards in all its purchases. The same is true of other commercial IC users, including the in-house users. Thus strenuous efforts to maintain high quality have been essential to the survival of the industry. In this respect, the human factor, the skill of Japanese engineers and the homogeneity of the workforce, has been of great importance, resulting in particular in the high yield rates. This is confirmed by the fact that of all the TI (Texas Instruments) plants throughout the world, Japan TI has the highest yield (20 to 40 per cent above the US plant), and user reject rates are only 0.2 to 0.3 per cent for Japanese products against 2 to 3 per cent for the US.

Finally, IC development is an area particularly suited to Japanese talents. It is technological progress, rather than new innovations, which accounts for the rapid scaling-up of integration (doubling annually) in the capacity of ICs. Although the 'core' processing machines are still imported from the US, their combination with Japanese know-how in production, and with Japanese concentrated efforts at both the technical and factory level to meet the high standards required, has created an efficient capacity hard to surpass.

The role of official policy

Because the mainspring of Japanese success in semiconductors is to be found within the industry, the direct influence of government policies has been relatively small in recent years, although in the early stages industrial policy played a part in creating a favourable environment in which the industry could grow.

The NTT laboratory initiated research on transistors in 1950, and Sony succeeded in production of them in 1954. The present IC producers all entered into mass production in the late 1950s. In that period, the Japanese industry was wholly dependent on foreign, mainly US, technology. As shown in Chapter 9, the US industry was then far ahead, in part as a result of the abundant governmental expenditure on R & D and procurement for military and space operations, advantages not available in Japan. It appeared uncertain at that time whether there could be an adequate market in Japan to support IC development, and until the late 1960s Japanese imports exceeded domestic production. Some policy measures were, however, adopted: the 'Provisional Law for the Development of the Electronics Industry' of 1957 applied to IC production, but the funds supplied were so small as to be hardly relevant.

In the mid-1960s, some leading American producers considered entry into the Japanese market by direct investment. Among others, Texas Instruments applied in 1964 to the Japanese government for permission to establish a wholly owned IC production company. TI also applied to the Japanese Patent Office for patent rights in Japan on the fundamental structure of the IC—rights granted in the mid-1960s. The young Japanese producers were greatly shocked, even fearing that TI, taking a rather stiff posture, would not release the patent. The Japanese government then announced conditions on which TI would be allowed to set up a firm in Japan: (a) it must be a joint venture with a Japanese company owning 50 per cent of the capital; (b) the fundamental IC patent must be released to other Japanese producers, with reasonable compensation; (c) there must be a temporary limit on production. TI at first expressed objections, especially to the first condition, but ultimately (in 1968) accepted all three. Thus TI Japan, a joint venture with Sony, was established and initiated IC production in 1969. (Today TI Japan is wholly owned by TI, as Sony withdrew its holding in 1971, and is the most successful of TI overseas subsidiaries.) At the same time, six of Japan's main producers bought the fundamental IC patent from TI.

Progressive liberalisation of imports was another policy measure setting the external conditions for the industry. Imports of technology were liberalised in 1968, and of ICs themselves between 1970 and 1974, in three stages, beginning with small-scale ICs (below 100 elements). Capital investment was liberalised in two stages starting in 1971 (but excluding IC production for computers), leading to the establishment of some joint ventures, and completed in 1974. This cautious approach is the reason why the Japanese industry was not seriously affected by liberalisation. Subsidies for smoothing the effects of liberalisation were granted but do not appear to have been important; indeed, they may have been superfluous. The import tariff has been kept at 12 per cent, higher than the US tariff of 6 per cent, but an accelerated reduction to the Tokyo Round target (4.2 per cent in 1988) is expected.

Technological development has also received some official assistance. In 1975, the progressive-minded public telecommunications enterprise NTT initiated a project for the development of VSLI (Very Large Scale Integrated Circuits) for telecommunication and data processing equipment. It took the form of assistance by Fujitsu, Hitachi and NEC to the research laboratory of NTT, with 20 billion yen (about $80 million) in 1975-8, followed by a similar amount for a second phase in 1978-81.

In 1976, a VLSI Technology Research Association was established on the initiative of MITI, with the sole object of developing VLSI for the computer[12] (following earlier MITI efforts to promote computer technology). MITI has long been interested in the 'restructuring' of the Japanese computer industry and the possible formation of a merger of the existing companies may have been MITI's hidden intention in promoting the Association. Such a merger being unfeasible, the combination of research efforts was probably the second-best choice from MITI's point of view. The core of the Association is a joint laboratory incorporating research staff from the Electronics Technology Laboratory (attached to MITI) and from five companies (the existing joint research laboratories: CDL—Fujitsu/Hitachi/Mitsubishi Electric; and NTIS–NEC/Toshiba). Expenditure of 72 billion yen ($300 million) was provided for 1976-80, of which 30 billion yen comes from the national budget but is to be returnable. Despite its somewhat ambitious aims, the influence of the scheme on the semiconductor industry is likely to be limited. The joint laboratory is responsible for basic technology in which all the participating companies have a common interest. The project will certainly have results in the long term, but the companies are not necessarily dependent on it. And in view of the nature of the Japanese IC industry and market, the Association is unlikely to lead to industrial 'restructuring'.

In the 1980s further policy initiatives (for example, for the 'Fifth Generation Computer Program) will be taken by MITI or other public bodies. The role of MITI in this is basically one of helping to form a consensus on the direction of technological development. Consensus formation is difficult to achieve in other industrial countries because they lack effective measures for implementing such a policy. It is effective in Japan because of the nature of Japanese society: this will be studied in the next section.

10.5 The limits to the role of industrial policy

Japanese society: the background

It was suggested at the beginning of this chapter that the form and effectiveness of industrial policy, and the interaction between government and industry, depend on the general social environment in which government and industry operate. A little more should be said about cultural factors which differentiate Japan from other industrial societies, and which are generally assumed to have fostered Japanese industrial success so far.

The feature of Japanese society most commonly stressed is its homogeneity and high degree of consensus in pursuing national objectives. This homogeneity embodies, too, a pervasive social pressure on individuals to improve their standing, a pressure irrespective of family, inherited position or academic qualifications, and carrying with it a certain contempt for those who fail. This driving force for advancement was reinforced by the social changes brought about first by the Meiji Restoration and, even more, by the social reformation after the Second World War. Such changes have produced a relatively egalitarian society—egalitarian in respect both of opportunities and of social prestige. (For example, it has been found that 70 or 80 per cent of Japanese citizens think of themselves as belonging to the 'middle class'.) At the same time, the general ambition for advancement means that the society is basically an 'unsatisfied' society.

Another element in the social structure is important. Nakane (1970) describes the structure as essentially 'vertical' rather than 'horizontal'. The groups or organisations are more important to the citizen than his individual personality. It is the group to which he owes loyalty, in which he feels at ease, and in which he is cared for. In the past, many such organisations commanded loyalty: the state, the local community, the employing corporation, the family. However, defeat in war has eroded much of the importance of the state as the object of loyalty, while urbanisation and the disappearance of the extended family system have diminished attachment to the local community and the family. There remains the corporation—often compared with the family—as the increasingly important focus of loyalty and of welfare. Those employed in these great organisations benefit from their systems of lifetime employment (Nenko) and from the opportunities of an 'internal labour market' in which advancement in pay and status can be sought. Labour unions are also organised on a company basis. Because the increasing size and diversification of the giant corporations allow absorption of workers displaced from outdated jobs, rationalisation and labour-saving technologies have generally been accepted.

The system worked well for both employers and workers during the period of fast expansion, reducing expensive labour turnover and facilitating adjustment to changing circumstances. It must be said, however, that the Nenko system has never covered the whole labour force—perhaps less than half; it does not normally apply to women, or to small- or medium-sized firms. Moreover, slower rates of industrial growth in Japan, together with competition from new sources, have called into question a system which imposes on the big corporations a costly obligation to hold surplus labour: a situation escaped by their competitors.

These features of the social and cultural background to a free enterprise system have hitherto been the driving force for Japan's industrial success. Managements have been in a position to free themselves from the short-term profit considerations to which shareholders in some other countries are so sensitive, and to plan strategies of investment and product development designed for the long-term prosperity of the company. It is doubtful whether government policy has been effective in such major business decision-making even though in some cases MITI has apparently offered 'guidance'.

The actual role of industrial policy

I take the view that the role of government in Japanese industrial development, although varying in importance with changing economic conditions, has been essentially auxiliary, and complementary to the operations of private business. In the immediate post-war years, it is true, the government put through strong measures for recovery of the economy. But the circumstances were exceptional: as the economy was normalised, the role of industrial policy shifted to modest intervention and then to the function of catalyst. Moreover, the scale of intervention varies from industry to industry. Two factors, the growth of the market and technological needs, have been significant. These factors are illustrated by the three industries examined above. In motor vehicles, with a growing but increasingly mature market with medium-level technological requirements, governmental intervention has, at least recently, been of only modest importance. In the fast-growing and competitive market for semiconductors, where technological requirements are predominant, intervention has been still less. But in depressed shipbuilding, government assistance has been substantial in helping the industry to meet the problems of declining demand.

The autonomy of Japanese industry, moreover, is reinforced by the existence of the *Zaibatsu*—the diversified corporations, with their interlocked shareholdings, covering a variety of industrial, banking, insurance and trading interests (Mitsubishi, Sumitomo, Mitsui).[13] The dominant power which they exercise in the economy is supported by their solidarity and sense of unity (exemplified by the prefixing of the *Zaibatsu*'s name to that of each of the consituent companies).

The autonomy and increasing power of these groups naturally limits the extent to which the state can influence events by industrial policy (illustrated above by the successful opposition of the *Zaibatsu* in 1963 to MITI's proposals for the regulation of certain domestic industries inc'uding motor vehicles).

At the beginning of the 1980s some business interests were suggesting that prohibition on holding companies, made after the war to curb the power of the *Zaibatsu*, should be ended. If this were to happen, it could considerably strengthen the *Zaibatsu* and limit the influence of industrial policy.

The future course of Japanese economic policy must be affected by deveiopments in the world environment. Because of Japan's heavy dependence on export markets, her economy is increasingly vulnerable. Should import penetration from Japan exceed politically tolerable ceilings, some countries could be tempted to adopt protectionist measures on a scale leading to a collapse of the world economy through declining international trade. To prevent such an outcome, Japan will need to exercise her economic potential with great caution. Unless Japanese industry itself behaves cautiously enough in pursuing its own immediate short-term interests, an industrial policy, designed for the long-term advantages of the parties concerned, may make its appearance. For example, from 1980 MITI monitored car exports to the US and Europe in an effort to keep such exports down to an 'appropriate' level. This involved MITI in exercising some implicit control on each producer, for which there was no legal basis. It might be suggested that MITI could use such measures to recover a degree of administrative authority over industry which could not otherwise be acquired. Could this be a step towards a stronger and legally based authority? I do not see any strong possibility of such a result.

At the same time, the danger exists that Japan will herself be tempted towards protectionism for industries with an uncertain future in the face of competition from newly industrialising countries. (This is illustrated by proposals put forward in parliament for protection against imported silk fabric.)

Another issue is the extent to which jurisdiction will need to be exercised in the field of energy. Difficulties over oil supplies and their distribution might call for some kind of mandatory schemes of allocation, thus strengthening governmental authority. Moreover, the question arises of the government's role in promoting alternative sources of energy, since these have hitherto been assumed to be in the private domain. Since energy must continue to be a determining factor for the future of the Japanese economy, we should watch whether efforts by MITI to ensure a stable energy supply will lead to a general recovery of its authority.

Conclusion

Although the Japanese economy as a whole may appear to enjoy international competitiveness, some industries are bound to mature or to decline. However, the experiences recorded earlier in this chapter do not suggest that industrial policy has so far been particularly successful in the management of structurally depressed industries. Yet it is possible that, in future, MITI might be armed with more comprehensive weapons for assisting over a limited period either the survival or the running down of such industries. This prompts the question of whether the increasing range of structurally depressed industries will trigger a general governmental control over industry. Past experience does not seem to indicate such a result. Much depends on the attitude taken in the industries concerned. I do not myself imagine that Japanese industry will be so feeble as to take refuge in administrative protection at the first sign of distress.

Notes

1. These economic programmes were drafted by the Economic Planning Agency. Although the agency has no jurisdiction over industry, it is concerned with industrial policy in that it proposes the economic forecasting framework in which the policy is to operate.
2. The Basic Law for Environmental Pollution Control was enacted in 1967 and the Environment Agency was established in 1971. Strong public pressure led in 1974 to proposals by the Fair Trading Commission for a stiffening of the Anti-Trust Law (which had been several times relaxed since its enactment in 1947). Despite persistent resistance from MITI and others, the Law was eventually revised in 1977.
3. The Law on Temporary Measures for the Stabilisation of Specific Depressed Industries and the Law of Temporary Measures for the Unemployed in Specific Depressed Areas were enacted in 1978. 1979 saw enaction of the Law for Rationalisation of Energy Consumption (known as the Energy Conservation Law), which provides for conservation targets to be set for several industrial areas.
4. Toyota, the largest firm, agreed on a link with Ford (US) early in 1950. But

the agreement never materialised because the US government prohibited the sending of technical experts overseas on account of the Korean war.

5. In 1956, Toyota presented a test car conforming to the programme, except that it was expected to cost double or more than double the price specified. The Publica model (announced by Toyota in 1961) originated from this test car.

6. Sometimes such a structure is called 'soft' (see Takeuchi, 1979). In such a structure, in Takeuchi's view, export industries can absorb among themselves difficulties such as exchange rate fluctuations; but this means simply that the car industry can shift to the components industry the loss of export earnings.

7. The 1979 regulations provide the following targets for fuel consumption in 1985:

| | Miles per gallon | | 1985 % improvement |
	Present level	1985 target	
Light cars	52.5	55.9	6.5
Popular—small size	32.45	36.7	13.0
Medium—large size	21.4	24.0	11.8
Average (weighted by present composition of sales)	32.2	36.1	12.3

8. Toyota's 'Kanban system' is a well-known example of production management. It aims at minimising inventories in the production process by programming the supply of components.

9. One example is 'quality control circles'—a system which has impressed several automobile companies outside Japan. The shop floor workers are divided into small teams in a limited form of workers' participation.

10. ICs can be classified according to the number of elements (transistor equivalents) on a chip (a square with sides about 3–5 mm):

LSI (large scale IC)	above 1,000 elements
MSI (medium scale)	100–1,000
SSI (small scale)	below 100
VLSI (very large scale)	no fixed definition, but possibly above 100,000

11. The President of Texas Instruments remarked that there is a 'fundamental difference' between TI and other American IC companies in that TI is the first non-Japanese company to understand and use fully the 'learning curve' (*Business Week*, 18 September 1978). This is an interesting comment on Japanese producers.

12. The purpose of the Association is to develop a computer to compete with IBM's 'future systems' computer. The research objectives are techniques for (a) refining treatment, (b) the crystal, (c) design, (d) processing, (e) test/evaluation, and (f) the final device. Apart from its basic elements, the practical technology is to be researched in the company-based laboratories. The patents derived from research within the Association, including those publicly owned, are to be released in full outside.

13. The *Zaibatsu* groups originated with single families (for example, the Iwasaki family in the case of Mitsubishi). But these families no longer play an important role in the management.

References and selected bibliography

General:
Abegglen, J. C. (1958), *The Japanese Factory*, Boston: MIT Press.
Doi, T. (1973), *Anatomy of Dependence*,* Tokyo: Kodansha International.
Nakane, C. (1970), *Japanese Society*,* New York: Penguin Books.
Ouchi, W. (1981), *Theory Z—How American Business can Meet the Japanese Challenge*, Reading: Addison-Wesley Publishing Company Inc.
Pascale, R. T., and Athos, A. G. (1982), *The Art of Japanese Management*, New York: Simon & Schuster.
Takeuchi, H. (1979), *Japan's Economy in Soft Structure* (in Japanese), Tokyo: Asahi Shimbun Press.
Vogel, E. F. (1979), *Japan as Number One,* Cambridge: Harvard University Press.

Policy:
Johnson, C. (1982), *MITI and the Japanese Miracle—The Growth of Industrial Policy, 1925-1975*,† San Francisco: Stanford University Press.
Tsuruta, T. (1982), *Industrial Policy of Japan after the War* (in Japanese), Tokyo: Japan Economic Journal Press.

Historical:
Ito, M. (1977), *Witness to Industrial History after the War*: Volume I, *Industrial Policy*, and Volume II, *The Age of Bigger Business* (in Japanese), Tokyo: Mainichi Shimbun Press.

Industry:
Amaya, S. (1978), *The Development of the Automobile Industry in Japan* (in Japanese), Tokyo: National Diet Library.
Daily Industrial Journal (1976), *The Car Industry in a Changing Period* (in Japanese), Tokyo: Daily Industrial Journal Press.
The Industrial Bank of Japan (1982), *New Developments in Japanese Industry,* ‡ (in Japanese), Tokyo: Nihon Keizai Shimbun.
Japan Economic Journal (annual), *Industrial Review of Japan* Tokyo: Japan Economic Journal Press.
Larsen, W. M. (1980), *Auto Grossmacht Japan*, Hamburg: Rudolf Augstein GmbH & Co.
Namiki, N. (1977), *The Automobile Industry in Japan* (in Japanese), Tokyo: Japan Economic Journal Press.

* Written by a Japanese author and recommended for clarifying aspects of Japanese society relevant to its industrial success.
† A thorough analysis of MITI and its policy.
‡ A comprehensive picture of Japanese industry in the most recent period.

Namiki, N. (1977), *The Electronics Industry in Japan* (in Japanese), Tokyo: Japan Economic Journal Press.

Noda, M. (1977), *The Shipbuilding Industry* (in Japanese), Tokyo: Kyoiku-Sha.

OECD, *Measures of Assistance to Shipbuilding*, edns of 1973 and 1976, Paris.

Shimura, S. (1979), *Warfare in the Integrated Circuit Industry* (in Japanese), Tokyo: Diamond Press.

INDEX